THE SECOND WORLD WAR
11. The Tide of Victory

This is the eleventh of twelve books which together make up the first complete paperback edition of Sir Winston Churchill's classic memoirs, The History of the Second World War. *Here, full and unabridged, is the greatest Englishman of our time, describing in unforgettable words, the follies which brought about the most terrible war known to mankind, and the sacrifices, determination and matchless courage by which it was brought to an end.*

The Moral of the Work

In War: RESOLUTION
In Defeat: DEFIANCE
In Victory: MAGNANIMITY
In Peace: GOODWILL

Winston S. Churchill

THE SECOND WORLD WAR

11. The Tide of Victory

CASSELL · LONDON

CASSELL & COMPANY LTD
35 Red Lion Square · London WC1

and at Melbourne, Sydney, Toronto,
Johannesburg, Cape Town, Auckland

The Tide of Victory
was first published as Book 1 of 'Triumph and Tragedy',
the sixth volume of Sir Winston Churchill's
The Second World War

First published 1954
All rights reserved
First published in this edition September 1964
Second edition March 1965

Set in 9 point Intertype Times and
printed in Great Britain by Cox and Wyman Ltd.,
London, Reading and Fakenham.
1064

Preface

(From the Preface to the original edition)

I must regard these volumes as a continuation of the story of the First World War which I set out in The World Crisis, The Eastern Front *and* The Aftermath. *Together they cover an account of another Thirty Years War.*

I have followed, as in previous volumes, the method of Defoe's Memoirs of a Cavalier, *as far as I am able, in which the author hangs the chronicle and discussion of great military and political events upon the thread of the personal experiences of an individual. I am perhaps the only man who has passed through both the two supreme cataclysms of recorded history in high executive office. Whereas however in the First World War I filled responsible but subordinate posts, I was in this second struggle with Germany for more than five years the head of His Majesty's Government. I write therefore from a different standpoint and with more authority than was possible in my earlier books. I do not describe it as history, for that belongs to another generation. But I claim with confidence that it is a contribution to history which will be of service for the future.*

These thirty years of action and advocacy comprise and express my life-effort, and I am content to be judged upon them. I have adhered to my rule of never criticising any measure of war or policy after the event unless I had before expressed publicly or formally my opinion or warning about it. Indeed in the afterlight I have softened many of the severities of contemporary controversy. It has given me pain to record these disagreements with so many men whom I liked or respected: but it would be wrong not to lay the lessons of the past before the future. Let no one look down on those honourable, well-meaning men whose actions are chronicled in these pages without searching his own heart, reviewing his own discharge of public duty, and applying the lessons of the past to his future conduct.

It must not be supposed that I expect everyone to agree with what I say, still less that I only write what will be popular. I give my testimony according to the lights I follow. Every possible care has been taken to verify the facts; but much is constantly coming to light from the disclosure of captured documents and other revelations which may present a new aspect to the conclusions which I have drawn.

One day President Roosevelt told me that he was asking publicly for suggestions about what the war should be called. I said at once 'The Unnecessary War'. There never was a war more easy to stop than that which has just wrecked what was left of the world from the previous struggle. The human tragedy reaches its climax in the fact that after all the exertions and sacrifices of hundreds of millions of people and the victories of the Righteous Cause we have still not found Peace or Security, and that we lie in the grip of even worse perils than those we have surmounted. It is my earnest hope that pondering upon the past may give guidance in days to come, enable a new generation to repair some of the errors of former years, and thus govern, in accordance with the needs and glory of man, the awful unfolding scene of the future.

WINSTON SPENCER CHURCHILL

Chartwell,
Westerham,
Kent.

March 1948

Acknowledgments

I have been greatly assisted in the establishment of the story in its military aspect by Lieutenant-General Sir Henry Pownall; in naval matters by Commodore G. R. G. Allen; in presenting the Air aspect by Air Chief Marshal Sir Guy Garrod; and on European and general questions by Colonel F. W. Deakin, of Wadham College, Oxford, who has helped me with my work Marlborough: His Life and Times. *I have had much assistance from the late Sir Edward Marsh, Mr. Denis Kelly, and Mr. C. C. Wood. I must in addition make my acknowledgments to the very large number of others who have kindly read these pages and commented upon them.*

Lord Ismay has also given me his invaluable aid, as have my other friends.

I record my obligations to Her Majesty's Government for the permission to reproduce the text of certain official documents of which the Crown Copyright is legally vested in the Controller of Her Majesty's Stationery Office. At the request of Her Majesty's Government, on security grounds, I have paraphrased some of the telegrams I have quoted. These changes have in no way altered the sense or substance of the telegrams.

I am indebted to the Roosevelt Trust for the use they have permitted me of the President's telegrams I have quoted; to Captain Samuel Eliot Morison, U.S.N.R., whose books on naval operations give a clear presentation of the actions of the United States Fleet; and also to others who have allowed their private letters to be published.

The publishers wish to thank the owners, named and unnamed, of the photographs used to illustrate this book.

Contents

Illustrations

Supply vehicles litter the Normandy beaches after D-Day

A glider lands on an improvised landing-strip

The destruction of the little Normandy town of St. Lô

Churchill and Montgomery inspect a 'Mulberry' harbour

Hidden collaborators shoot at civilians in Paris after the liberation

Churchill and de Gaulle at the head of a procession in the Champs-Elysées

The remains of Warsaw after the sixty-day rising

A Japanese suicide aircraft shot down

American trucks on their way from the Chinese front

British transport moves over the Nijmegen bridge

The last phase of the mopping up of the Scheldt estuary

British troops fighting in Athens

Maps and Diagrams

Theme of the Book

HOW THE GREAT
DEMOCRACIES TRIUMPHED,
AND SO WERE ABLE TO RESUME
THE FOLLIES WHICH HAD SO
NEARLY COST THEM THEIR
LIFE

CHAPTER 1

D-Day

The Normandy Landings – My Report to the House of Commons, June 6 – Important News from Stalin – His Telegram of June 11 – Enemy Dispositions on the Atlantic Wall – The German Warning System is Paralysed – Rundstedt's Mistake – I Visit the Beaches and Lunch with Montgomery, June 10 – Cruise in H.M.S. 'Kelvin' – General Marshall's Message – My Telegrams to Stalin and Roosevelt, June 14.

Our long months of preparation and planning for the greatest amphibious operation in history ended on D-Day, June 6, 1944. During the preceding night the great armadas of convoys and their escorts sailed, unknown to the enemy, along the swept channels from the Isle of Wight to the Normandy coast. Heavy bombers of the Royal Air Force attacked enemy coast-defence guns in their concrete emplacements, dropping 5,200 tons of bombs. When dawn broke the United States Air Force came on the scene to deal with other shore defences, followed by medium and fighter-bombers. In the twenty-four hours of June 6 the Allies flew over 14,600 sorties. So great was our superiority in the air that all the enemy could put up during daylight over the invasion beaches was a mere hundred sorties. From midnight three airborne divisions were alighting, the British 6th Airborne Division north-east of Caen to seize bridgeheads over the river between the town and the sea, and two American airborne divisions north of Carentan to assist the seaborne assault on the beaches and to check the movement of enemy reserves into the Cotentin peninsula. Although in places the airborne divisions were more widely scattered than had been intended, the object was in every case achieved.

As dawn came and the ships, great and small, began to file into their prearranged positions for the assault the scene might almost have been a review. Immediate opposition was limited to an attack by torpedo-boats, which sank a Norwegian destroyer. Even when the naval bombardment began the reply from the coastal batteries was desultory and ineffective. There was no doubt that we had achieved a tactical surprise. Landing and support craft with infantry, with tanks, with self-propelled artillery, and a great variety of weapons, and engineer demolition teams to deal with the beach obstacles, all formed up into groups and moved towards the beaches. Among them were the D.D. ('swimming') tanks, which made their first large-scale appearance in battle. It was still very rough from the bad weather of the day before, and a good many of the 'swimming' tanks foundered on the way.

Destroyers and gun and rocket batteries mounted on landing-craft pounded the beach defences, while farther to seaward battleships and cruisers kept down the fire of the defending batteries. Ground opposition was slight until the first landing-craft were a mile from the shore, but then mortar and machine-gun fire grew. Surf and the partly submerged obstacles and mines made the landings hazardous, and many craft were wrecked after setting down their troops, but the advance went on.

As soon as the foremost infantry got ashore they dashed forward towards their objectives, and in every case except one made good progress. On 'Omaha' beach, north-west of Bayeux, the Vth American Corps ran into severe resistance. By an unlucky chance the enemy defences in this sector had recently been taken over by a German division in full strength and on the alert. Our Allies had a very stiff fight all day to make any lodgment at all, and it was not until the 7th that, after losing several thousand men, they were able to force their way inland. Although we did not gain all we sought, and in particular Caen remained firmly in enemy hands, the progress made on the first two days of the assault was judged very satisfactory.

From the Biscay ports a stream of U-boats, facing all risks and moving on the surface at high speed, sought to break up the invasion. We were well prepared. The western approaches to the Channel were guarded by numerous aircraft, forming our first line of defence. Behind them were the naval forces covering the landings. Meeting the full blast of our defence, the U-boats fared badly. In the first crucial four days six were sunk by air attack and a similar number damaged. They were not able to make any impression on the invasion convoys, which continued to move to their objectives with trifling loss. Thereafter they were more cautious, but no more successful.

*   *   *

At noon on June 6 I asked the House of Commons to 'take

formal cognisance of the liberation of Rome by the Allied Armies under the command of General Alexander', the news of which had been released the night before. There was intense excitement about the landings in France, which everyone knew were in progress at the moment. Nevertheless I devoted ten minutes to the campaign in Italy and in paying my tribute to the Allied Armies there. After thus keeping them on tenterhooks for a little I said:

I have also to announce to the House that during the night and the early hours of this morning the first of the series of landings in force upon the European continent has taken place. In this case the liberating assault fell upon the coast of France. An immense armada of upwards of 4,000 ships, to-gether with several thousand smaller craft, crossed the Channel. Massed airborne landings have been successfully effected behind the enemy lines, and landings on the beaches are proceeding at various points at the present time. The fire of the shore batteries has been largely quelled. The obstacles that were constructed in the sea have not proved so difficult as was apprehended. The Anglo-American Allies are sustained by about 11,000 first-line aircraft, which can be drawn upon as may be needed for the purposes of the battle. I cannot of course commit myself to any particular details. Reports are coming in in rapid succession. So far the commanders who are engaged report that everything is proceeding according to plan. And what a plan! This vast operation is undoubtedly the most complicated and difficult that has ever taken place. It involves tides, winds, waves, visibility, both from the air and the sea standpoint, and the combined employment of land, air, and sea forces in the highest degree of intimacy and in contact with conditions which could not and cannot be fully foreseen.

There are already hopes that actual tactical surprise has been attained, and we hope to furnish the enemy with a suc-cession of surprises during the course of the fighting. The battle that has now begun will grow constantly in scale and in intensity for many weeks to come, and I shall not attempt to speculate upon its course. This I may say however. Complete unity prevails through the Allied Armies. There is a brother-hood in arms between us and our friends of the United States. There is complete confidence in the Supreme Commander, General Eisenhower, and his lieutenants, and also in the com-mander of the Expeditionary Force, General Montgomery. The ardour and spirit of the troops, as I saw myself, embark-ing in these last few days was splendid to witness. Nothing that equipment, science, or forethought could do has been neglected, and the whole process of opening this great new front will be pursued with the utmost resolution both by the commanders and by the United States and British Governments whom they serve.

By the afternoon I felt justified in reporting to Stalin.

6 June 44

Everything has started well. The mines, obstacles, and land batteries have been largely overcome. The air landings were very successful, and on a large scale. Infantry landings are proceeding rapidly, and many tanks and self-propelled guns are already ashore. Weather outlook moderate to good.

His answer was prompt, and contained welcome news of highest importance.

Marshal Stalin to Prime Minister   6 June 44

I have received your communication about the success of the beginning of the 'Overlord' operations. It gives joy to us all and hope of further successes.

The summer offensive of the Soviet forces, organised in accordance with the agreement at the Teheran Conference, will begin towards the middle of June on one of the important sectors of the front. The general offensive of the Soviet forces will develop by stages by means of the successive bringing of armies into offensive operations. At the end of June and during July offensive operations will become a general offensive of the Soviet forces.

I shall not fail to inform you in due course of the progress of the offensive operations.

I was actually sending Stalin a fuller account of our progress when his telegram arrived.

Prime Minister to Marshal Stalin   7 June 44

I am well satisfied with the situation up to noon to-day, 7th. Only at one American beach has there been serious difficulty, and that has now been cleared up. 20,000 airborne troops are safely landed behind the flanks of the enemy's lines, and have made contact in each case with the American and British seaborne forces. We got across with small losses. We had expected to lose about 10,000 men. By to-night we hope to have the best part of a quarter of a million men ashore, including a considerable quantity of armour (tanks), all landed from special ships or swimming ashore by themselves. In this latter class of tanks there have been a good many casualties, especially on the American front, owing to the waves overturning the swimming tanks. We must now expect heavy counter-attacks, but we expect to be stronger in armour, and of course overwhelming in the air whenever the clouds lift.

2. There was a tank engagement of our newly landed armour with fifty enemy tanks of the 21st Panzer-Grenadier Division late last night towards Caen, as the result of which the enemy quitted the field. The British 7th Armoured Division is now going in, and should give us superiority for a few days. The question is, how many can they bring against us in the next week? The weather outlook in the Channel does not seem to impose any prohibition on our continued landings. Indeed, it seems more promising than before. All the commanders are satisfied that in the actual landing things have gone better than we expected.

3. Most especially secret. We are planning to construct very quickly two large synthetic harbours on the beaches of this wide, sandy bay of the Seine estuary. Nothing like these has ever been seen before. Great ocean liners will be able to discharge and run by numerous piers supplies to the fighting troops. This must be quite unexpected by the enemy, and will enable the build-up to proceed with very great independence of weather conditions. We hope to get Cherbourg at an early point in the operations.

4. On the other hand, the enemy will concentrate rapidly and heavily and the fighting will be continuous and increasing in scale. Still, we hope to have by D plus 30 about twenty-five divisions deployed, with all their corps troops, with both flanks of the second front resting on the sea and possessed of at least three good harbours—Cherbourg and the two synthetic harbours. This front will be constantly nourished and expanded, and we hope to include later the Brest peninsula. But all this waits on the hazards of war, which, Marshal Stalin, you know so well.

5. We hope that this successful landing and the victory of Rome, of which the fruits have still to be gathered from the cut-off Hun divisions, will cheer your valiant soldiers after all the weight they have had to bear, which no one outside your country has felt more definitely than I.

6. Since dictating the above I have received your message about the successful beginning of 'Overlord', in which you speak of the summer offensive of the Soviet forces. I thank you cordially for this. I hope you will observe that we have never asked you a single question, because of our full confidence in you, your nation, and your armies.

He replied:

9 June 44

I have received your message of June 7 with the information of the successful development of the operation 'Overlord'. We all greet you and the valiant British and American Armies and warmly wish you further successes.

The preparation of the summer offensive of the Soviet armies is concluding. To-morrow, June 10, the first stage will open in our summer offensive on the Leningrad front.

I repeated this at once to Roosevelt.
Stalin telegraphed again on June 11:

As is evident, the landing, conceived on a grandiose scale has succeeded completely. My colleagues and I cannot but admit that the history of warfare knows no other like undertaking from the point of view of its scale, its vast conception, and its masterly execution. As is well known, Napoleon in his time failed ignominiously in his plan to force the Channel. The hysterical Hitler, who boasted for two years that he would effect a forcing of the Channel, was unable to make up his mind even to hint at attempting to carry out his threat. Only our Allies have succeeded in realising with honour the grandiose plan of the forcing of the Channel. History will record this deed as an achievement of the highest order.

The word 'grandiose' is the translation from the Russian text which was given me. I think 'majestic' was probably what Stalin meant. At any rate, harmony was complete.

*   *   *

Let us survey the enemy's dispositions and plans as we now know them. Marshal Rundstedt, with sixty divisions, was in command of the whole Atlantic Wall, from the Low Countries to the Bay of Biscay, and from Marseilles along the southern French shore. Under him Rommel held the coast from Holland to the Loire. His Fifteenth Army with nineteen divisions held the sector about Calais and Boulogne, and his Seventh Army had nine infantry and one Panzer division at hand in Normandy. The ten Panzer divisions on the whole Western Front were spreadeagled from Belgium to Bordeaux. How strange that the Germans, now on the defensive, made the same mistake as the French in 1940 and dispersed their most powerful weapon of counter-attack !

When Rommel took up his command in late January he had been displeased with the defences he found, and his energy improved them greatly. Along the coast there was a line of concrete works with all-round defence, many mines and difficult obstacles of various patterns, especially below high-water mark. Fixed guns pointed seawards, and field artillery covered the beaches. While there was no complete second line of defence, villages in rear were strongly fortified. Rommel was not content with the progress made, and had more time been left him our task would have been harder. Our opening bombardment by sea and air did not destroy many of the concrete works, but by stunning their defenders reduced their fire and also upset their Radar.

The German warning system had been completely paralysed. From Calais to Guernsey the Germans had no fewer than one hundred and twenty major pieces of Radar equipment for finding our convoys and directing the fire of their shore batteries. These were grouped in forty-seven stations. We discovered them all, and attacked them so successfully with rocket-firing aircraft that on the night before D-Day not one in six was working. The serviceable ones were deceived by the device of tin-foil strips known as 'Window',* which simulated a convoy heading east of Fécamp, and they thus failed to detect the real landings. One piece of equipment near Caen managed to keep going and discovered the approach of the British force, but its reports were ignored by the plotting centre as they were not corroborated by any of the other stations. Nor was this the only menace which was overcome. Encouraged by their success two years before in concealing the passage up the Channel of the *Scharnhorst* and *Gneisenau*, the enemy had built many more jamming stations for thwarting both the ships which directed our night fighters and the Radar beams upon which many of our forces depended for an accurate landfall. But they too were discovered, and Bomber Command made some highly concentrated raids upon them. All were obliterated, and our radio and Radar aids were secure. It may be mentioned that all the Allied effort in the radio war for D-Day was British.

It is indeed remarkable that the vast, long-planned assault fell on the enemy as a surprise both in time and place. The German High Command was told that the weather would be too rough that day for amphibious operations, and had received no recent air reports of the assembly of our thousands of ships along the English shore. Early on June 5 Rommel left his

* See Books 7, Chapter 16, and 10, Chapter 12.

headquarters to visit Hitler at Berchtesgaden, and was in Germany when the blow fell. There had been much argument about which front the Allies would attack. Rundstedt had consistently believed that our main blow would be launched across the Straits of Dover, as that was the shortest sea route and gave the best access to the heart of Germany. Rommel for long agreed with him. Hitler and his staff however appear to have had reports indicating that Normandy would be the principal battleground.* Even after we had landed uncertainties continued. Hitler lost a whole critical day in making up his mind to release the two nearest Panzer divisions to reinforce the front. The German Intelligence Service grossly overestimated the number of divisions and the amount of suitable shipping available in England. On their showing there were ample resources for a second big landing, so Normandy might be only a preliminary and subsidiary one. On June 19 Rommel reported to von Rundstedt, '. . . a large-scale landing is to be expected on the Channel front on both sides of Cap Gris Nez or between the Somme and Le Havre,'† and he repeated the warning a week later. Thus it was not until the third week in July, six weeks after D-Day, that reserves from the Fifteenth Army were sent south from the Pas de Calais to join the battle. Our deception measures both before and after D-Day had aimed at creating this confused thinking. Their success was admirable and had far-reaching results on the battle.

* * *

On June 10 General Montgomery reported that he was sufficiently established ashore to receive a visit. I therefore set off in my train to Portsmouth, with Smuts, Brooke, General Marshall, and Admiral King. All three American Chiefs of Staff had flown to the United Kingdom on June 8 in case any vital military decision had to be taken at short notice. A British and an American destroyer awaited us. Smuts, Brooke, and I embarked in the former, and General Marshall and Admiral King, with their staffs, in the latter, and we crossed the Channel without incident to our respective fronts. Montgomery, smiling and confident, met me at the beach as we scrambled out of our landing-craft. His army had already penetrated seven or eight miles inland. There was very little firing or activity. The weather

---

* Blumentritt, *Von Rundstedt*, pp. 218, 219.
† Chester Wilmot, *The Struggle for Europe*, p. 318.

was brilliant. We drove through our limited but fertile domain in Normandy. It was pleasant to see the prosperity of the countryside. The fields were full of lovely red and white cows basking or parading in the sunshine. The inhabitants seemed quite buoyant and well nourished and waved enthusiastically. Montgomery's headquarters, about five miles inland, were in a château with lawns and lakes around it. We lunched in a tent looking towards the enemy. The General was in the highest spirits. I asked him how far away was the actual front. He said about three miles. I asked him if he had a continuous line. He said, 'No.' 'What is there then to prevent an incursion of German armour breaking up our luncheon?' He said he did not think they would come. The staff told me the château had been heavily bombed the night before, and certainly there were a good many craters around it. I told him he was taking too much of a risk if he made a habit of such proceedings. Anything can be done once or for a short time, but custom, repetition, prolongation, is always to be avoided when possible in war. He did in fact move two days later, though not till he and his staff had had another dose.

It continued fine, and apart from occasional air alarms and anti-aircraft fire there seemed to be no fighting. We made a considerable inspection of our limited bridgehead. I was particularly interested to see the local ports of Port-en-Bessin, Courseulles, and Ouistreham. We had not counted much on these little harbours in any of the plans we had made for the great descent. They proved a most valuable acquisition, and soon were discharging about two thousand tons a day. I dwelt on these agreeable facts as we drove or walked round our interesting but severely restricted conquest.

Smuts, Brooke, and I went home in the destroyer *Kelvin*. Admiral Vian, who now commanded all the flotillas and light craft protecting the Arromanches harbour, was on board. He proposed that we should go and watch the bombardment of the German position by the battleships and cruisers protecting the British left flank. Accordingly we passed between the two battleships, which were firing at twenty thousand yards, and through the cruiser squadron, firing at about fourteen thousand yards, and soon we were within seven or eight thousand yards of the shore, which was thickly wooded. The bombardment was leisurely and continuous, but there was no reply from the enemy. As we were about to turn I said to Vian, 'Since we are so near, why shouldn't we have a plug at them ourselves before we go home?' He said, 'Certainly,' and in a minute or two all our guns fired on the silent coast. We were of course well within the range of their artillery, and the moment we had fired Vian made the destroyer turn about and depart at the highest speed. We were soon out of danger and passed through the cruiser and battleship lines. This is the only time I have ever been on board a naval vessel when she fired 'in anger'—if it can be so called. I admired the Admiral's sporting spirit. Smuts too was delighted. I slept soundly on the four-hour voyage to Portsmouth. Altogether it had been a most interesting and enjoyable day.

*   *   *

At our train we found the three American Chiefs of Staff. They were highly pleased with all they had seen on the American beaches, and full of confidence in the execution of our long-cherished design. We dined together in a happy mood. During the dinner I noticed General Marshall writing industriously, and presently he handed me a message he had written to Admiral Mountbatten, which he suggested we should all sign.

10 June 44

To-day we visited the British and American armies on the soil of France. We sailed through vast fleets of ships, with landing-craft of many types pouring more and more men, vehicles, and stores ashore. We saw clearly the manœuvre in process of rapid development. We have shared our secrets in common and helped each other all we could. We wish to tell you at this moment in your arduous campaign that we realise that much of this remarkable technique, and therefore the success of the venture, has its origin in developments effected by you and your staff of Combined Operations.

ARNOLD, BROOKE, CHURCHILL, KING,
MARSHALL, SMUTS

Mountbatten must indeed have valued this tribute. The vast, intricate operation, with all its novel and ingenious devices, could not have been achieved without the devoted efforts of the staff of Combined Operations, the organisation which had been created in 1940 under Admiral Keyes, and had been carried by his successor to full fruition.

*   *   *

When time permitted I reported again to my two great companions.

Prime Minister to Marshal Stalin   14 June 44

I visited the British sector of the front on Monday, as you may have seen from the newspapers. The fighting is continuous, and at that time we had fourteen divisions operating on a front of about seventy miles. Against this the enemy have thirteen divisions, not nearly so strong as ours. Reinforcements are hurrying up from their rear, but we think we can pour them in much quicker from the sea. It is a wonderful sight to see this city of ships stretching along the coast for nearly fifty miles and apparently secure from the air and the U-boats which are so near. We hope to encircle Caen, and perhaps to make a capture there of prisoners. Two days ago the number of prisoners was 13,000, which is more than all the killed and wounded we had lost up to that time. Therefore it may be said that the enemy have lost nearly double what we have, although we have been continuously on the offensive. During yesterday the advances were quite good, though the enemy resistance is stiffening as his strategic reserves are thrown into the battle. I should think it quite likely that we should work up to a battle of about a million a side, lasting through June and July. We plan to have about two million there by mid-August.

Every good wish for your successes in Karelia.

To the President I wrote on the same day about various questions, including the visit of de Gaulle to France, which I had arranged without consulting Roosevelt beforehand. I added:

I had a jolly day on Monday on the beaches and inland. There is a great mass of shipping extended more than fifty miles along the coast. It is being increasingly protected against weather by the artificial harbours, nearly every element of which has been a success, and will soon have effective shelter against bad weather. The power of our air and of our anti-U-boat forces seems to ensure it a very great measure of protection. After doing much laborious duty we went and had a plug at the Hun from our destroyer, but although the range was 6,000 yards he did not honour us with a reply.

Marshall and King came back in my train. They were greatly reassured by all they saw on the American side, and Marshall wrote out a charming telegram to Mountbatten, saying how many of these new craft had been produced under his organisation and what a help they had been. You used the word 'stupendous' in one of your early telegrams to me. I must admit that what I saw could only be described by that word, and I think your officers would agree as well. The marvellous efficiency of the transportation exceeds anything that has ever been known in war. A great deal more has to be done, and I think more troops are needed. We are working up to a battle which may well be a million a side. The Chiefs of Staff are searching about for the best solution of these problems as between the Mediterranean and 'Overlord'.

How I wish you were here!

Normandy to Paris

Once ashore the first need of the Allies was to consolidate the immediate defence of their beaches and form a continuous front by expanding from them. The enemy fought stubbornly and were not easily overcome. In the American sector the marshes near Carentan and at the mouth of the river Vire hampered our movements, and everywhere the country was suited to infantry defence. The *bocage* which covers much of Normandy consists of a multitude of small fields divided by banks, with ditches and very high hedges. Artillery support for an attack is thus hindered by lack of good observation and it was extremely difficult to use tanks. It was infantry fighting all the way, with every little field a potential strong-point. Nevertheless good progress was made, except for the failure to capture Caen.

This small but famous town was to be the scene of bitter struggles over many days. To us it was important, because, apart from the fact that there was good ground to the east for constructing air-strips, it was the hinge on which our whole plan turned. Montgomery's intention was to make a great left wheel by the American forces, with Caen as their left-hand pivot. It was equally important for the Germans. If their lines were pierced there the whole of their Seventh Army would be forced south-eastwards towards the Loire, opening a gap between it and the Fifteenth Army in the north. The way to Paris would then be open. Thus in the following weeks Caen became the scene of ceaseless attacks and the most stubborn defence, drawing towards it a great part of the German divisions, and especially their armour. This was a help as well as a hindrance.

The Germans, though the reserve divisions of their Fifteenth Army were still held intact north of the Seine, had of course been reinforced from elsewhere, and by June 12 twelve divisions were in action, four of them Panzers. This was less than we had expected. The tremendous air offensive had hampered all the enemy's communications. Every bridge across the Seine below Paris and the principal bridges across the river Loire were by now destroyed. Most of the reinforcing troops had to use the roads and railways running through the gap between Paris and Orleans, and were subjected to continuous and damaging attacks by day and night from our air forces. A German report of July 8 said, 'From Paris to the west and south-west all rail communications are broken.' Not only were the enemy unable to reinforce quickly, but their divisions arrived piecemeal, short of equipment, and fatigued by long night marches, and they were thrown into the line as they came. The German command had no chance to form a striking force behind the battle for a powerful, well-concerted counter-offensive.

By June 11 the Allies had formed a continuous front inland, and our fighters were operating from half a dozen forward airstrips. The next task was to secure a lodgment area big enough to hold sufficient forces for the decisive break-out. The Americans thrust westward across the Cherbourg peninsula towards Barneville, on the western coast, which they reached on June 17. Simultaneously they advanced northwards, and after sharp fighting stood before the outer defences of Cherbourg on the 22nd. The enemy resisted stoutly till the 26th in order to carry out demolitions. These were so thorough that heavy loads could not be brought in through the port till the end of August.

*　　*　　*

Beyond the battlefield other events influenced the future. On the night of June 12–13 the first flying bombs fell on London. They were launched in Northern France from places remote from our landed armies. Their early conquest would bring relief to our civil population, once again under bombardment. Part of the Strategic Air Force renewed attacks on these sites, but there could of course be no question of distorting the land battle on this account. As I said in Parliament, the people at home could feel they were sharing the perils of their soldiers.

On June 17, at Margival, near Soissons, Hitler held a conference with Rundstedt and Rommel. His two generals pressed on him strongly the folly of bleeding the German Army to death in Normandy. They urged that before it was destroyed the Seventh Army should make an orderly withdrawal towards the Seine, where, together with the Fifteenth Army, it could fight a defensive but mobile battle with at least some hope of success. But Hitler would not agree. Here, as in Russia and Italy, he demanded that no ground should be given up and all should fight where they stood. The generals were of course right. Hitler's method of fighting to the death at once on all fronts lacked the important element of selection.

In the battle area along the coast our consolidation was making headway. Bombarding ships of all types, including battleships, continued to support the armies on shore, particularly in the eastern sector, where the enemy concentrated the bulk of his armour and where his batteries were most troublesome. U-boats and light surface vessels tried to attack, though with little success, but sea mines, which were mostly laid by aircraft, took a serious toll of Allied shipping and delayed our build-up. Attacks from enemy bases to the eastward, particularly from Havre, were warded off, and in the west an Allied naval bombarding squadron later co-operated with the American Army in the capture of Cherbourg. Across the beaches progress was good. In the first six days 326,000 men, 54,000 vehicles, and 104,000 tons of stores were landed. In spite of serious losses among landing-craft an immense supply organisation was rapidly taking shape. An average of more than two hundred vessels and craft of all types was arriving daily with supplies. The gigantic problem of handling such a volume of shipping was aggravated by bad weather. Nevertheless remarkable progress was made. The Merchant Navy played an outstanding part. Their seamen cheerfully accepted all the risks of war and weather, and their staunchness and fidelity played an impressive part in the vast enterprise.

By June 19 the two 'Mulberry' harbours, one at Arromanches, the other ten miles farther west, in the American sector, were making good progress. The submarine pipe-lines ('Pluto') were to come into action later, but meanwhile Port-en-Bessin was being developed as the main supply port for petrol.* But then a four-day gale began which almost entirely prevented the landing of men and material, and did great damage to the newly sunk breakwaters. Many floating bombardons which were not designed for such conditions broke from their moorings and crashed into other breakwaters and the anchored shipping. The harbour in the American sector was ruined, and its serviceable parts were used to repair Arromanches. This gale, the like of which had not been known in June for forty years, was a severe misfortune. We were already behind our programme of unloading. The break-out was equally delayed, and on June 23 we stood only on the line we had prescribed for the 11th.

*   *   *

The Soviet offensive had now begun, and I kept Stalin constantly informed of our fortunes.

Prime Minister to Marshal Stalin   25 June 44
We now rejoice in the opening results of your immense operations, and will not cease by every human means to broaden our fronts engaged with the enemy and to have the fighting kept at the utmost intensity.

2. The Americans hope to take Cherbourg in a few days. The fall of Cherbourg will soon set three American divisions free to reinforce our attack southwards, and it may be 25,000 prisoners will fall into our hands at Cherbourg.

3. We have had three or four days of gale—most unusual in June—which has delayed the build-up and done much injury to our synthetic harbours in their incomplete condition. We have provided the means to repair and strengthen them. The roads leading inland from the two synthetic harbours are being made with great speed by bulldozers and steel networks unrolled. Thus, with Cherbourg, a large base will be established from which very considerable armies can be operated irrespective of weather.

* The 'Pluto' project included first the laying of pipe-lines in the assault area through which seagoing tankers could discharge petrol direct to the shore. Submarine pipe-lines across the Channel were laid later from the Isle of Wight to Cherbourg and from Dungeness to Boulogne.

4. We have had bitter fighting on the British front, where four out of the five Panzer divisions are engaged. The new British onslaught there has been delayed a few days by the bad weather, which delayed the completion of several divisions. The attack will begin to-morrow.

5. The advance in Italy goes forward with great rapidity, and we hope to be in possession of Florence in June and in contact with the Pisa–Rimini line by the middle or end of July. I shall send you a telegram presently about the various strategic possibilities which are open in this quarter. The overriding principle which, in my opinion, we should follow is the continuous engagement of the largest possible number of Hitlerites on the broadest and most effective fronts. It is only by hard fighting that we can take some of the weight off you.

6. You may safely disregard all the German rubbish about the results of their flying bomb. It has had no appreciable effect upon the production or life of London. Casualties during the seven days it has been used are between ten and eleven thousand. The streets and parks remain full of people enjoying the sunshine when off work or duty. Parliament debates continually throughout the alarms. The rocket development may be more formidable when it comes. The people are proud to share in a small way the perils of our own soldiers and of your soldiers, who are so highly admired in Britain. May all good fortune attend your new onfall.

Stalin sent me his congratulations on the fall of Cherbourg, and gave further information about his own gigantic operation.

Marshal Stalin to Prime Minister   27 June 44
The Allied forces have liberated Cherbourg, thus crowning their efforts in Normandy wi'h another great victory. I greet the increasing successes of the brave British and American forces, who have developed their operations both in Northern France and Italy.

If the scale of military operations in Northern France is becoming increasingly powerful and dangerous for Hitler, the successful development of the Allies' offensive in Italy is also worthy of every attention and applause. We wish you new successes.

Concerning our offensive, it can be said that we shall not give the Germans a breathing-space, but shall continue to widen the front of our offensive operations by increasing the strength of our onslaught against the German armies. You will of course agree with me that this is indispensable for our common cause.

As regards the Hitlerite flying bombs, this expedient, it is clear, can have no serious importance either for operations in Normandy or for the population of London, whose bravery is known to all.

I replied:

Prime Minister to Marshal Stalin   1 July 44

This is the moment for me to tell you how immensely we are all here impressed with the magnificent advances of the Russian armies, which seem, as they grow in momentum, to be pulverising the German armies which stand between you and Warsaw, and afterwards Berlin. Every victory that you gain is watched with eager attention here. I realise vividly that all this is the second round you have fought since Teheran, the first of which regained Sebastopol, Odessa, and the Crimea and carried your vanguards to the Carpathians, Sereth, and Pruth.

The battle is hot in Normandy. The June weather has been tiresome. Not only did we have a gale on the beaches worse than any in the summer-time records of many years, but there has been a great deal of cloud. This denies us the full use of our overwhelming air superiority, and also helps the flying bombs to get through to London. However, I hope that July will show an improvement. Meanwhile the hard fighting goes in our favour, and although eight Panzer divisions are in action against the British sector we still have a good majority of tanks. We have well over three-quarters of a million British and Americans ashore, half and half. The enemy is burning and bleeding on every front at once, and I agree with you that this must go on to the end.

*   *   *

In the last week of June the British established a bridgehead across the river Odon south of Caen. Efforts to extend it southward and eastward across the river Orne were repelled. The southern sector of the British front was twice attacked by several Panzer divisions. In violent conflicts the Germans were severely defeated, with heavy losses from our air and powerful artillery.* It was now our turn to strike, and on July 8 a strong attack on Caen was launched from the north and north-west. The first of the tactical bombardments by Allied heavy bombers, which henceforward were a marked feature, prepared the way. Royal Air Force heavy bombers dropped more than 2,000 tons

* These attacks were the result of Hitler's instructions at the Soissons conference. On July 1 Keitel telephoned Rundstedt and asked, 'What shall we do?' Rundstedt answered, 'Make peace, you idiots. What else can you do?'

on the German defences, and at dawn British infantry, hampered
unavoidably by the bomb-craters and the rubble of fallen buildings, made good progress. By July 10 all of Caen on our side of
the river was gained and I could say to Montgomery, 'Many
congratulations on your capture of Caen.' He replied:

General Montgomery to Prime Minister   **11 July 44**
Thank you for your message. We wanted Caen badly. We
used a great weight of air-power to ensure quick success, and
the whole battle area leading up to Caen is a scene of great
destruction. The town itself also suffered heavily. All to-day
the 9th and 10th Panzer Divisions have been attacking furi-
ously to retake Pt. 112, to the [north-east] of Évrecy, and another division has been assaulting the 30th U.S. Division to
the north-west of St. Lô. Very heavy losses have been inflicted
on all three divisions, and the more they will attack us in this
way the better. All goes well.

Smuts, who had now returned to South Africa, sent a pres-
cient and suggestive telegram.

      10 July 44
In view of the spectacular Russian advance, and of the capture of Caen, which forms a welcome pendant, the Germans
cannot, as things are now developing, face both fronts. They
will soon have to decide whether to throw their main weight
against the attack from the east or that from the west. *Knowing what to expect from a Russian invasion, it is likely that
they will decide for concentrating on the Russian front. This
will help to ease our task in the west.**
Having broken through at Caen, it is essential that we should
maintain the initiative and offensive without pause, and that
we should advance to the rear of the German flying bomb
bases as soon as possible.
I must express my regret at the decision affecting Alexander's
advance.† Considering however your success in coping with
similar obstructions in the past, I continue to hope that in the
end your strategy will again prove successful, backed as it is
by every sound military as well as political consideration.

Stalin, who followed our fortunes with daily attention, also
sent his 'congratulations on the occasion of the splendid new
victory of the British forces in the liberation of the town of
Caen'.

* Author's italics.
† The decision to make a landing in Southern France.

North-West Europe

By the middle of July thirty Allied divisions were ashore. Half
are American and half British and Canadian. Against these the
ermans had gathered twenty-seven divisions. But they had
ready suffered 160,000 casualties, and General Eisenhower
stimated their fighting value as no higher than sixteen
visions.

An important event now occurred. On July 17 Rommel was
verely wounded. His car was attacked by our low-flying
ghters, and he was carried to hospital in what was thought a
ing condition. He made a wonderful recovery, in time to meet
s death later on at Hitler's orders. In early July Rundstedt was
placed in the overall command of the Western Front by von
luge, a general who had won distinction in Russia.

* * *

Montgomery's general offensive, planned for July 18, now
proached. 'God with you,' I said. He replied:

17 July 44
Thank you for your message. General conditions for big
attack to-morrow now very favourable, as main enemy weight
has moved to west of Orne, as was intended, to oppose my
attacks in Évrecy area, and these attacks will be continued to-
day and to-night.
For complete success to-morrow good flying weather
essential. Am determined to loose the armoured divisions to-
morrow if in any way possible, and will delay zero hour up to
3 p.m. if necessary.

The British Army attacked with three corps, with the aim of
larging their bridgeheads and carrying them well beyond the
ver Orne. The operation was preceded by an even greater
mbardment by the Allied air. The German Air Force was
tally prevented from interfering. Good progress was made to
e east of Caen, until clouded skies began to hamper our planes
d led to a week's delay in launching the break-out from the
merican sector. I thought this was an opportunity to visit
erbourg and to spend a few days in the 'Mulberry' harbour.
n the 20th I flew direct in an American Army Dakota to
eir landing-ground on the Cherbourg peninsula, and was taken
round the harbour by the United States commander. Here I
w for the first time a flying bomb launching-point. It was a
ry elaborate affair. I was shocked at the damage the Germans

had done to the town, and shared the staff disappointment at th
inevitable delay in getting the port to work. The basins of th
harbour were thickly sown with contact mines. A handful o
devoted British divers were at work day and night disconnectin
these at their mortal peril. Warm tributes were paid to them b
their American comrades. After a long and dangerous drive t
the United States beach-head known as Utah Beach I wer
aboard a British motor torpedo-boat, and thence had a roug
passage to Arromanches. As one gets older sea-sickness retreat
I did not succumb, but slept soundly till we were in the cal
waters of our synthetic lagoon. I went aboard the cruiser *Enter
prise*, where I remained for three days, making myse
thoroughly acquainted with the whole working of the harbou
on which all the armies now almost entirely depended, and a
the same time transacting my London business.

The nights were very noisy, there being repeated raids b
single aircraft, and more numerous alarms. By day I studied th
whole process of the landing of supplies and troops, both at th
piers, in which I had so long been interested, and on the beache
On one occasion six tank landing-craft came to the beach i
line. When their prows grounded their drawbridges fell forwar
and out came the tanks, three or four from each, and splashe
ashore. In less than eight minutes by my stop-watch the tank
stood in column of route on the highroad ready to move int
action. This was an impressive performance, and typical of th
rate of discharge which had now been achieved. I was fascinate
to see the D.U.K.W.s swimming through the harbour, waddlin
ashore, and then hurrying up the hill to the great dump whe
the lorries were waiting to take their supplies to the vario
units. Upon the wonderful efficiency of this system, now yieldir
results far greater than we had ever planned, depended the hop
of a speedy and victorious action.

On the first night when I visited the wardroom the office
were singing songs. At the end they sang the chorus of 'Ru
Britannia'. I asked them what were the words. Nobody kne
them. So I recited some of Thomson's noble lines myself, an
for the benefit and the instruction of the reader (if he nee
any) I reprint them here:

> The nations not so blest as thee
>   Must in their turn to tyrants fall:
> While thou shalt flourish great and free,
>   The dread and envy of them all.

The Muses still, with freedom found,
   Shall to thy happy coasts repair ;
Blest isle, with matchless beauty crowned,
   And manly hearts to guard the fair.

*   *   *

On my last day at Arromanches I visited Montgomery's headquarters, a few miles inland. The Commander-in-Chief was in the best of spirits on the eve of his largest operation, which he explained to me in all detail. He took me into the ruins of Caen and across the river, and we also visited other parts of the British front. Then he placed at my disposal his captured Storch aeroplane, and the Air Commander himself piloted me all over the British positions. This aircraft could land at a pinch almost anywhere, and consequently one could fly at a few hundred feet from the ground, gaining a far better view and knowledge of the scene than by any other method. I also visited several of the air stations, and said a few words to gatherings of officers and men. Finally I went to the field hospital, where, though it was a quiet day, a trickle of casualties was coming in. One poor man was to have a serious operation, and was actually on the table about to take the anæsthetic. I was slipping away when he said he wanted me. He smiled wanly and kissed my hand. I was deeply moved, and very glad to learn later on that the operation had been entirely successful.

I flew back home that evening, July 23, and arrived before dark. To Captain Hickling, the naval officer in charge of Arromanches, I paid the tribute that was due.

25 July 44

I send you and all under your command my warmest congratulations on the splendid work that has been done at Arromanches. This miraculous port has played, and will continue to play, a most important part in the liberation of Europe. I hope to pay you another visit before long.

The above message should be promulgated to all concerned, in such a way that it does not become known to the enemy, who are as yet ignorant of the capacity and potentialities of Arromanches.

They wanted to call the harbour 'Port Churchill'. But this for various reasons I forbade.

*   *   *

At this time the orders which had held the German Fifteenth Army behind the Seine were cancelled, and several fresh divisions were sent to reinforce the hard-pressed Seventh Army. Their transference, by rail or road, or across the Seine by the ferry system which had replaced the broken bridges, was greatly delayed and injured by our air forces. The long-withheld aid reached the field too late to turn the scale.

During the pause in the fighting in Normandy there took place on July 20 a renewed, unsuccessful attempt on Hitler's life. According to the most trustworthy story, Colonel von Stauffenberg had placed under Hitler's table, at a staff meeting, a small case containing a time-bomb. Hitler was spared from the full effect of the explosion by the heavy table-top and its supporting cross-pieces, and also by the light structure of the building itself, which allowed an instantaneous dispersal of the pressures. Several officers present were killed, but the Fuehrer, though badly shaken and wounded, arose exclaiming, 'Who says I am not under the special protection of God?' All the fury of his nature was aroused by this plot, and the vengeance which he inflicted on all suspected of being in it makes a terrible tale.

*   *   *

The hour of the great American break-out under General Omar Bradley came at last. On July 25 their VIIth Corps struck southwards from St. Lô, and the next day the VIIIth Corps, on their right, joined the battle. The bombardment by the United States Air Force had been devastating, and the infantry assault prospered. Then the armour leaped through and swept on to the key point of Coutances. The German escape route down that coast of Normandy was cut, and the whole German defence west of the Vire was in jeopardy and chaos. The roads were jammed with retreating troops, and the Allied bombers and fighter-bombers took a destructive toll of men and vehicles. The advance drove forward. Avranches was taken on July 31, and soon afterwards the sea corner, opening the way to the Brittany peninsula, was turned. The Canadians, under General Crerar, made a simultaneous attack from Caen down the Falaise road. This was effectively opposed by four Panzer divisions. Montgomery, who still commanded the whole battle line, thereupon transferred the weight of the British attack to the other front, and gave orders to the British Second Army, under General Dempsey, for a new thrust from Caumont to Vire. Preceded again by heavy air bombing, this started on July 30, and Vire was reached a few days later.

*   *   *

When the main American offensive began and the Canadian Corps was checked on the Falaise road some invidious comparisons were made at our expense.

Prime Minister to General Montgomery   27 July 44
It was announced from S.H.A.E.F. last night that the British had sustained 'quite a serious setback'. I am not aware of any facts that justify such a statement. It seems to me that only minor retirements of, say, a mile have taken place on the right wing of your recent attack, and that there is no justification for using such an expression. Naturally this has created a good deal of talk here. I should like to know exactly what the position is, in order to maintain confidence among wobblers or critics in high places.
2. For my own most secret information, I should like to know whether the attacks you spoke of to me, or variants of them, are going to come off. It certainly seems very important for the British Army to strike hard and win through ; otherwise there will grow comparisons between the two armies which will lead to dangerous recrimination and affect the fighting value of the Allied organisation. As you know, I have the fullest confidence in you and you may count on me.

Montgomery replied:

27 July 44
I know of no 'serious setback'. Enemy has massed great strength in area south of Caen to oppose our advance in that quarter. Very heavy fighting took place yesterday and the day before, and as a result the troops of Canadian Corps were forced back 1,000 yards from farthest positions they had reached. . . .
My policy since the beginning has been to draw the main enemy armoured strength on to my eastern flank and to fight it there, so that our affairs on western flank could proceed the easier. In this policy I have succeeded ; the main enemy armoured strength is now deployed on my eastern flank, to east of the river Odon, and my affairs in the west are proceeding the easier and the Americans are going great guns.
As regards my future plans. The enemy strength south of Caen astride the Falaise road is now very great, and greater than anywhere else on the whole Allied front. I therefore do

not intend to attack him there. Instead I am planning to keep the enemy forces tied to that area and to put in a very heavy blow with six divisions from Caumont area, where the enemy is weaker. This blow will tend to make the American progress quicker.

Montgomery's optimism was justified by events and on August 3 I telegraphed:

Prime Minister to General Montgomery   3 Aug 44
 I am delighted that the unfolding of your plan, which you explained to me, has proceeded so well. It is clear that the enemy will hold on to his eastern flank and hinge with desperate vigour. I am inclined to feel that the Brest peninsula will mop up pretty cheaply. I rejoice that our armour and forward troops have taken Vire. It looks on the map as if you ought to have several quite substantial cops. Naturally I earnestly desire to see the Second Army armour, which cannot be far short of 2,500, loose on the broad plains. In this war by-passing has become a brand-new thing on land as well as at sea. I may come to you for a day in the course of the next week, before I go to Italy. Every good wish.

General Montgomery to Prime Minister   4 Aug 44
 Thank you for your message.
 2. I fancy we will now have some heavy fighting on eastern flank, and especially on that part from Villers-Bocage to Vire which faces due east. The enemy has moved considerable strength to that part from area south and south-east of Caen.
 3. I am therefore planning to launch a heavy attack with five divisions from Caen area directed towards Falaise. Am trying to get this attack launched on August 7.
 4. I have turned only one American corps westward into Brittany, as I feel that will be enough.
 The other corps of Third United States Army will be directed on Laval and Angers. The whole weight of First United States Army will be put into the swing round the south flank of Second Army and directed against Domfront and Alençon.
 5. Delighted to welcome you here next week or at any time.

Prime Minister to General Montgomery   6 Aug 44
 I was sorry I could not reach you yesterday. If possible I will come to-morrow, Monday. Please make no special arrangements on my account or inconvenience yourself in any way. Eisenhower, with whom I spent yesterday afternoon, suggested I should also visit Bradley at his headquarters,

which I should like to do in the afternoon if you see no objection. The party would consist of self, General Hollis, and Tommy only.

Accordingly, on the 7th I went again to Montgomery's headquarters by air, and after he had given me a vivid account with his maps an American colonel arrived to take me to General Bradley. The route had been carefully planned to show me the frightful devastation of the towns and villages through which the United States troops had fought their way. All the buildings were pulverised by air bombing. We reached Bradley's headquarters about four o'clock. The General welcomed me cordially, but I could feel there was great tension, as the battle was at its height and every few minutes messages arrived. I therefore cut my visit short and motored back to my aeroplane, which awaited me. I was about to go on board when, to my surprise, Eisenhower arrived. He had flown from London to his advanced headquarters, and, hearing of my movements, intercepted me. He had not yet taken over the actual command of the army in the field from Montgomery; but he supervised everything with a vigilant eye, and no one knew better than he how to stand close to a tremendous event without impairing the authority he had delegated to others.

*   *   *

The Third United States Army, under General Patton, had now been formed and was in action. He detached two armoured and three infantry divisions for the westward and southerly drive to clear the Brittany peninsula. The cut-off enemy at once retreated towards their fortified ports. The French Resistance Movement, which here numbered 30,000 men, played a notable part, and the peninsula was quickly overrun. By the end of the first week in August the Germans, amounting to 45,000 garrison troops and remnants of four divisions, had been pressed into their defensive perimeters at St. Malo, Brest, Lorient, and St. Nazaire. Here they could be penned and left to wither, thus saving the unnecessary losses which immediate assaults would have required. The damage done to Cherbourg had been enormous, and it was certain that when the Brittany ports were captured they would take a long time to repair. The fertility of the 'Mulberry' at Arromanches, the sheltered anchorages, and the unforeseen development of smaller harbours on the Normandy coast had lessened the urgency of capturing the Brittany

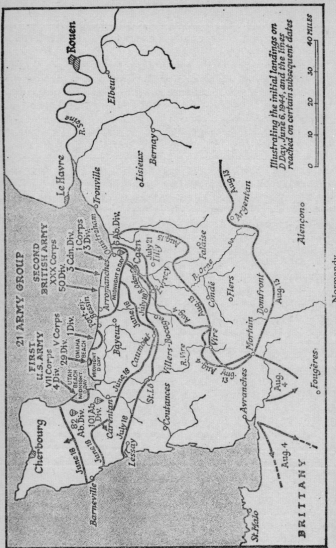

Normandy

ports, which had been so prominent in our early plans. More-over, with things going so well we could count on gaining soon the far better French ports from Havre to the north. Brest, however, which held a large garrison, under an active com-mander, was dangerous, and had to be eliminated. It surrendered on September 19 to violent attacks by three U.S. divisions.

* * *

While Brittany was thus being cleared or cooped the rest of Patton's Third Army drove eastward in the 'long hook' which was to carry them to the gap between the Loire and Paris and down the Seine towards Rouen. The town of Laval was entered on August 6, and Le Mans on August 9. Few Germans were found in all this wide region, and the main difficulty was supply-ing the advancing Americans over long and ever-lengthening distances. Except for a limited air-lift, everything had still to come from the beaches of the original landing and pass down the western side of Normandy through Avranches to reach the front. Avranches therefore became the bottle-neck, and offered a tempting opportunity for a German attack striking westward from the neighbourhood of Falaise. The idea caught Hitler's fancy, and he gave orders for the maximum possible force to attack Mortain, burst its way through to Avranches, and thus cut Patton's communications. The German commanders were unanimous in condemning the project. Realising that the battle for Normandy was already lost, they wished to use four divisions which had just arrived from the Fifteenth Army in the north to carry out an orderly retreat to the Seine. They thought that to throw any fresh troops westward was merely to 'stick out their necks', with the certain prospect of having them severed. Hitler insisted on having his way, and on August 7 five Panzer and two infantry divisions delivered a vehement attack on Mortain from the east.

The blow fell on a single U.S. division, but it held firm and three others came to its aid. After five days of severe fighting and concentrated bombing from the air the audacious onslaught was thrown back in confusion, and, as the enemy generals had predicted, the whole salient from Falaise to Mortain, full of German troops, was at the mercy of converging attacks from three sides. To the south of it one corps of the Third United States Army had been diverted northwards through Alençon to Argentan, which they reached on August 13. The First United

States Army, under General Hodges, thrust southwards from Vire, and the Second British Army towards Condé. The Canadian Army, supported again by heavy bombers, continued to press down the road from Caen to Falaise, and this time with greater success, for they reached their goal on August 17. The Allied air forces swept on to the crowded Germans within the long and narrow pocket, and with the artillery inflicted fearful slaughter. The Germans held stubbornly on to the jaws of the gap at Falaise and Argentan, and, giving priority to their armour, tried to extricate all that they could. But on August 17 command and control broke down and the scene became a shambles. The jaws closed on August 20, and although by then a considerable part of the enemy had been able to scramble eastwards no fewer than eight German divisions were annihilated. What had been the Falaise pocket was their grave. Von Kluge reported to Hitler: 'The enemy air superiority is terrific and smothers almost all our movements. Every movement of the enemy however is prepared and protected by his air forces. Losses in men and material are extraordinary. The morale of the troops has suffered very heavily under constant murderous enemy fire.'

*   *   *

The Third United States Army, besides clearing the Brittany peninsula and contributing with their 'short hook' to the culminating victory at Falaise, thrust three corps eastwards and north-eastwards from Le Mans. On August 17 they reached Orleans, Chartres, and Dreux. Thence they drove north-westwards down the left bank of the river to meet the British advancing on Rouen. Our Second Army had experienced some delay. They had to reorganise after the Falaise battle, and the enemy found means to improvise rearguard positions. However, the pursuit was pressed hotly, and all the Germans south of the Seine were soon seeking desperately to retreat across it, under destructive air attacks. None of the bridges destroyed by previous air bombardments had been repaired, but there were a few pontoon bridges and a fairly adequate ferry service. Very few vehicles could be saved. South of Rouen immense quantities of transport were abandoned. Such troops as escaped were in no condition to resist on the farther bank of the river.

Eisenhower, who had taken up supreme command, was determined to avoid a battle for Paris. Stalingrad and Warsaw had proved the horrors of frontal assaults and patriotic risings, and he therefore resolved to encircle the capital and force the garrison to surrender or flee. By August 20 the time for action had come. Patton had crossed the Seine near Mantes, and his right flank had reached Fontainebleau. The French Underground had revolted. The police were on strike. The Prefecture was in Patriot hands. An officer of the Resistance reached Patton's headquarters with vital reports, and on the morning of Wednesday, August 23, these were delivered to Eisenhower at Le Mans.

Attached to Patton was the French 2nd Armoured Division, under General Leclerc, which had landed in Normandy on August 1, and played an honourable part in the advance.* De Gaulle arrived the same day, and was assured by the Allied Supreme Commander that when the time came—and as had been long agreed—Leclerc's troops would be the first in Paris. That evening the news of street-fighting in the capital decided Eisenhower to act, and Leclerc was told to march. At 7.15 p.m. General Bradley delivered these instructions to the French commander, whose division was then quartered in the region of Argentan. The operation orders, dated August 23, began with the words, 'Mission (1) s'emparer de Paris . . .'

Leclerc wrote to de Gaulle: 'I have had the impression . . . of living over again the situation of 1940 in reverse—complete disorder on the enemy side, their columns completely surprised.' He decided to act boldly and evade rather than reduce the German concentrations. On August 24 the first detachments moved on the city from Rambouillet, where they had arrived from Normandy the day before. The main thrust, led by Colonel Billotte, son of the commander of the First French Army Group, who was killed in May 1940, moved up from Orleans. That night a vanguard of tanks reached the Porte d'Orléans, and at 9.22 precisely entered the square in front of the Hôtel de Ville. The main body of the division got ready to enter the capital on the following day. Early next morning Billotte's armoured columns held both banks of the Seine opposite the Cité. By the afternoon the headquarters of the German commander, General von Cholitz, in the Hôtel Meurice, had been surrounded, and Cholitz surrendered to a French lieutenant, who brought him to Billotte. Leclerc had meanwhile arrived and established himself at the Gare Montparnasse, moving down in the afternoon to the

* See Book 10, Chapter 18.

Prefecture of Police. About four o'clock von Cholitz was taken before him. This was the end of the road from Dunkirk to Lake Chad and home again. In a low voice Leclerc spoke his thoughts aloud: 'Maintenant, ça y est', and then in German he introduced himself to the vanquished. After a brief and brusque discussion the capitulation of the garrison was signed, and one by one their remaining strong-points were occupied by the Resistance and the regular troops.

The city was given over to a rapturous demonstration. German prisoners were spat at, collaborators dragged through the streets, and the liberating troops fêted. On this scene of long-delayed triumph there arrived General de Gaulle. At 5 p.m. he reached the Rue St. Dominique, and set up his headquarters in the Ministry of War. Two hours later at the Hôtel de Ville he appeared for the first time as the leader of Free France before the jubilant population in company with the main figures of the Resistance and Generals Leclerc and Juin. There was a spontaneous burst of wild enthusiasm. Next afternoon, on August 26, de Gaulle made his formal entry on foot down the Champs Élysées to the Place de la Concorde, and then in a file of cars to Notre Dame. There was some firing from inside and outside the cathedral by hidden collaborators. The crowd scattered, but after a short moment of panic the solemn dedication of the liberation of Paris proceeded to its end.

*   *   *

By August 30 our troops were crossing the Seine at many points. Enemy losses had been tremendous: 400,000 men, half of them prisoners, 1,300 tanks, 20,000 vehicles, 1,500 field-guns. The German Seventh Army, and all divisions that had been sent to reinforce it, were torn to shreds. The Allied break-out from the beach-head had been delayed by bad weather and Hitler's mistaken resolve. But once that battle was over everything went with a run, and the Seine was reached six days ahead of the planned time. There has been criticism of slowness on the British front in Normandy, and the splendid American advances of the later stages seemed to indicate greater success on their part than on ours. It is therefore necessary to emphasise again that the whole plan of campaign was to pivot on the British front and draw the enemy's reserves in that direction in order to help the American turning movement. The object of the Second British Army was described in its original plan as 'to protect the flank of the U.S. armies while the latter captured Cherbourg, Angers, Nantes, and the Brittany ports'. By determination and hard fighting this was achieved. General Eisenhower, who fully comprehended the work of his British comrades, wrote in his official report: 'Without the great sacrifices made by the Anglo-Canadian armies in the brutal, slugging battles for Caen and Falaise the spectacular advances made elsewhere by the Allied forces could never have come about.'

CHAPTER 3

The Pilotless Bombardment

The long-studied assault on England by unmanned missiles now began. The target was Greater London. For more than a year we had argued among ourselves about the character and scale of the attack, and every preparation which our wits could devise and our resources permit had been made in good time.

In the early hours of June 13, exactly a week after D-Day, four pilotless aircraft crossed our coast. They were the premature result of a German order, sent urgently on D-Day in reaction to our successes in Normandy. One reached Bethnal Green, where it killed six people and injured nine; the others caused no casualties. Nothing further happened until late on June 15, when the Germans started their campaign of 'Retaliation' (*Vergeltung*) in earnest. More than two hundred of the missiles came against us within twenty-four hours, and over three thousand were to follow in the next five weeks.

The flying bomb, as we came to call it, was named V1 by Hitler, since he hoped—with some reason—that it was only the first of a series of terror weapons which German research would provide. To Londoners the new weapon was soon known as the 'doodle-bug,' or 'buzz bomb', from the strident sound of its engine, which was a jet of new and ingenious design. The bomb flew at speeds up to four hundred miles an hour, and at heights around three thousand feet, and it carried about a ton of explosive. It was steered by a magnetic compass, and its range was governed by a small propeller, which was driven round by the passage of the bomb through the air. When the propeller had revolved a number of times which corresponded to the distance of London from the launching site the controls of the missile were tripped to make it dive to earth. The blast damage was all the more vicious because the bomb usually exploded before penetrating the ground.

This new form of attack imposed upon the people of London a burden perhaps even heavier than the air raids of 1940 and 1941. Suspense and strain were more prolonged. Dawn brought no relief, and cloud no comfort. The man going home in the evening never knew what he would find ; his wife, alone all day or with the children, could not be certain of his safe return. The blind, impersonal nature of the missile made the individual on the ground feel helpless. There was little that he could do, no human enemy that he could see shot down.

* * *

My daughter Mary was still serving in the Hyde Park Anti-Aircraft Battery. On the morning of Sunday, June 18, when I was at Chequers, Mrs. Churchill told me she would pay the battery a visit. She found it in action. One bomb had passed over it and demolished a house in the Bayswater Road. While my wife and daughter were standing together on the grass they saw a tiny black object dive out of the clouds, which looked as if it would fall very near Downing Street. My car had gone to collect the letters, and the driver was astonished to see all the passers-by in Parliament Square fall flat on their faces. There was a dull explosion near by and everyone went on their business. The bomb had fallen on the Guards Chapel at Wellington Barracks. A special service for which a large number of members of the Brigade, active and retired, had gathered was going on. There was a direct hit. The whole building was demolished in a second, and nearly two hundred Guardsmen, including many distinguished officers, and their relations and friends were left killed or maimed under the ruins. This was a tragic event. I was still in bed working at my boxes when my wife returned. 'The battery has been in action,' she said, 'and the Guards Chapel is destroyed.'

36

I gave directions at once that the Commons should retire again into the Church House, whose modern steel structure offered somewhat more protection than the Palace of Westminster. This involved a lot of messages and rearrangement. We had a brief interlude in Secret Session, and a Member indignantly asked, 'Why have we come back here?' Before I could reply another Member intervened. 'If the hon. gentleman will walk a few hundred yards to Birdcage Walk he will see the reason.' There was a long silence and the matter dropped.

As the days passed, every borough in London was hit. The worst damage lay in a belt extending from Stepney and Poplar south-westwards to Wandsworth and Mitcham. Of individual boroughs Croydon suffered most hits, including eight bombs in a single day, followed by Wandsworth, Lewisham, Camberwell, Woolwich and Greenwich, Beckenham, Lambeth, Orpington, Coulsdon and Purley, West Ham, Chislehurst, and Mitcham.* About three-quarters of a million houses were damaged, twenty-three thousand of them beyond repair. But although London was the worst sufferer the casualties and the damage spread well outside its bounds. Parts of Sussex and Kent, popularly known as 'Bomb Alley' because they lay on the line of route, paid a heavy toll; and bombs, although all were aimed at Tower Bridge, fell far and wide over the countryside from Hampshire to Suffolk. One landed near my home at Westerham, killing, by a cruel mischance, twenty-two homeless children and five grown-ups collected in a refuge made for them in the woods.

* * *

Our Intelligence had accurately foretold six months before how the missiles would perform, but we had not found it easy to prepare fighter and gun defences of adequate quality. Hitler had in fact believed, from trials he had witnessed of a captured Spitfire against a flying bomb, that our fighters would be useless. Our timely warning enabled us to disappoint him, but only by a narrow margin. Our fastest fighters, specially stripped and with added power, could barely overtake the speediest missiles. Many bombs did not fly as fast as their makers intended, but even so it was often difficult for our fighters to catch them in time. To make things worse, the enemy fired the bombs in

* In order of intensity—*i.e.*, bombs per 100 acres—the order was different: first the City of London area, and then Penge, Bermondsey, Deptford, Greenwich, Camberwell, Lewisham, Stepney, Poplar, Lambeth, Battersea, Mitcham, and Wandsworth.

salvoes, in the hope of saturating our defences. Our normal procedure of 'scrambling' was too slow, and so the fighters had to fly standing patrols, finding and chasing their quarry with the help of instructions and running commentaries from Radar stations and Observer Corps posts on the ground. The flying bombs were much smaller than normal aircraft, and so they were difficult either to see or hit. There were poor chances of a 'kill' from much more than three hundred yards; but it was dangerous to open fire from less than two hundred yards, because the exploding bomb might destroy the attacking fighter.

The red flame of their exhausts made the bombs easier to see in the dark, and during the first two nights our anti-aircraft batteries in London fired on them and claimed to have brought many down. This tended to serve the enemy's purpose, since some of the missiles might otherwise have fallen in open country beyond the capital. Firing in the Metropolitan area was therefore stopped, and by June 21 the guns had moved to the advanced line on the North Downs. Many of the bombs flew at heights which we at first thought would be awkward for the guns, rather too low for the heavies and too high for the others; but fortunately it proved possible to use the heavies against lower targets than we had previously thought. We had realised of course that some bombs would escape both fighters and guns, and these we tried to parry by a vast balloon barrage deployed to the south and south-east of London. In the course of the campaign the barrage did in fact catch 232 bombs, each of which would almost inevitably have fallen somewhere in the London area.

Nor had we been content with defensive measures. The original 'ski sites', ninety-six in number, from which the bombs were to have been launched in France, had been heavily attacked by our bombers from December 1943 onwards and substantially eliminated.* But, despite all our efforts, the enemy had succeeded in launching the assault from new and less pretentious sites, and bombs were penetrating our defences in numbers which, although far smaller than the enemy had originally hoped, were presenting us with many problems. For the first week of the bombardment I kept the control in my own hands; but on June 20 I passed it to an Inter-Service Committee under Duncan Sandys which was known by the code-name of 'Crossbow'.

* See Book 9, Chapter 13.

Prime Minister to Home Secretary, Sir Edward   22 June 44
Bridges, and General Ismay, for C.O.S. Committee

Now that we can see our way a little clearer, and after consultation with the Chiefs of Staff, I have decided that the 'Crossbow' Committee, over which I have hitherto presided, should consist of a smaller group charged with the responsibility for reporting the effects of the flying bomb and the flying rocket and the progress of counter-measures and precautions to meet it. The Joint Parliamentary Secretary, Ministry of Supply [Mr. Duncan Sandys], will be chairman, and the membership should be kept as small as possible. . . .

This Committee will report daily, or as often as may be necessary, to me, the Home Secretary, the Secretary of State for Air, and the Chiefs of Staff.

The Home Secretary, the Secretary of State for Air, and I will attend together should occasion arise.

The committee included Air Marshal Bottomley, Deputy Chief of the Air Staff, Air Marshal Hill, Air Officer Commanding Air Defence of Great Britain, and General Pile, General Officer Commanding Anti-Aircraft Command.

*   *   *

On July 6 I unfolded to the House of Commons, many of whose constituencies were feeling the strain of the attack, the preparation and action the Government had taken since early in 1943. At any rate, no one could say that we had been caught by surprise. There was no complaint. Everyone saw we just had to lump it, an ordeal made easier by our hopes of a successful advance in Normandy. My account was detailed.

The total weight of bombs so far dropped by us on flying bomb and rocket targets in France and Germany, including Peenemünde, has now reached about fifty thousand tons, and the number of reconnaissance flights totals many thousands. The scrutiny and interpretation of the tens of thousands of air photographs obtained for this purpose has alone been a stupendous task, discharged by the Air Reconnaissance and Photographic Interpretation units of the Royal Air Force. These efforts have been exacting to both sides, friends and foes. Quite a considerable proportion of our flying power has been diverted for months past from other forms of offensive activity. The Germans for their part have sacrificed a great deal of manufacturing strength which would have increased their fighter and bomber forces working in conjunction with their hard-pressed armies on every front. It has yet to be decided who has suffered and will suffer most in the process. There has in fact been in progress for a year past an unseen battle into which great resources have been poured by both sides. This invisible battle has now flashed into the open, and we shall be able, and indeed obliged, to watch its progress at fairly close quarters. . . .

We must neither underrate nor exaggerate. In all up to six o'clock this morning about two thousand seven hundred and fifty flying bombs have been discharged from the launching stations along the French coast. A very large proportion of these have either failed to cross the Channel or have been shot down and destroyed by various methods. . . . The weather however during June has been very unfavourable to us for every purpose. In Normandy it has robbed us in great part of the use of our immense superiority. . . . In Britain it has made more difficult the work and combination of the batteries and aircraft. It has also reduced the blows we strike at every favourable opportunity at the launching sites and suspected points on the other side of the Channel. Nevertheless the House will, I think, be favourably surprised to learn that the total number of flying bombs launched from the enemy's stations has killed exactly one person per bomb. . . . Actually the latest figures up to six o'clock this morning are 2,754 flying bombs launched and 2,752 fatal casualties sustained. . . . A very high proportion of the casualties, somewhere around 10,000, not always severe or mortal, has fallen upon London, which presents to the enemy a target eighteen miles wide by over twenty miles deep. It is therefore the unique target of the world for the use of a weapon of such proved inaccuracy. The flying bomb is a weapon literally and essentially indiscriminate in its nature, purpose, and effect. The introduction by the Germans of such a weapon obviously raises some grave questions, upon which I do not propose to trench to-day.

* * *

Arrangements had been made to evacuate mothers and children and to open the deep shelters which had hitherto been held in reserve, and I explained that everything in human power would be done to defeat this novel onslaught ; but I ended on a note which seemed appropriate to the mood of the hour.

We shall not allow the battle operations in Normandy nor the attacks we are making against special targets in Germany to suffer. They come first, and we must fit our own domestic arrangements into the General scheme of war operations. There can be no question of allowing the slightest weakening of the battle in order to diminish in scale injuries which, though they may inflict grievous suffering on many people and change to some extent the normal, regular life and industry of London will never stand between the British nation and their duty in the van of a victorious and avenging world. It may be a comfort to some to feel that they are sharing in no small degree the perils of our soldiers overseas, and that the blows which fall on them diminish those which in other forms would have smitten our fighting men and their allies. But I am sure of one thing, that London will never be conquered and will never fail and that her renown, triumphing over every ordeal, will long shine among men.

We now know that Hitler had thought that the new weapon would be 'decisive' in fashioning his own distorted version of peace. Even his military advisers, who were less obsessed than their master, hoped that London's agony would cause some of our armies to be diverted to a disastrous landing in the Pas de Calais in an attempt to capture the launching sites. But neither London nor the Government flinched, and I had been able to assure General Eisenhower on June 18 that we would bear the ordeal to the end, asking for no change in his strategy in France.

*   *   *

Our bombing attacks on launching sites went on for a time, but it was clear before the end of June that these were now poor targets. Bomber Command, anxious to share more effectively in relieving London, sought better ones; and they were soon found. The main storage depots for the flying bombs in France now lay in a few large natural caverns around Paris, long exploited by French mushroom-growers. One of these caverns, at St. Leu d'Esserent, in the Oise valley, was rated by the Germans to store two thousand bombs, and it had supplied 70 per cent. of all the bombs fired in June. Early in July it was largely destroyed by Bomber Command, using some of their heaviest bombs to crush the roof in. Another, rated to hold one thousand, was smashed by American bombers. We know that at least three hundred flying bombs were irretrievably buried in this one cavern. London was spared all these, and the Germans were forced to use bombs of a type which they had previously condemned as unsatisfactory.

Our bombers did not achieve their success without loss. Of all our forces they were the earliest engaged against the flying bombs. They had attacked research centres and factories in Germany, and launching sites and supply depots in France. By the end of the campaign nearly two thousand airmen of British and Allied bombers had died in London's defence.

* * *

At the headquarters of Air Defence of Great Britain much thought had been given to the *rôles* of fighters and guns. Our dispositions had seemed sensible enough: fighters ranging out over the sea and over most of Kent and Sussex, where the bombs were dispersed, and guns concentrated in a belt nearer London, where the bombs drew into a more compact front as they approached their target. This seemed to give each method of defence its best chance, and it was no surprise that in the first few weeks of the campaign, as indeed in all other campaigns previously, the fighters had much more success than the guns. By the second week of July however General Pile and some discerning experts came to the conclusion that the guns could do very much better without undue prejudice to the success of the fighters if the batteries were moved on to the coast. Their Radar for fire control would have more scope, and it would be safer to use the proximity-fused shells which were now arriving from America.* We had not been sure if the guns could use their Radar on the coast, owing to the danger of enemy jamming, but so good had been our Intelligence, and so accurate our bombing, that by D-Day we had put all the German jamming stations out of action. It was nevertheless a grave decision to uproot the enormous Anti-Aircraft organisation from the North Downs and to redeploy it on the coast, knowing that this might spoil the success of the fighters.

On July 17 Duncan Sandys, who had pressed strongly for this change, reported to the War Cabinet:

The lay-out of our defences against the flying bomb has been reviewed in the light of the results obtained during the past few weeks. Experience has shown that under the original plan fighters and guns frequently interfered with one another and that an unnecessarily large proportion of the flying bombs destroyed were brought down over land. It has accordingly

* These shells, which were designed to explode as they passed near the target, were dangerous to use over land, since if they missed the target badly they did not explode until they fell to earth.

been decided to re-deploy our defences in four distinct belts
as follows:

(i) *Fighter Belt at Sea*

Fighter aircraft will operate under close radio control at a
distance of not less than 10,000 yards from the shore.

(ii) *Coastal Gun Belt*

All anti-aircraft guns allotted for defence against the flying
bomb will be deployed in a narrow strip 5,000 yards in width
extending along the coast from Beachy Head to St. Margaret's
Bay. These guns will fire out to sea up to the 10,000-yard
limit.

(iii) *Inland Fighter Belt*

Inland, between the coastal gun zone and the balloon barrage, there will be a second fighter belt in which aircraft will
operate under running commentary control. The bursts of
anti-aircraft fire in the gun belt should be a great help to the
pilots in spotting the line of flight of approaching bombs. By
night they will have the additional assistance of searchlights
over the whole of the inland fighter zone.

(iv) *Balloon Belt*

There will be no important changes in the boundaries of
the balloon barrage.

The re-deployment of the anti-aircraft guns on to their new
sites along the coast was carried out over the week-end, and
the new defence plan came into operation at six o'clock this
morning.

The new deployment was a vast undertaking, and it was executed with the most praiseworthy speed. Nearly four hundred
heavy and six hundred Bofors guns had to be moved and re-
sited. Three thousand miles of telephone cable were laid.
Twenty-three thousand men and women were moved, and the
vehicles of Anti-Aircraft Command travelled two and three-
quarter million miles in a week. In four days the move to the
coast was completed.

This whole operation was decided upon and carried out on
their own responsibility by Air Marshal Hill and General Pile
with the approval of Duncan Sandys. For a few days after the
re-deployment our combined defences destroyed far fewer
bombs, mainly because the fighters were much hampered by the
new restrictions on their movement. But this setback did not last
long. The guns soon got their grip, and the results improved
rapidly. With the new Radar and predicting equipment, and
above all with the new proximity fuses, all of which we had
asked for from America six months before, the performance of

the gunners exceeded all our hopes. By the end of August not more than one bomb in seven got through to the London area. The record 'bag' was on August 28, when ninety-four bombs approached our coast and all but four were destroyed. The balloons caught two, the fighters twenty-three, and the guns sixty-five. The V1 had been mastered.

The Germans, who keenly watched the performance of our guns from across the Channel, were completely bewildered by the success of our artillery. They had still not solved the mystery when their launching sites were overwhelmed in the first week of September by the victorious and rapid advance of the British and Canadian armies from Normandy to Antwerp. The success of the armies released London and its defenders from the intense strain of the previous three months, and on September 6 Mr. Herbert Morrison, Home Secretary and Minister of Home Security, was able to announce, 'The Battle of London is won'. Although the Germans thereafter irritated us from time to time with flying bombs launched from aircraft, and with a few long-range bombs from Holland, the threat was thenceforward insignificant. In all about eight thousand bombs were launched against London, and about two thousand four hundred got through.* Our total civilian casualties were 6,184 killed and 17,981 seriously injured. These figures do not tell the whole story. Many people, though wounded, did not have to stay in hospital, and their sufferings have gone unrecorded.

Our Intelligence had played a vital part. The size and performance of the weapon, and the intended scale of attack, were known to us in excellent time. This enabled our fighters to be made ready. The launching sites and the storage caverns were found, enabling our bombers to delay the attack and mitigate its violence. Every known means of getting information was employed, and it was pieced together with great skill. To all our sources, many of whom worked amid deadly danger, and some of whom will be for ever unknown to us, I pay my tribute.

But good Intelligence alone would have been useless. Fighters, bombers, guns, balloons, scientists, Civil Defence, and all the organisation that lay behind them, had each played their parts to the full. It was a great and concerted defence, made absolute by the victory of our armies in France.

*   *   *

* The exact German figure for flying bombs launched against London from sites in France was 8,564, of which 1,006 crashed soon after launching.

A second threat drew near. This was the long-range rocket, or V2, with which we had been so preoccupied twelve months before. The Germans however had found it difficult to perfect, and in the meantime it had been overtaken by the flying bomb. But almost as soon as the bombs began to hit us the signs appeared that a rocket assault was also approaching. The weight of the rocket and its war-head became subjects of high dispute. Certain early but doubtful Intelligence reports had suggested war-heads of five to ten tons, and these were seized upon by those of our experts who believed on other grounds that such weights were reasonable. Some believed that the rocket would weigh eighty tons, with a ten-ton war-head. Lord Cherwell, now strongly vindicated in his stand for the flying bomb in June 1943,* even before there were any indications of it from Intelligence was very doubtful whether we should ever see the rocket in operation at all, and certainly not the monster of eighty tons. Between the extremes there were a few Intelligence reports which suggested a much lighter rocket than eighty tons ; but, with all the controversy, anxiety remained acute.

We knew that work was continuing at Peenemünde, and sparse reports from the Continent renewed our concern about the scale and imminence of the attack. On July 18 Dr. Jones informed the Crossbow Committee that there might well be a thousand rockets already in existence. On July 24 Sandys reported to the Cabinet: 'Although we have as yet no reliable information about the movement of projectiles westwards from Germany, it would be unwise to assume from this negative evidence that a rocket is not imminent.' In a minute to me the following day the Chiefs of Staff wrote: 'The Air Staff agree with this statement, and the Chiefs of Staff consider that the War Cabinet should be warned.' The situation was discussed by the Cabinet on July 27, and we considered proposals by Mr. Herbert Morrison which would have involved evacuating about a million people from London.

Every effort was made to complete the remaining gaps in our knowledge about the size, performance, and characteristics of the rocket. Fragmentary evidence from many sources was pieced together by our Intelligence services and presented to the Crossbow Committee. From this it was deduced that the rocket weighed twelve tons, with a one-ton war-head. This light weight explained many things that had puzzled us, such as the

* See Book 9, Chapter 13.

absence of elaborate launching arrangements. These calculations were confirmed when the Royal Aircraft Establishment had the opportunity to examine the wreckage of an actual rocket. It came into our hands as the result of a lucky and freak error in the trials at Peenemünde on June 13, and according to a prisoner the explanation was as follows. For some time the Germans had been using glider bombs against our shipping. These were launched from aircraft and guided to the target by radio. It was now decided to see whether a rocket could be steered in the same way. An expert operator was obtained, and placed in a good position to watch the missile from the start. The Peenemünde experimenters were well accustomed to seeing a rocket rise, and it had not occurred to them that the glider-bomb expert would be surprised by the spectacle. But surprised he was, so much so that he forgot his own part in the procedure. In his astonishment he pushed the control lever well off to the left and held it there. The rocket obediently kept turning to the left, and by the time the operator had pulled himself together it was out of control range and heading for Sweden. There it fell. We soon heard about it, and after some negotiations the remains were brought to Farnborough, where our experts sorted out the battered fragments with noteworthy success.

Before the end of August we knew exactly what to expect. This is shown by the following tables, which compare figures given in a Scientific Intelligence report dated August 26 with those discovered after the war in German records.

—	British Estimate on August 26, 1944	German Figures
Total weight	11½–14 tons Probably 12–13	12·65 tons
Weight of war-head— i.e., amount of explosive	1 ton	1 ton (sometimes ·97 ton)
Range	200–210 miles	207 miles

The rocket was an impressive technical achievement. Its thrust was developed in a jet from the combustion of alcohol and liquid oxygen, nearly four tons of the former and five of the latter being consumed in about a minute. To force these fuels into the jet chamber at the required rate needed a special pump

TOTAL STOCKS AND MONTHLY PRODUCTION

—	British Estimate on August 26, 1944	German Figures
Total stocks	Perhaps 2,000	1,800
Mothly production	About 500	300 in May 1944. Average from Sept. 1944 to March 1945, 618

of nearly a thousand horse-power. The pump in its turn was worked by a turbine driven by hydrogen peroxide. The rocket was controlled by gyroscopes or by radio signals operating on large graphite vanes placed behind the jet to deflect the exhaust gases and so steer the rocket. The rocket first rose vertically for six miles or so, and automatic controls then turned it over to climb with increasing speed at about forty-five degrees. When the speed was sufficient for the desired range further controls cut off the fuels from the jet, and the missile then flew in a gigantic parabola, reaching a height of about fifty miles and falling about two hundred miles away from the launching point. Its maximum speed was about four thousand miles an hour, and the whole flight took no more than three or four minutes.

*   *   *

At the end of August it seemed that our armies might expel the enemy from all territory within the two-hundred-mile range of the rocket from London, but he managed to hold Walcheren and The Hague. On September 8, a week after the main V1 bombardment ceased, the Germans launched their first two rockets against London.* The first V2 fell at Chiswick at seventeen minutes to seven in the evening, the other at Epping sixteen seconds later. About thirteen hundred† were fired against England in the seven months before our armies could liberate The Hague, whence most rockets were launched. Many fell short, but about five hundred hit London. The total casualties caused by the V2 in England were 2,724 killed and 6,476 seriously in-

* The first long-range rocket to be successfully fired in war had been launched about ten hours earlier, against Paris, but this, as it turned out, was of minor consequence.

† The German records show that 1,190 rockets were successfully launched against London, out of 1,359 attempts.

jured. On the average each rocket caused about twice as many casualties as a flying bomb. Although the war-heads were of much the same size, the strident engine of the flying bomb warned people to take cover. The rocket approached in silence.

Many counter-measures were tried, and still more explored. The raid on Peenemünde over a year before did more than everything else to alleviate the threat. The V2 attack would otherwise have started at least as early as the V1 attack, and it would have been from a shorter range, and therefore more accurate in June than it was in September and after the United States Air Force continued to bomb Peenemünde in July and August, and both they and Bomber Command attacked factories making rocket components. We owe it to our armies that they had pushed the rocket back to the limit of its range before the Germans were at last ready to open fire. Our fighters and tactical bombers continually worried the launching points near The Hague. We made ready to jam the radio control of the rockets, should the Germans use it, and we even considered attempting to burst the rockets in the air by gunfire as they fell.

Our efforts confined the attack to four or five hundred rockets a month, shared between London and the Continent, compared with an intended rate of nine hundred. Thus, although we could do little against the rocket once it was launched, we postponed and substantially reduced the weight of the onslaught. About two hundred rockets a month were aimed against London, most of the rest against Antwerp, and a few against other Continental targets. The enemy made no mention of his new missiles until November 8, and I did not feel the need for a public statement until November 10. I was then able to assure the House that the scale and effects of the attack had not hitherto been serious. This fortunately continued to be true throughout the remaining months of the war.

Despite the great technical achievements, Speer, the highly competent German Minister of Munitions, deplored the effort that had been put into making rockets. He asserted that each one took as long to produce as six or seven fighters, which would have been far more useful, and that twenty flying bombs could have been made for the cost of one rocket. This post-war information confirms the views Lord Cherwell had so often expressed before the event.

It was fortunate that the Germans spent so much effort on rockets instead of on bombers. Even our Mosquitoes, each of which was probably no dearer than a rocket, dropped on the average 125 tons of bombs per aircraft within one mile of the target during their life, whereas the rocket dropped one ton only, and that with an average error of fifteen miles.

* * *

Hitler had hoped to have yet another 'V' weapon. This was to have been a multi-barrel long-range gun installation dug into the ground near the village of Mimoyecques, in the Pas de Calais. Each of the fifty smooth-bore barrels was about four hundred feet long, and it was to fire a shell about six inches in diameter, and stabilised, not by spin, but by fins like a dart. Explosive charges were placed in side-tubes at frequent intervals up the barrel, and were ignited in succession as the projectile accelerated. The shell was intended to emerge from the barrel with a speed of at least five thousand feet per second, and with so many barrels the designers hoped to fire a shell at London every few minutes. This time however Hitler's hopes were completely disappointed: all the trial projectiles 'toppled' in flight, and range and accuracy were therefore very poor. A hundred scientists, technicians, and serving officers met in Berlin on May 4, 1944, and came to the unpleasant conclusion that the Fuehrer would have to be told of the failure. We did not know this until afterwards, and as a precaution our bombers repeatedly smashed the concrete structure at Mimoyecques, which five thousand workmen laboured as repeatedly to repair.

* * *

While I have recorded the story of Hitler's 'Retaliation' campaign against England, we must not forget that Belgium suffered with equal bitterness when the Germans attempted to use the same vindictive weapons against her liberated cities. We did not of course allow the German attack to go unparried. Our bombing of German production centres, and other targets, happily reduced the scale of effort against Belgium as much as against ourselves ; but it was not easy to re-deploy fighter and gun defences, with all their elaborate control, in the newly won territories. German records show that by the end of the war Antwerp had been the target for 8,696 flying bombs and 1,610 rockets. 5,960 of all these fell within eight miles of the city centre, and between them they killed 3,470 Belgian citizens and 682 Allied Service-men. A further 3,141 flying bombs were aimed against Liége, and 151 rockets against Brussels. The people of Belgium bore this senseless bombardment in a spirit equal to our own.

*   *   *

The German 'V' weapons, though in the event unsuccessful, impressed us with the potentialities of these new methods. In a report to the Cabinet Duncan Sandys emphasised the decisive importance which guided missiles might have in future wars, and pointed out the need for devoting substantial resources to their development. The following extract may be deemed significant:

> The advent of the long-range, radio-controlled, jet-propelled projectile has opened up vast new possibilities in the conduct of military operations. In future the possession of superiority in long-distance rocket artillery may well count for as much as superiority in naval or air power. High-grade scientific and engineering staff, together with extensive research facilities, will have to be maintained as a permanent part of our peace-time military organisation.

We began to design our own guided missiles, and by the end of the war we had founded a permanent organisation for this purpose.

*   *   *

Such is the tale of the new weapons on which Hitler pinned his stubborn hopes for many months, and of their defeat by the foresight of the British Administration, the skill of the Services, and the fortitude of the people who, by their conduct for the second time in this war, gave 'Greater London' a prouder meaning.

CHAPTER 4

Attack on the South of France?

The Strategic Decisions of the Teheran Conference – The Plan to Land in the South of France – Delay in the Capture of Rome – General Marshall's Visit to England and the Mediterranean – 'Overlord's' Need for More Ports in the South or West – A Telegram from Smuts, June 23 – Opposing Views of the British and American Chiefs of Staff – Correspondence with President Roosevelt – General Wilson is Ordered to Attack the French Riviera – My Plan for a Landing on the Atlantic Coast – A Visit to Eisenhower and a Conference at Portsmouth, August 7 – Mr. Roosevelt's Adverse Telegram.

Liberating Normandy was a supreme event in the European campaign of 1944, but it was only one of several concentric strokes upon Nazi Germany. In the east the Russians were flooding into Poland and the Balkans, and in the south Alexander's armies in Italy were pressing towards the river Po. Decisions had now to be taken about our next move in the Mediterranean, and it must be recorded with regret that these occasioned the first important divergence on high strategy between ourselves and our American friends.

The design for final victory in Europe had been outlined in prolonged discussion at the Teheran Conference in November 1943. Its decisions still governed our plans, and it would be well to recall them. First and foremost we had promised to carry out 'Overlord'. Here was the dominating task, and no one disputed that here lay our prime duty. But we still wielded powerful forces in the Mediterranean, and the question had remained, what should they do? We had resolved that they should capture Rome, whose near-by airfields were needed for bombing Southern Germany. This accomplished, we planned to advance up the peninsula as far as the Pisa–Rimini line, and there hold as many enemy divisions as possible in Northern Italy. This however was not all. A third operation was also agreed upon, namely, an amphibious landing in the south of France, and it was on this project that controversy was about to descend. It was originally conceived as a feint or threat to keep German troops on the

Riviera and stop them joining the battles in Normandy, but in Cairo the Americans had pressed for a real attack by ten divisions, and at Teheran Stalin had supported them. I accepted the change, largely to prevent undue diversions to Burma, although I contemplated other ways of exploiting success in Italy, and the plan had been given the code-name 'Anvil'.

One thing was plain: it was no use landing in the south of France unless we did so at the right time. The mere threat of an assault would suffice to keep German troops in the region; a real invasion might induce the enemy to reinforce them; but once we joined battle in Normandy 'Anvil's' value was much reduced, because Hitler was not likely to detach troops from the main struggle in the north for the sake of keeping his hold on Provence. If we invaded the Riviera at all we must do so at the same time as or just before we landed in Normandy, and this was what we intended to do when we made our plans at Teheran.

A second condition also governed 'Anvil's' usefulness. Many of the forces needed for the operation—that is to say, for the full-scale invasion as opposed to a feint or threat—would have to come from our armies in Italy. But these had first to accomplish the arduous and important task of seizing Rome and the airfields. Until this was done little could be spared or taken from Alexander's forces. Rome must fall before 'Anvil' could start.

All turned on the capture of Rome. If we could seize it quickly all would be well. Troops could then be withdrawn from the Italian front and 'Anvil' launched in good time. If not, a feint landing would suffice. If we landed in earnest, but after 'Overlord' had started, our forces would have a long way to go before they could reach Eisenhower's armies, and by then the battle of the beaches would be over. They would be too late to help. This in fact was what happened, and indeed already seemed likely to happen early in 1944.

At Teheran we had confidently expected to reach Rome early in the spring, but this had proved impossible. The important descent at Anzio to accelerate the capture of Rome had drawn eight or ten German divisions away from the vital theatre, or more than was expected to be attracted to the Riviera by 'Anvil'. This in effect superseded it by achieving its object. Nevertheless the Riviera project went forward as if nothing had happened.

Apart from 'Anvil' hanging somewhat vaguely in the future,

some of the finest divisions of the armies in Italy had rightly been assigned to the main operation of 'Overlord' and had sailed for England before the end of 1943. Alexander had thus been weakened and Kesselring had been strengthened. The Germans had sent reinforcements to Italy, had parried the Anzio swoop, and had stopped us entering Rome until just before D-Day. The hard fighting had of course engulfed important enemy reserves which might otherwise have gone to France, and it certainly helped 'Overlord' in its critical early stages, but none the less our advance in the Mediterranean had been gravely upset. Landing-craft were another obstacle. Many of them had been sent to 'Overlord'. 'Anvil' could not be mounted until they came back, and this depended on events in Normandy. These facts had been long foreseen, and as far back as March 21 General Maitland Wilson, the Supreme Commander in the Mediterranean, reported that 'Anvil' could not be launched before the end of July. Later he put it at mid-August, and declared that the best way to help 'Overlord' was to abandon any attack on the Riviera and concentrate on Italy.

When Rome fell on June 4 the problem had to be reviewed. Should we go on with 'Anvil' or should we make a new plan?

General Eisenhower naturally wanted to strengthen his attack in North-West Europe by all available means. Strategic possibilities in Northern Italy did not attract him, but he consented to return the landing-craft as soon as possible if this would lead to a speedy 'Anvil'. The American Chiefs of Staff agreed with Eisenhower, holding rigidly to the maxim of concentration at the decisive point, which in their eyes meant only North-West Europe. They were supported by the President, who was mindful of the agreements made with Stalin many months before at Teheran. Yet all was changed by the delay in Italy.

*   *   *

Soon after D-Day General Marshall came to England and expressed his concern about yet another problem. Enormous forces were accumulating in the United States, and should join the battle as soon as possible. This they could do either by sailing direct to France or by coming through the United Kingdom, and arrangements had been made accordingly, but so great was the promised influx that Marshall doubted whether our ports would suffice. At this period we held only a few harbours along the French coast of the Channel, and although

Eisenhower intended to capture Brest, and other landing-places in the Bay of Biscay might also fall to us if things went well, we could not be sure of seizing them, and still less of clearing them, in sufficient time. Yet a full and speedy build-up was vital to the success of 'Overlord'. The solution which General Marshall proposed was to capture entirely new bases in either the west or the south of France, and preferably in the west because this was the more quickly reached from America.

I was fully alive to all this, and had for some time contemplated a descent on the Biscay coast from North Africa, even though this could not be achieved before the end of July or early in August. But I was equally anxious not to wreck Alexander's victory in Italy. I considered that the options might still remain open and all preparations should be made to move in whatever direction seemed best.

On June 14 the Combined Chiefs of Staff decided to prepare an amphibious operation in the Mediterranean which might strike either in the south of France or in the Bay of Biscay or at the head of the Adriatic. Its destination could be left open for the moment. Three days later General Marshall visited the Mediterranean to confer with the commanders. General Wilson was impressed with 'Overlord's' need for more ports, of which he then learnt for the first time, but he did not alter his judgment against 'Anvil', and on June 19 told the Combined Chiefs of Staff that he still thought his best contribution to the common end would be to press forward with all his resources into the Po valley. Thereafter, with the help of an amphibious operation against the Istrian peninsula, at the head of the Adriatic, which is dominated by and runs south from Trieste, there would be attractive prospects of advancing through the Ljubljana Gap into Austria and Hungary and striking at the heart of Germany from another direction. Alexander agreed.

Smuts was in Italy at the time and telegraphed to me:

Field-Marshal Smuts to Prime Minister   23 June 44
I have discussed with Wilson and Alexander the future employment of latter's forces, and summarise results for your information. Neither of them favours any of present 'Anvil' proposals, as their results will be at least doubtful in directly helping Eisenhower, and in any case would involve very serious loss of time when time is so important to us. The success already achieved by Alexander and present high morale of his army tells strongly against any break-up of his forces

and interruption of their victorious advance. With the reinforcements forthcoming for Eisenhower he should be able not only to hold his own and extend his right flank to the Loire, but also to advance eastwards towards or beyond Paris. The extension of his left flank is a matter for Staff consideration and report, but this ought not to delay a decision on present question of the switch-over, which is both most urgent and critical.

As regards plan for Alexander's advance, he and Wilson agree that there will be no difficulty in his break-through to the Po and thereafter swinging east towards Istria, Ljubljana, and so on to Austria. Alexander favours an advance both by land and sea, while Wilson favours the latter and thinks three seaborne divisions with one or two airborne divisions would suffice and make possible capture of Trieste by beginning of September. Thereafter the advance will reopen eastward, gathering large Partisan support and perhaps forcing the enemy out of the Balkans. The co-operation between our and the Russian advance towards Austria and Germany would constitute as serious a threat to the enemy as Eisenhower's advance from the west, and the three combined are most likely to produce early enemy collapse.

Alexander, who has just held a meeting with his commanders, is sending C.I.G.S. separately his views. I would only add that considered views of two such competent and experienced leaders as Wilson and Alexander weigh heavily with me, and should not lightly be set aside by Combined Chiefs of Staff, whose planning in any case does not exclude alternative now pressed by both of them. Both have impressed on me urgency of a decision on many grounds, if possible before end of next week.

* * *

On June 23 General Eisenhower advised the Combined Chiefs of Staff to concentrate our forces in direct support of the decisive battle in Northern France. He admitted that an advance through the Ljubljana Gap might contain German troops, but it would not draw any of their divisions from France. As for a descent in the Bay of Biscay, he agreed that Bordeaux was closer to the United States than Marseilles, but maintained that the latter could be captured more quickly by forces already in the Mediterranean, and would furnish a direct route northwards to join in the battle for the Ruhr. He therefore urged that 'Anvil' should be undertaken, at the expense of course of our armies in Italy, since 'in my view the resources of Great Britain and the United States will not permit us to maintain two major theatres in the European war, each with decisive missions'.

We were all agreed that 'Overlord' took priority; the point was how the armies in the second theatre, Italy, could best help to overthrow Germany. The American Chiefs of Staff strongly supported Eisenhower. They condemned what they called the 'commitment of Mediterranean resources to large-scale operations in Northern Italy and into the Balkans'. Our own Chiefs of Staff took the opposite view. On June 26 they declared that the Allied forces in the Mediterranean could best help 'Overlord' by destroying the Germans who faced them. In order to launch 'Anvil' on August 15 withdrawals from the Italian front would have to begin at once, and rather than land on the Riviera they preferred to send troops by sea direct to Eisenhower. With much prescience they remarked: 'We think that the mounting of "Anvil" on a scale likely to achieve success would hamstring General Alexander's remaining forces to such an extent that any further activity would be limited to something very modest.'

They urged that Alexander should develop his offensive in Italy so as to engage and destroy all the German forces opposed to him, that General Wilson should do all he could to emphasise *the threat of an assault** on the south of France, and that Wilson should prepare to send Eisenhower one or more American divisions and/or all the French divisions which he was capable of receiving and which our shipping resources would permit.

This direct conflict of opinions, honestly held and warmly argued by either side, could only be settled, if at all, between the President and myself, and an interchange of telegrams now took place.

'The deadlock,' I said on June 28, 'between our Chiefs of Staff raises most serious issues. Our first wish is to help General Eisenhower in the most speedy and effective manner. But we do not think this necessarily involves the complete ruin of all our great affairs in the Mediterranean, and we take it hard that this should be demanded of us. ... I most earnestly beg you to examine this matter in detail for yourself. ... Please remember how you spoke to me at Teheran about Istria, and how I introduced it at the full Conference. This has sunk very deeply into my mind, although it is not by any means the immediate issue we have to decide.'

Later I summed up my conclusions to Mr. Roosevelt.

---

* Author's italics.

(*a*) Let us reinforce 'Overlord' directly, to the utmost limits of landings from the west.

(*b*) Let us next do justice to the great opportunities of the Mediterranean commanders, and confine ourselves to minor diversions and threats to hold the enemy around the Gulf of Lions.

(*c*) Let us leave General Eisenhower all his landing-craft as long as he needs them to magnify his landing capacity.

(*d*) Let us make sure of increasing to the maximum extent the port capacity in the 'Overlord' battle area.

(*e*) Let us resolve not to wreck one great campaign for the sake of another. Both can be won.

The President's reply was prompt and adverse. He was resolved to carry out what he called 'the grand strategy' of Teheran, namely, exploiting 'Overlord' to the full, 'victorious advances in Italy, and an early assault on Southern France'. Political objects might be important, but military operations to achieve them must be subordinated to striking at the heart of Germany by a campaign in Europe. Stalin himself had favoured 'Anvil', and had classified all other operations in the Mediterranean as of lesser importance, and Mr. Roosevelt declared he could not abandon it without consulting him. The President continued:

My interest and hopes centre on defeating the Germans in front of Eisenhower and driving on into Germany, *rather than on limiting this action for the purpose of staging a full major effort in Italy*.* I am convinced we will have sufficient forces in Italy, with 'Anvil' forces withdrawn, to chase Kesselring north of Pisa–Rimini and maintain heavy pressure against his army at the very least to the extent necessary to contain his present force. I cannot conceive of the Germans paying the price of ten additional divisions, estimated by General Wilson, in order to keep us out of Northern Italy.

We can—and Wilson confirms this—immediately withdraw five divisions (three United States and two French) from Italy for 'Anvil'. *The remaining twenty-one divisions, plus numerous separate brigades, will certainly provide Alexander with adequate ground superiority*. . . .

Mr. Roosevelt contended that a landing in the Bay of Biscay would be a waste of shipping. If Eisenhower wanted more

* Author's subsequent italics throughout.

troops they were ready in the United States and he had only to ask for them. But it was his objections to a descent on the Istrian peninsula and a thrust against Vienna through the Ljubljana Gap that revealed both the rigidity of the American military plans and his own suspicion of what he called a campaign 'in the Balkans'. He claimed that Alexander and Smuts, 'for several natural and very human reasons', were inclined to disregard two vital considerations. First, the operation infringed 'the grand strategy'. Secondly, it would take too long and we could probably not deploy more than six divisions. 'I cannot agree,' he wrote, 'to the employment of United States troops against Istria *and into the Balkans*, nor can I see the French agreeing to such use of French troops. . . . For purely political considerations over here, I should never survive even a slight setback in "Overlord" *if it were known that fairly large forces had been diverted to the Balkans.*'

No one involved in these discussions had ever thought of moving armies *into the Balkans*; but Istria and Trieste were strategic and political positions, which, as he saw very clearly, might exercise profound and widespread reactions, especially after the Russian advances.

The President suggested at one point that we should lay our respective cases before Stalin. I said I did not know what he would say if the issue were put to him to decide. On military grounds he might have been greatly interested in the eastward movement of Alexander's army, which, without entering the Balkans, would profoundly affect all the forces there, and which, in conjunction with any attacks Stalin might make upon Roumania or with Roumania against Transylvania, might produce the most far-reaching results. On a long-term political view he might prefer that the British and Americans should do their share in France in the very hard fighting that was to come, and that East, Middle, and Southern Europe should fall naturally into his control. But I felt it was better to settle the matter for ourselves and between ourselves. I was sure that if we could have met, as I so frequently proposed, we should have reached a happy agreement.

On July 2 the President declared that he and his Chiefs of Staff were still convinced that 'Anvil' should be launched at the earliest possible date, and he asked us to direct General Wilson accordingly. He said that at Teheran he had only contemplated a series of raids in force in Istria if the Germans started a general retirement from the Dodecanese and Greece. But this had not happened yet.

'Therefore,' he concluded, 'I am compelled by the logic of not dispersing our main efforts to a new theatre to agree with my Chiefs of Staff.

'I honestly believe that God will be with us as He has in "Overlord" and in Italy and in North Africa. I always think of my early geometry—"a straight line is the shortest distance between two points".'

For the time being I resigned myself, and the same day General Wilson was ordered to attack the south of France on August 15. Preparations began at once, but the reader should note that 'Anvil' was renamed 'Dragoon'. This was done in case the enemy had learnt the meaning of the original code-word.

* * *

By early August however a marked change had come over the battlefield in Normandy and great developments impended. On the 4th I reopened with the President the question of switching 'Dragoon' to the west.

Prime Minister to President Roosevelt   4 Aug 44
  The course of events in Normandy and Brittany, and especially the brilliant operations of the United States Army, give good prospects that the whole Brittany peninsula will be in our hands within a reasonable time. I beg you will consider the possibility of switching 'Dragoon' into the main and vital theatre, where it can immediately play its part at close quarters in the great and victorious battle in which we are now engaged.

  2. I cannot pretend to have worked out the details, but the opinion here is that they are capable of solution. Instead of having to force a landing against strong enemy defences we might easily find welcoming American troops at some point or other from St. Nazaire north-westward along the Brittany peninsula. I feel that we are fully entitled to use the extraordinary flexibility of sea- and air-power to move with the moving scene. The arrival of the ten divisions assigned to 'Dragoon', with their L.S.T.s, might be achieved rapidly, and if this came off it would be decisive for Eisenhower's victorious advance by the shortest route right across France.

  3. I most earnestly ask you to instruct your Chiefs of Staff to study this proposal, on which our people here are already at work.

I also hoped that Hopkins might be able to help.

Prime Minister to Mr. Harry Hopkins   6 Aug 44

I am grieved to find that even splendid victories and widening opportunities do not bring us together on strategy. The brilliant operations of the American Army have not only cut off the Brest peninsula, but in my opinion have to a large extent demoralised the scattered Germans who remain there. St. Nazaire and Nantes, one of your major disembarkation ports in the last war, may be in our hands at any time. Quiberon Bay, Lorient, and Brest will also soon fall into our hands. It is my belief that the German troops on the Atlantic shore south of the Cherbourg peninsula are in a state of weakness and disorder and that Bordeaux could be obtained easily, cheaply, and swiftly. The possession of these Atlantic ports, together with those we have now, will open the way for the fullest importation of the great armies of the United States still awaiting their opportunity. In addition the ten divisions now mounted for 'Dragoon' could be switched into St. Nazaire as soon as it is in Allied possession, in this case American possession. Thus Eisenhower might speedily be presented with a new great port, as well as with a new army to operate on his right flank in the march towards the Seine.

2. I repeat that the above is additional to anything that has been foreshadowed in the schedules of transportation either from Great Britain or the United States. Instead of this we are to be forced to make a heavy attack from the sea on the well-fortified Riviera coast and to march westward to capture the two fortresses of Toulon and Marseilles, thus opening a new theatre where the enemy will at the outset be much stronger than we are, and where our advance runs cross-grained to the country, which abounds in most formidable rocky positions, ridges, and gullies.

3. Even after taking the two fortresses of Toulon and Marseilles we have before us the lengthy advance up the Rhone valley before we even get to Lyons. None of this operation can influence Eisenhower's battle for probably ninety days after the landings.* We start 500 miles away from the main battlefield instead of almost upon it at St. Nazaire. There is no correlation possible between our armies in the Brest and Cherbourg peninsulas and the troops operating against Toulon and Marseilles. When Marseilles is gained the turn-round from the United States is about fourteen days longer than the straight run across the Atlantic.

4. Of course we are going to win anyway, but these are

* The first major operations in which the 'Dragoon' armies took part after their junction with General Eisenhower's forces were in mid-November.

very hard facts. When 'Anvil' was raised at Teheran it was to be a diversionary or holding operation a week before or a week later than 'Overlord' D-Day, in the hope of drawing about eight German divisions away from the main battle. The decision to undertake Anzio and the delays at Cassino forced us to continue putting off 'Anvil', until its successor 'Dragoon' bears no relation to the original conception. However, out of evil came good, and the operations in Italy being persevered in drew not fewer than twelve divisions from the German reserves in North Italy and elsewhere, and they have been largely destroyed. The coincidence that the defeat of Kesselring's army and the capture of Rome occurred at the exact time of launching 'Overlord' more than achieved all that was ever foreseen from 'Anvil', and, to those who do not know the inner history, wears the aspect of a great design. Thus I contend that what 'Anvil' was meant for is already gained.

5. Bowing to the United States Chiefs of Staff under recorded protest and the overriding of our views, we have done everything in human power, including the provision of nearly one-half the naval forces about to be engaged. If nothing can be done to save the situation I earnestly pray the American view may be right. But now an entirely new situation has developed through the victories that have been won in France and the greater victories that seem possible. It is in these circumstances that I have thought it right, on the recommendation of the British Chiefs of Staff, to reopen the question. There are still three or four days in which the decision to send to St. Nazaire the forces now destined and largely loaded for 'Dragoon' could be reconsidered. I admit the arguments against late changes in plans, but they ought to be fairly weighed against what seems to us to be the overwhelming case for strengthening the main battle, and thus possibly finishing up Hitler this year.

6. You know the great respect and regard which I have for Marshall, and if you feel able to embroil yourself in these matters I should be glad if you would bring my views before him, especially the later paragraphs, which are my reply to any complaint he may have made that I supported 'Anvil' at Teheran and have turned against it since.

7. Let me know also whether my last speech was satisfactory from the American military standpoint and whether there were any points which you would rather I had stated differently. I set the good relations of our Armies above everything else.

Kindest regards.

The reply was far from comforting.

Mr. Harry Hopkins to Prime Minister   7 Aug 44
Your wire received. While there has been no reply as yet
from the President to your message relative to the same matter,
I am sure his answer will be in the negative. While I have seen
no analysis of logistics involved, I am absolutely certain you
will find the supply problem insurmountable. Divisions are
already available for Eisenhower's immediate build-up which
will tax the ports to the limit. Then, too, no one knows the
condition of the Brittany ports. It seems to me that our
tactical position to-day in 'Overlord' is precisely as planned
and as we anticipated it would be when 'Anvil' was laid on.
To change the strategy now would be a great mistake, and I
believe would delay rather than aid in our sure conquest of
France. I believe too the movement north from 'Anvil' will be
much more rapid than you anticipate. They have nothing to
stop us. The French will rise and abyssiniate large numbers of
Germans, including, I trust, Monsieur Laval. A tremendous
victory is in store for us.

*   *   *

That day I visited Eisenhower at his headquarters near Portsmouth and unfolded to him my last hope of stopping the 'Dragoon' operation. After an agreeable luncheon we had a long
and serious conversation. Eisenhower had with him Bedell
Smith and Admiral Ramsay. I had brought the First Sea Lord,
as the movement of shipping was the key. Briefly, what I proposed was to continue loading the 'Dragoon' expedition, but
when the troops were in the ships to send them through the
Straits of Gibraltar and enter France at Bordeaux. The matter
had been long considered by the British Chiefs of Staff, and the
operation was considered feasible. I showed Eisenhower the
telegram I had sent to the President, whose reply I had not yet
received, and did my best to convince him. The First Sea Lord
strongly supported me. Admiral Ramsay argued against any
change of plan. Bedell Smith, on the contrary, declared himself
strongly in favour of this sudden deflection of the attack, which
would have all the surprise that sea-power can bestow. Eisenhower in no way resented the views of his Chief of Staff. He
always encouraged free expression of opinion in council at the
summit, though of course whatever was settled would receive
every loyalty in execution.
However, I was quite unable to move him, and the next day I
received the President's reply.

President Roosevelt to Prime Minister   8 Aug 44

I have consulted by telegraph with my Chiefs of Staff, and am unable to agree that the resources allocated to 'Dragoon' should be considered available for a move into France via ports on the coast of Brittany.

On the contrary, it is my considered opinion that 'Dragoon' should be launched as planned at the earliest practicable date, and I have full confidence that it will be successful and of great assistance to Eisenhower in driving the Huns from France.

There was no more to be done about it. It is worth noting that we had now passed the day in July when for the first time in the war the movement of the great American armies into Europe and their growth in the Far East made their numbers in action greater than our own. Influence on Allied operations is usually increased by large reinforcements. It must also be remembered that had the British views on this strategic issue been accepted the tactical preparations might well have caused some delay, which again would have reacted on the general argument.

Prime Minister to President Roosevelt   8 Aug 44

I pray God that you may be right. We shall of course do everything in our power to help you achieve success.

CHAPTER 5

Balkan Convulsions
The Russian Victories

The Need for Political Agreement with Russia in Central and Eastern Europe – Mr. Eden's Suggestion about Greece and Roumania, May 18 – My Telegram to the President, May 31 – Nervousness in the State Department – Mr. Roosevelt's Telegram of June 11, and My Reply – My Message to the President of June 23 – An Argument Between Friends – I Telegraph Stalin about Turkey, July 11 – His Non-committal Answer – The Russian Summer Campaign – The Finns Sue for an Armistice, August 25 – Advance to the Niemen – Twenty-five German Divisions Cease to Exist – The Red Army Crosses the Vistula – Revolution in Roumania.

The advance of the Soviet armies into Central and Eastern Europe in the summer of 1944 made it urgent to come to a political arrangement with the Russians about those regions. Post-war Europe seemed to be taking shape. Difficulties in Italy had already begun owing to Russian intrigues. We were striving to reach a balanced result in Yugoslav affairs by direct negotiation with Tito. But no progress had as yet been made with Moscow about Poland, Hungary, Roumania, and Bulgaria. The whole subject had been surveyed at the meeting of the Imperial Conference in London in May, and I had then minuted to the Foreign Secretary:

4 May 44

A paper should be drafted for the Cabinet, and possibly for the Imperial Conference, setting forth shortly—for that is essential—the brute issues between us and the Soviet Government which are developing in Italy, in Roumania, in Bulgaria, in Yugoslavia, and above all in Greece. It ought to be possible to get this on one page.

2. I cannot say there is much in Italy, but broadly speaking the issue is: are we going to acquiesce in the Communisation of the Balkans and perhaps of Italy? Mr. Curtin touched upon this this morning, and I am of opinion on the whole that we ought to come to a definite conclusion about it, and that if our

conclusion is that we resist the Communist infusion and invasion we should put it to them pretty plainly at the best moment that military events permit. We should of course have to consult the United States first.

And again on the same day:

Evidently we are approaching a showdown with the Russians about their Communist intrigues in Italy, Yugoslavia, and Greece. I think their attitude becomes more difficult every day.

On May 18 the Soviet Ambassador in London called at the Foreign Office to discuss a general suggestion which Mr. Eden had made that the U.S.S.R. should temporarily regard Roumanian affairs as mainly their concern under war conditions while leaving Greece to us. The Russians were prepared to accept this, but wished to know if we had consulted the United States. If so they would agree. I minuted on the record of this conversation: 'I should like to telegraph to the President about this. He would like the idea, especially as we should keep in close touch with him.'

On May 31 I accordingly sent a personal telegram to Mr. Roosevelt.

Prime Minister to President Roosevelt　　　　31 May 44
There have recently been disquieting signs of a possible divergence of policy between ourselves and the Russians in regard to the Balkan countries, and in particular towards Greece. We therefore suggested to the Soviet Ambassador here that we should agree between ourselves as a practical matter that the Soviet Government would take the lead in Roumanian affairs, while we would take the lead in Greek affairs, each Government giving the other help in the respective countries. Such an arrangement would be a natural development of the existing military situation, since Roumania falls within the sphere of the Russian armies and Greece within the Allied command under General Wilson in the Mediterranean.

2. The Soviet Ambassador here told Eden on May 18 that the Soviet Government agreed with this suggestion, but before giving any final assurance in the matter they would like to know whether we had consulted the United States Government and whether the latter had also agreed to this arrangement.

3. I hope you may feel able to give this proposal your blessing. We do not of course wish to carve up the Balkans

into spheres of influence, and in agreeing to the arrangement we should make it clear that it applied only to war conditions and did not affect the rights and responsibilities which each of the three Great Powers will have to exercise at the peace settlement and afterwards in regard to the whole of Europe. The arrangement would of course involve no change in the present collaboration between you and us in the formulation and execution of Allied policy towards these countries. We feel however that the arrangement now proposed would be a useful device for preventing any divergence of policy between ourselves and them in the Balkans.

4. Meanwhile Halifax has been asked to raise this matter with the State Department on the above lines.

The first reactions of the State Department were cool. Mr. Hull was nervous of any suggestion that 'might appear to savour of the creation or acceptance of the idea of spheres of influence'.

On June 8 I sent the following message to Lord Halifax in Washington:

Prime Minister to Lord Halifax (Washington) 8 June 44
There is no question of spheres of influence. We all have to act together, but someone must be playing the hand. It seems reasonable that the Russians should deal with the Roumanians and Bulgarians, upon whom their armies are impinging, and that we should deal with the Greeks, who are in our assigned theatre, who are our old allies, and for whom we sacrificed 40,000 men in 1941. I have reason to believe that the President is in entire agreement with the line I am taking about Greece. The same is true of Yugoslavia. I keep him constantly informed, but on the whole we, His Majesty's Government, are playing the hand, and have to be very careful to play it agreeably with the Russians. No fate could be worse for any country than to be subjected in these times to decisions reached by triangular or quadrangular telegraphing. By the time you have got one thing settled three others have gone astray. Moreover, events move very rapidly in these countries.

2. On the other hand, we follow the lead of the United States in South America as far as possible, as long as it is not a question of our beef and mutton. On this we naturally develop strong views on account of the little we get.

On June 11 Mr. Roosevelt cabled:

... Briefly, we acknowledge that the military responsible Government in any given territory will inevitably make decisions required by military developments, but are convinced that the natural tendency for such decisions to extend

66

to other than military fields would be strengthened by an agreement of the type suggested. In our opinion, this would certainly result in the persistence of differences between you and the Soviets and in the division of the Balkan region into spheres of influence despite the declared intention to limit the arrangement to military matters.

We believe efforts should preferably be made to establish consultative machinery to dispel misunderstandings and restrain the tendency toward the development of exclusive spheres.

Prime Minister to President Roosevelt   11 June 44

I am much concerned to receive your message. Action is paralysed if everybody is to consult everybody else about everything before it is taken. Events will always outstrip the changing situations in these Balkan regions. Somebody must have the power to plan and act. A Consultative Committee would be a mere obstruction, always overridden in any case of emergency by direct interchanges between you and me, or either of us and Stalin.

2. See, now, what happened at Easter. We were able to cope with this mutiny of the Greek forces entirely in accordance with your own views. This was because I was able to give constant orders to the military commanders, who at the beginning advocated conciliation, and above all no use or even threat of force. Very little life was lost. The Greek situation has been immensely improved, and, if firmness is maintained, will be rescued from confusion and disaster. The Russians are ready to let us take the lead in the Greek business, which means the E.A.M. and all its malice can be controlled by the national forces of Greece. Otherwise civil war and ruin to the land you care about so much. I always reported to you, and I always will report to you. You shall see every telegram I send. I think you might trust me in this.

3. If in these difficulties we had had to consult other Powers and a set of triangular or quadrangular telegrams got started the only result would have been chaos or impotence.

4. It seems to me, considering the Russians are about to invade Roumania in great force and are going to help Roumania recapture part of Transylvania from Hungary, provided the Roumanians play, which they may, considering all that, it would be a good thing to follow the Soviet leadership, considering that neither you nor we have any troops there at all and that they will probably do what they like anyhow. Moreover, I thought their terms, apart from indemnity, very sensible, and even generous. The Roumanian Army has inflicted many injuries upon the Soviet troops, and went into the

war against Russia with glee. I see no difficulty whatever in our addressing the Russians at any time on any subject, but please let them go ahead upon the lines agreed as they are doing all the work.

5. Similarly with us in Greece. We are an old ally of Greece. We had 40,000 casualties in trying to defend Greece against Hitler, not counting Crete. The Greek King and the Greek Government have placed themselves under our protection. They are at present domiciled in Egypt. They may very likely move to the Lebanon, which would be a better atmosphere than Cairo. Not only did we lose the 40,000 men above mentioned in helping Greece, but a vast mass of shipping and warships, and by denuding Cyrenaica to help Greece we also lost the whole of Wavell's conquests in Cyrenaica. These were heavy blows to us in those days. Your telegrams to me in the recent crisis worked wonders. We were entirely agreed, and the result is entirely satisfactory. Why is all this effective direction to be broken up into a committee of mediocre officials such as we are littering about the world? Why can you and I not keep this in our own hands, considering how we see eye to eye about so much of it?

6. To sum up, I propose that we agree that the arrangements I set forth in my message of May 31 may have a trial of three months, after which it must be reviewed by the three Powers.

On June 13 the President agreed to this proposal, but added: 'We must be careful to make it clear that we are not establishing any post-war spheres of influence.'

I shared his view, and replied the next day:

I am deeply grateful to you for your telegram. I have asked the Foreign Secretary to convey the information to Molotov and to make it clear that the reason for the three months' limit is in order that we should not prejudge the question of establishing post-war spheres of influence.

I reported the situation to the War Cabinet that afternoon, and it was agreed that, subject to the time-limit of three months, the Foreign Secretary should inform the Soviet Government that we accepted this general division of responsibility. This was done on June 19. The President however was not happy about the way we had acted, and I received a pained message saying 'we were disturbed that your people took this matter up with us only after it had been put up to the Russians'. On June 23 accordingly I outlined to the President, in reply to his rebuke, the situation as I saw it from London.

Prime Minister to President Roosevelt   23 June 44

The Russians are the only Power that can do anything in Roumania, and I thought it was agreed between you and me that on the basis of their reasonable armistice terms, excepting indemnities, they should try to give coherent direction to what happened there. In point of fact we have all three co-operated closely in handling in Cairo the recent Roumanian peace-feelers. On the other hand, the Greek burden rests almost entirely upon us, and has done so since we lost 40,000 men in a vain endeavour to help them in 1941. Similarly, you have let us play the hand in Turkey, but we have always consulted you on policy, and I think we have been agreed on the line to be followed. It would be quite easy for me, on the general principle of slithering to the Left, which is so popular in foreign policy, to let things rip, when the King of Greece would probably be forced to abdicate and E.A.M. would work a reign of terror in Greece, forcing the villagers and many other classes to form Security Battalions under German auspices to prevent utter anarchy. The only way I can prevent this is by persuading the Russians to quit boosting E.A.M. and ramming it forward with all their force. Therefore I proposed to the Russians a temporary working arrangement for the better conduct of the war. This was only a proposal, and had to be referred to you for your agreement.

2. I cannot admit that I have done anything wrong in this matter. It would not be possible for three people in different parts of the world to work together effectively if no one of them may make any suggestion to either of the others without simultaneously keeping the third informed. A recent example of this is the message you have sent quite properly to Uncle Joe about your conversations with the Poles, of which as yet I have heard nothing from you. I am not complaining at all of this, because I know we are working for the general theme and purposes, and I hope you will feel that has been so in my conduct of the Greek affair.

3. I have also taken action to try to bring together a union of the Tito forces with those in Serbia, and with all adhering to the Royal Yugoslav Government, which we have both recognised. You have been informed at every stage of how we are bearing this heavy burden, which at present rests mainly on us. Here again nothing would be easier than to throw the King and the Royal Yugoslav Government to the wolves and let a civil war break out in Yugoslavia, to the joy of the Germans. I am struggling to bring order out of chaos

in both cases and concentrate all efforts against the common foe. I am keeping you constantly informed, and I hope to have your confidence and help within the spheres of action in which initiative is assigned to us.

The President's reply of June 27 settled this argument between friends. 'It appears,' he said, 'that both of us have inadvertently taken unilateral action in a direction that we both now agree to have been expedient for the time being. It is essential that we should always be in agreement on matters bearing on our Allied war effort.'

I replied the same day: 'You may be sure I shall always be looking to our agreement in all matters before, during, and after.'

The difficulties however continued on a Governmental level. The Russians insisted on consulting the Americans direct.

* * *

Another issue also claimed our attention. The Russian armies were now poised on the borders of Roumania. Here was Turkey's last chance to enter the war on the Allied side, and her entry at this stage would have a potent influence on the future of South-Eastern Europe. She now offered to go as far as breaking off relations with the Axis.

I gave Stalin my views on these events.

Prime Minister to Marshal Stalin   11 July 44
    Some weeks ago it was suggested by Eden to your Ambassador that the Soviet Government should take the lead in Roumania, and the British should do the same in Greece. This was only a working arrangement to avoid as much as possible the awful business of triangular telegrams, which paralyses action. Molotov then suggested very properly that I should tell the United States, which I did, and always meant to, and after some discussion the President agreed to a three months' trial being made. These may be three very important months, Marshal Stalin, July, August, and September. Now however I see that you find some difficulty in this. I would ask whether you should not tell us that the plan may be allowed to have its chance for three months. No one can say it affects the future of Europe or divides it into spheres; but we can get a clear-headed policy in each theatre, and we will all report to the others what we are doing. However, if you tell me it is hopeless I shall not take it amiss.
    2. There is another matter I should like to put to you.

Turkey is willing to break relations immediately with the Axis Powers. I agree with you that she ought to declare war, but I fear that if we tell her to do so she will defend herself by asking both for aircraft to protect her towns, which we shall find it hard to spare or put there at the present moment, and also for joint military operations in Bulgaria and the Ægean, for which we have not at present the means. And in addition to all this she will demand once again all sorts of munitions, which we cannot spare because the stocks we had ready for her at the beginning of the year have been drawn off in other directions. It seems to me therefore wiser to take this breaking off relations with Germany as a first instalment. We can then push a few things in to help her against a vengeance attack from the air, and out of this, while we are together, her entry into the war might come. The Turkish alliance in the last war was very dear to the Germans, and the fact that Turkey had broken off relations would be a knell to the German soul. This seems to be a pretty good time to strike such a knell.

3. I am only putting to you my personal thoughts on these matters, which are also being transmitted by Eden to M. Molotov.

4. We have about a million and fifty thousand men in Normandy, with a vast mass of equipment, and rising by 25,000 a day. The fighting is very hard, and before the recent battles, for which casualties have not yet come in, we and the Americans had lost 64,000 men. However, there is every evidence that the enemy has lost at least as many, and we have besides 51,000 prisoners in the bag. Considering that we have been on the offensive and had the landing from the sea to manage, I consider that the enemy has been severely mauled. The front will continue to broaden and the fighting will be unceasing.

5. Alexander is pushing very hard in Italy also. He hopes to force the Pisa–Rimini line and break into the Po valley. This will either draw further German divisions on to him or yield up valuable strategic ground.

6. The Londoners are standing up well to the bombing, which has amounted to 22,000 casualties so far and looks like becoming chronic.

7. Once more, congratulations on your glorious advance to Vilna.

His reply was non-committal.

Marshal Stalin to Prime Minister　　　　　　　　15 July 44
As regards the question of Roumania and Greece. . . . One thing is clear to me: it is that the American Government have

some doubts regarding this question, and that it would be better to revert to this matter when we receive the American reply to our inquiry. As soon as the observations of the American Government are known I shall not fail to write to you further on this question.

2. The question of Turkey should be considered in the light of those facts which have been well known to the Governments of Great Britain, the Soviet Union, and the U.S.A. from the time of the last negotiations with the Turkish Government at the end of last year. You of course will remember how insistently the Governments of our three countries proposed to Turkey that she should enter the war against Hitlerite Germany on the side of the Allies as long ago as in November and December of 1943. Nothing came of this. As you know, on the initiative of the Turkish Government in May–June of this year we again entered into negotiations with the Turkish Government, and twice we proposed to them the same thing that the three Allied Governments had proposed to them at the end of last year. Nothing came of this either. As regards these or other half-measures on the part of Turkey, at the present time I see no benefit in them for the Allies. In view of the evasive and vague attitude with regard to Germany adopted by the Turkish Government, it is better to leave Turkey in peace and to her own free will and not to exert fresh pressure on Turkey. This of course means that the claims of Turkey, who has evaded war with Germany, to special rights in post-war matters also lapse. . . .

We were thus unable to reach any final agreement about dividing responsibilities in the Balkan peninsula. Early in August the Russians dispatched from Italy by a subterfuge a mission to E.L.A.S. in Northern Greece. In the light of American official reluctance and of this instance of Russian bad faith, we abandoned our efforts to reach a major understanding until I met Stalin in Moscow two months later. By then much had happened on the Eastern Front.

*　　　*　　　*

The Russian summer campaign was a tale of sweeping success. I can but summarise it here.

The advance opened with a secondary offensive against the Finns. Between Lake Ladoga and the sea they had deepened and strengthened the original Mannerheim Line into a formidable defensive system. However, the Russian troops, very different in quality and armament from those who had fought here in

1940, broke through after twelve days of hard fighting and captured Viborg on June 21. Operations were begun the same day to clear the north shore to Lake Ladoga, and at the end of the month they had thrown their opponents back and reopened the railway from Leningrad to Murmansk, the terminal of our Arctic convoys. The Finns struggled on for a while, supported by German troops, but they had had enough, and on August 25 sued for an armistice.

The attack on the German front between Vitebsk and Gomel began on June 23. These, with Bobruisk, Mogilev, and many other towns and villages, had been turned into strong positions, with all-round defence, but they were successively surrounded and disposed of, while the Russian armies poured through the gaps between. Within a week they had broken through to a depth of eighty miles. Taking swift advantage of their success, they captured Minsk on July 6, and closed the retreating enemy along a hastily organised line running southwards from Vilna to the Pripet Marshes, from which the Germans were soon swept by the irresistible Russian flood. At the end of July the Red armies had reached the Niemen at Kovno and Grodno. Here, after an advance of 250 miles in five weeks, they were brought to a temporary halt to replenish. The German losses had been crushing. Twenty-five divisions had ceased to exist, and an equal number were cut off in Courland.* On July 17 alone 57,000 German prisoners were marched through Moscow—who knows whither?

South of the Pripet Marshes the Russian successes were no less magnificent. On July 13 a series of attacks were launched on the front between Kovel and Stanislav. In ten days the whole German front was broken and the Russians had reached Jaroslav, on the San river, 120 miles farther west. Stanislav, Lemberg, and Przemysl, isolated by this advance, were soon accounted for, and on July 30 the triumphant Russians crossed the Vistula south of Sandomir. Here supply imposed a halt. The crossing of the Vistula was taken by the Polish Resistance Movement in Warsaw as a signal for the ill-fated rising which is recorded in another chapter.

There was still a further far-reaching Russian success in this great campaign. To the southward of their victories lay Roumania. Till August was far advanced the German line from Cernowitz to the Black Sea barred the way to Roumania, the

* Guderian, *Panzer Leader*, p. 352.

Legend:
Russian front, June 1944
Major Russian attacks
Approx. front, Feb. 1, 1945
Surrounded enemy garrisons, Feb. 1945

1939 frontiers
0   100   200   300 MILES

To Murmansk
L. Onega
FINLAND
L. Ladoga
Viborg
G. of Finland
Leningrad
Tallinn
ESTONIA
L. Peipus
Pskov
SWEDEN
BALTIC SEA
Riga
COURLAND
LATVIA
U. S. S. R.
Vitebsk
Smolensk
LITHUANIA
Tilsit
R. Niemen
Kovno
Vilna
Minsk
Mogilev
Königsberg
Grodno
Danzig
E. PRUSSIA
Bobruisk
Gomel
Stettin
Schneidemühl
Pinsk
R. Pripet
MARSHES
Berlin
Posen
R. Vistula
Warsaw
R. Oder
POLAND
Kiev
UPPER
Breslau
SILESIA
Oppeln
Sandomir
Kovel
Prague
Cracow
R. San
Jaroslav
Lemberg
R. Dnieper
R. Bug
CZECHOSLOVAKIA
Przemysl
CARPATHIAN MOUNTAINS
Stanislav
Cernowitz
R. Danube
Vienna
Jassy
R. Dniester
AUSTRIA
Budapest
R. Pruth
Odessa
HUNGARY
TRANSYLVANIAN ALPS
L. Balaton
ROUMANIA
Crimea
Belgrade
Bucharest
Ploesti
BLACK SEA
YUGOSLAVIA
R. Danube
BULGARIA

Operations on the Russian Front, June 1944–January 1945

Ploesti oilfields, and the Balkans. It had been weakened by withdrawal of troops to sustain the sagging line farther north, and under violent attacks, beginning on August 22, it rapidly disintegrated. Aided by landings on the coast, the Russians made short work of the enemy. Sixteen German divisions were lost. On August 23 a *coup d'état* in Bucharest, organised by the young King Michael and his close advisers, led to a complete reversal of the whole military position. The Roumanian armies followed their King to a man. Within three days before the arrival of the Soviet troops the German forces had been disarmed or had retired over the northern frontiers. By September 1 Bucharest had been evacuated by the Germans. The Roumanian armies disintegrated and the country was overrun. The Roumanian Government capitulated. Bulgaria, after a last-minute attempt to declare war on Germany, was overwhelmed. Wheeling to the west, the Russian armies drove up the valley of the Danube and through the Transylvanian Alps to the Hungarian border, while their left flank, south of the Danube, lined up on the frontier of Yugoslavia. Here they prepared for the great westerly drive which in due time was to carry them to Vienna.

Italy and the Riviera Landing

After Rome fell on June 4 Kesselring's broken armies streamed northwards in disorder, harassed and disorganised by continuous air attacks and closely pursued on land. General Clark's Fifth U.S. Army took the coastal roads towards Pisa, while our Eighth Army followed up astride the Tiber, heading for Lake Trasimene. The pace was hot.

Prime Minister to General Alexander   9 June 44

All our information here goes to reinforce your estimate of the ruin you have wrought on the German armies in Italy. Your whole advance is splendid, and I hope the remnants of what were once the German armies will be collected.

Alexander hoped greatly that the 'Anvil' plan to land in the south of France would be put aside and that he would be allowed to keep intact his battle-trained troops, now flushed with victory. If so, he was confident of breaking through the Apennines into the valley of the Po and beyond within a few months. He failed by a very narrow margin, as this story will show, and it seems certain that but for the deprivations and demands of 'Anvil' the campaign in Italy could have been over by Christmas.

In any case there was hard fighting ahead. Nineteen German divisions had been involved in the battles of May and early June. Three of them had ceased to exist ; most of the others were gravely stricken and hurrying northwards in confused retreat. But Kesselring was a good general, with a competent staff. His problem was to delay our advance until he had re organised his troops and occupied his next prepared position the so-called Gothic Line, which ran from the west coast beyond Pisa, curved along the mountains north of Florence, and then struck off to the Adriatic at Pesaro. The Germans had been working on this line for more than a year, but it was still un finished. Kesselring had to fight for time to complete and man it and to receive the eight divisions which were being sent him from Northern Europe, the Balkans, Germany, and Russia.

After ten days of pursuit German resistance began to stiffen and the Eighth Army had a hard fight to overcome a strong position on the famous shores of Lake Trasimene. It was not till June 28 that the enemy were ejected and fell back on Arezzo On the west coast American troops of the Fifth Army took Cecina, not without difficulty, on July 1, and on their right the French Corps also under General Clark's command, reached Siena soon afterwards. The enemy made a corresponding with drawal on the Adriatic coast, enabling the Polish Corps swiftly to occupy Pescara and drive on towards Ancona. At this time too a French colonial division, transhipped from Corsica, took Elba, with two thousand prisoners, after a couple of days' sharp fighting, in which they received strong naval and air support.

In early July, as a result of the discussions which had been proceeding with the United States, Alexander was ordered to detach forces amounting finally to seven divisions, for 'Anvil' The Fifth Army alone was thereby reduced from nearly 250,000 men to 153,000. Despite this blow Alexander persevered with vigour in his pursuit and plan. The Germans, re-formed and re built to the equivalent of fourteen divisions, faced him on a line from Rosignano to Arezzo and thence to the Adriatic south of Ancona. This was one of a succession of covering positions which the enemy were to hold with increasing obstin acy to stop us reaching their Gothic Line. Arezzo fell to the British on July 16, after heavy air and artillery bombardment On the 18th the Americans reached the river Arno east of Pisa and the next day entered the port of Leghorn, while the Poles who had been pressing hard along the Adriatic shore, took Ancona. These two ports, though severely damaged, eased the strain on our now much-extended line of communications. In the last week of the month further advances gave the Americans the whole line of the Arno from Empoli to Pisa. The Eighth

Northern Italy

Ljubljana Main lines of Allied advance,
June–August 1944
German Gothic Line
Mountainous areas
0 25 50 75 100 MILES

YUGOSLAVIA

Trieste
Fiume
Pola

ADRIATIC SEA

Vis

Venice
Ravenna
Forlì
Rimini
Pesaro
Ancona

Verona
L. Garda
Cremona
Pavia
Capua
River- Po
Modena
Bologna
Faenza
GOTHIC LINE
Apennine
Florence
Pistoia
R. Arno
Empoli
Leghorn
Rossignano
Cecina
Spezia
Genoa

Mountains
POLISH
CORPS
L. Trasimene
Arezzo
EIGHTH
ARMY
R. Tiber
ROME
Anzio
Pescara
Siena
FIFTH
ARMY
Civitavecchia
Cassino
Caserta
Naples

Elba

CORSICA
Ajaccio

SARDINIA

Turin

Army cleared all the mountain country south of Florence, and the New Zealanders, breaking into the defence, forced the enemy to withdraw through the city, where they destroyed behind them all the bridges except the venerable but inadequate Ponte Vecchio.

In less than two months the Allied armies had advanced over 250 miles. After the first fortnight it had been hard going all the way, with many vexatious supply problems. The Germans had their share of these. All their rearward communications ran across the wide river Po on a score of road and rail bridges. Towards the end of July these were incessantly attacked by the Allied air forces, and every one of them was cut, although, thanks to the skill of Kesselring's engineer's, some supplies still got through.

* * *

I now decided to go myself to Italy, where many questions could be more easily settled on the spot than by correspondence. It would be a great advantage to see the commanders and the troops from whom so much was being demanded, after so much had been taken. The 'Anvil' operation was about to be launched. Alexander, though sorely weakened, was preparing his armies for a further offensive. I was anxious to meet Tito, who could easily come to Italy from the island of Vis, where we were still protecting him. M. Papandreou and some of his colleagues could come from Cairo, and plans could be made to help them back to Athens when the Germans departed. Finally there was the Italian political tangle of which Rome was now the centre. On July 30 I telegraphed to General Wilson at Caserta:

> I am hoping, if the ['doodle-bug'] bombardment here does not flare up unduly, to come to Italy for ten days or a fortnight, starting August 6 or 7. It would be a pity for me to miss Tito, with whom I am quite prepared to discuss political matters of all kinds. Could you therefore stage your meeting with him so that he will be at Caserta at dates including the 8th or 9th?

And on August 4 to General Alexander:

> I thought it would be better for us to make our plans [for my visit] together when I arrive. Mind you do not let me get in your way. I do not want a heavy programme, nor to engage myself to see anybody except you, Wilson, and Tito. I have

no doubt I shall find plenty to do when I am on the spot.

* * *

The days were so crowded with Cabinet business that my dates receded. On August 9 I telegraphed to Mr. Duff Cooper that I hoped to arrive at the Maison Blanche airfield, outside Algiers, about 6.30 a.m. on Friday, August 11, and would stay there for about three hours on my way to Naples. I added, 'You may tell de Gaulle in case he wishes to see me at your house or the Admiral's villa. The visit is quite informal.'

We arrived punctually. Duff Cooper met me, and took me to his house, which his wife had made most comfortable. He told me he had conveyed my invitation or suggestion to de Gaulle, and that the General had refused. He did not wish to intrude upon the repose I should need at this brief halt on my journey.

I thought this needlessly haughty, considering all the business I've had in hand and what I could have told him. He was however still offended by what had happened at 'Overlord', and thought this was a good chance of marking his displeasure. I did not in fact see him again for several months.

I reached Naples that afternoon, and was installed in the palatial though somewhat dilapidated Villa Rivalta, with a glorious view of Vesuvius and the bay. Here General Wilson explained to me that all arrangements had been made for a conference next morning with Tito and Subašić, the new Yugoslav Prime Minister of King Peter's Government in London. They had already arrived in Naples, and would dine with us the next night.

On the morning of August 12 Marshal Tito came up to the villa. He wore a magnificent gold and blue uniform which was very tight under the collar and singularly unsuited to the blazing heat. The uniform had been given him by the Russians, and, as I was afterwards informed, the gold lace came from the United States. I joined him on the terrace of the villa, accompanied by Brigadier Maclean and an interpreter.

I suggested that the Marshal might first like to see General Wilson's War Room, and we moved inside. The Marshal, who was attended by two ferocious-looking bodyguards, each carrying automatic pistols, wanted to bring them with him in case of treachery on our part. He was dissuaded from this with some difficulty, and proposed to bring them to guard him at dinner instead.

I led the way into a large room, where maps of the battle fronts covered the walls. I began by displaying the Allied front in Normandy and indicating our broad strategic moves against the German armies in the West. I pointed out Hitler's obstinacy in refusing to yield an inch of territory, how numerous divisions were locked up in Norway and in the Baltic provinces, and said that his correct strategy would be to withdraw his troops from the Balkans and concentrate them on the main battle-fronts. Allied pressure in Italy and the Russian advance from the east might force him to go but we must reckon on the possibility of his staying. As I talked I pointed on the map to the Istrian peninsula, and asked Tito where, if we were able to reach it from the east coast of Italy, his forces could be sent to co-operate with us. I explained that it would help if a small port could be opened on the Yugoslav coast so that we could send in war material by sea. In June and July we had sent nearly two thousand tons of stores to his forces by air, but could do much more if we had a port. Tito said that although German opposition had intensified lately, and Yugoslav losses increased, he was able to raise considerable forces in Croatia and Slovenia, and he would certainly favour an operation against the Istrian peninsula, in which Yugoslav forces would join.

We now moved into a small sitting-room, and I began to question him about his relations with the Royal Yugoslav Government. He said that violent fighting still continued between the Partisans and Mihailović, whose power rested on German and Bulgar help. Reconciliation was unlikely. I replied that we had no desire to intervene in internal Yugoslav affairs, but wanted his country to be strong, united, and independent. Dr Subašić was very loyal to this idea. Moreover we ought not to let the King down. Tito said that he understood our obligation towards King Peter, but was not able to do anything about it until after the war, when the Yugoslav people themselves would decide.

I then turned to the future, and suggested that the right solution for Yugoslavia would be a democratic system based on the peasantry, and perhaps some gradual measure of agrarian re-form where the holdings were too small. Tito assured me that, as he had stated publicly, he had no desire to introduce the Communist system into Yugoslavia, if only because most European countries after the war would probably be living under a democratic régime. Developments in small countries depended on

elations between the Great Powers. Yugoslavia should be able
o profit by the growing improvement in these relations and
develop along democratic lines. The Russians had a mission
with the Partisans, but its members, far from expressing any
dea of introducing the Soviet system into Yugoslavia, had
spoken against it.

I asked Tito if he would reaffirm his statement about Communism in public, but he did not wish to do this as it might seem
o have been forced upon him. It was agreed that he should
however discuss the suggestion with Dr. Subašić, whom he was
meeting for the first time that afternoon.

We then lunched together, and arranged that if the talks with
Dr. Subašić made favourable progress we should meet again
the following evening. In the meantime I undertook to draft a
memorandum on Yugoslav affairs and the Marshal promised to
send me a letter on certain specific matters about supplies.

*   *   *

Early in the day Tito had met General Gammell, Chief of
Staff to General Wilson, and been given an important memorandum on Allied projects in Istria and thereabouts. It read as
follows:

In the event of Allied forces occupying Northern Italy,
Austria, or Hungary it is the Supreme Allied Commander's
intention to impose Allied military government in the area
which was under Italian rule at the outbreak of war, which
automatically suspends Italian sovereignty. The Military
Governor will be the General Officer Commanding the Allied
armies in the area. It is intended that the area shall remain
under direct Allied administration until its disposition has been
determined by negotiations between the Governments concerned.

2. This direct Allied military government is necessary in
order to safeguard the bases and lines of communication of
the Allied troops of occupation in Central Europe.

3. As the Allied forces of occupation will have to be supplied through the port of Trieste, it will be necessary for them
to have secure lines of communication protected by British
troops on the route through Ljubljana–Maribor–Graz.

4. The Supreme Allied Commander looks to the Yugoslav
authorities to co-operate with him in carrying out this policy,
and he intends to maintain the closest liaison with them.

Tito had grumbled at these proposals in a letter to me, and

when we met again on the afternoon of August 13, Mr. Stevenson, our Ambassador to Yugoslavia, and Dr. Subašić being present, I said that it was an operational question which needed careful study, and also close consultation with the American President. The status of Istria, which still remained Italian, could not be prejudged. It might be a good thing to remove it from Italian sovereignty, but this must be decided at the Peace Conference, or, if there were none, by a meeting of the principal Powers, at which Yugoslavia could state her claim. The United States Government was against territorial changes in time of war, and we ought not to discourage the Italians more than could be helped because they were now making a useful contribution to the war. The best solution might therefore be for the territory to be administered under Allied military government when it was freed from the Germans.

Tito said that he could not accept an Italian civil administration and pointed out that his National Liberation Movement already controlled many of these areas and should at least be associated in their administration. He and Subašić agreed to send us a joint memorandum on Istria, and there the matter rested for the moment.

We then discussed how to produce a united Yugoslav Navy and how to send him light tanks, gunboats, and artillery. I said that we would do what we could, but I warned him that we should lose interest if the fighting in Yugoslavia developed into mere civil war and the struggle against the Germans became only a side issue.

I had referred to this in a note which I had sent to Tito on August 12. We now considered the wider implications of this document, which ran as follows:

The desire of His Majesty's Government is to see a united Yugoslav Government, in which all Yugoslavs resisting the enemy are represented, and a reconciliation between the Serbian people and the National Liberation Movement.

2. His Majesty's Government intend to continue, and if possible to increase, the supply of war material to Yugoslav forces now that an agreement has been reached between the Royal Yugoslav Government and the National Liberation Movement. They expect, in return, that Marshal Tito will make a positive contribution to the unification of Yugoslavia by including in the declaration which he has already agreed with the Yugoslav Prime Minister to make, not only a state-

ment regarding his intention not to impose Communism on
the country, but also a statement to the effect that he will not
use the armed strength of the Movement to influence the free
expression of the will of the people on the future *régime* of
the country.

3. Another contribution which Marshal Tito could make
to the common cause is to agree to meet King Peter, preferably
on Yugoslav soil.

4. If it should turn out that any large quantities of ammunition sent by His Majesty's Government are used for fratricidal
strife other than in self-defence, it would affect the whole
question of Allied supplies, because we do not wish to be
involved in Yugoslav political differences.

5. We should like to see the Royal Yugoslav Navy and Air
Force working all out for national liberation, but this cannot
be agreed unless first of all due consideration is paid to the
King, the constitutional flag, and the closer unity of the
Government and the Movement.

6. His Majesty's Government, while regarding Marshal Tito
and his brave men with the utmost admiration, are not satisfied
that sufficient recognition has been given to the power and
rights of the Serbian people, or to the help which has been
given, and will be continued, by His Majesty's Government.

The Yugoslavs objected to my suggestion that the Partisan
movement was divorced from the Serbian people. I did not
ress this point, particularly as Tito had said that he was pre-
ared later on to make a public statement about not introducing
ommunism into Yugoslavia after the war. We then discussed a
ossible meeting between him and King Peter. I said that demo-
racy had flowered in England under constitutional monarchy,
nd thought that Yugoslavia's international position would be
ronger under a king than as a republic. Tito said his country
ad had an unfortunate experience with her King, and it would
ke time for King Peter to live down his connection with
Mihailović. He had no objection in principle to meeting the
ing, but thought that the moment had not yet come. We there-
ore agreed to leave it to him and Dr. Subašić to decide on the
ost opportune occasion.

* * *

Later I entertained Tito to dinner. He was still confined in his
old-lace strait-jacket. I was so glad to be wearing only a white
uck suit.

I now reported the results of these talks to the President.

T—s.w.w.—11—D

Prime Minister to President Roosevelt   14 Aug

I have had meetings during the last two days with Marsh
Tito and the Yugoslav Prime Minister. I told both the Yug
slav leaders that we had no thought but that they should co
bine their resources so as to weld the Yugoslav people in
one instrument in the struggle against the Germans. Our a
was to promote the establishment of a stable and independe
Yugoslavia, and the creation of a united Yugoslav Gover
ment was a step towards this end.

2. The leaders reached a satisfactory agreement on a numb
of practical questions. They agreed that all the Yugosl
naval forces will now be united in the struggle under
common flag. This agreement between the Yugoslav Prir
Minister and Marshal Tito will enable us with more confiden
to increase our supplies of war material to the Yugoslav forc

3. They agreed between themselves to issue simultaneou
a statement in a few days' time, which I hope will strength
and intensify the Yugoslav war effort. They are going off t
gether to-day to Vis to continue their discussions.

4. I am informing Marshal Stalin of the result of the
meetings.

*   *   *

On all these three days at Naples I mingled pleasure with t
Admiral Morse, who commanded the naval forces, took me ea
day in his barge on an expedition, of which the prime featu
was a bathe. On the first we went to the island of Ischia, with
hot springs, and on the return we ran through an immen
United States troop convoy sailing for the landing on the Rivie
All the ships were crowded with men, and as we passed alo
their lines they cheered enthusiastically. They did not know th
if I had had my way they would be sailing in a different directio
However, I was proud to wave to these gallant soldiers. We al
visited Capri. I had never seen the Blue Grotto before. It
indeed a miracle of transparent, sparkling water of a most i
tense, vivid blue. We bathed in a small, warm bay, and repair
to luncheon at a comfortable inn. I summoned up in my mind
I could remember about the Emperor Tiberius. Certainly
Capri he had chosen an agreeable headquarters from which
rule the world.

These days, apart from business, were a sunshine holiday.

*   *   *

On the afternoon of August 14 I flew in General Wilso

Dakota to Corsica in order to see the landing at 'Anvil' which I had tried so hard to stop, but to which I wished all success. We had a pleasant flight to Ajaccio, in the harbour of which General Wilson and Admiral Sir John Cunningham had posted themselves on board a British headquarters ship. The airfield was very small and not easily approached. The pilot was excellent. He had to come in between two bluffs, and his port wing was scarcely fifteen feet from one of them. The General and the Admiral brought me aboard, and we spent a long evening on our affairs. I was to start at daylight in the British destroyer *Kimberley*. I took with me two members of the American Administration, General Somervell and Mr. Patterson, the Assistant Secretary of War, who were on the spot to see their venture. Captain Allen, whose help in these Books I have acknowledged, was sent by the Admiral to see that we did not get into trouble. We were five hours sailing before we reached the line of battleships bombarding at about fifteen thousand yards. I now learned from Captain Allen that we were not supposed to go beyond the ten-thousand-yard limit for fear of mines. If I had known this when we passed the *Ramillies*, which was firing at intervals, I could have asked for a picket-boat and gone ashore. As it was we did not go nearer than about seven thousand yards. Here we saw the long rows of boats filled with American storm troops steaming in continuously to the Bay of St. Tropez. As far as I could see or hear not a shot was fired either at the approaching flotillas or on the beaches. The battleships had now stopped firing, as there seemed to be nobody there. We then returned to Ajaccio. I had at least done the civil to 'Anvil', and indeed I thought it was a good thing I was near the scene to show the interest I took in it. On the way back I found a lively novel, *Grand Hotel*, in the captain's cabin, and this kept me in good temper till I got back to the Supreme Commander and the Naval Commander-in-Chief, who had passed an equally dull day sitting in the stern cabin.

On August 16 I got back to Naples, and rested there for the night before going up to meet Alexander at the front. I telegraphed to the King, from whom I had received a very kind message.

Prime Minister to the King   17 Aug 44

    With humble duty.

    From my distant view of the 'Dragoon' operation, the landing seemed to be effected with the utmost smoothness. How much time will be taken in the advance first to Marseilles an then up the Rhone valley, and how these operations will rela themselves to the far greater and possibly decisive operatio in the north [Normandy], are the questions that now arise.

I am proceeding to-day to General Alexander's hea quarters. It is very important that we ensure that Alexander army is not so mauled and milked that it cannot have a then or plan of campaign. This will certainly require a conferenc on something like the 'Quadrant' scale, and at the same plac [Quebec].

My vigour has been greatly restored by the change an movement and the warm weather. I hope to see various peopl including Mr. Papandreou, in Rome, where I expect to be o the 21st.

May I express to Your Majesty the pleasure and encourag ment which Your Majesty's gracious message gave me.

And to General Eisenhower:

Prime Minister to General Eisenhower (*France*) 18 Aug 4

I am following with thrilled attention the magnificer developments of operations in Normandy and Anjou. I off you again my sincere congratulations on the truly marvellou results achieved, and hope for surpassing victory. You hav certainly among other things effected a very important diver sion from our attack at 'Dragoon'. I watched this landin yesterday from afar. All I have learnt here makes me admir the perfect precision with which the landing was arranged an the intimate collaboration of British-American forces an organisations. I shall hope to come and see you and Mon gomery before the end of the month. Much will have hap pened by then. It seems to me that the results might we eclipse all the Russian victories up to the present. All goo wishes to you and Bedell.

*   *   *

This chapter may close with an outline of the 'Anvil' 'Dragoon' operations themselves.

The Seventh Army, under General Patch, had been forme to carry out the attack. It consisted of seven French and thre U.S. divisions, together with a mixed American and British ai borne division. The three American divisions comprised Genera Truscott's VIth Corps, whch had formed an important part o General Clark's Fifth Army in Italy. In addition, up to fou French divisions and a considerable part of the Allied air force were withdrawn from Alexander's command.

The new expedition was mounted from both Italy and North Africa, Naples, Taranto, Brindisi, and Oran being used as the chief loading ports. Great preparations had been made throughout the year to convert Corsica into an advanced air base and to use Ajaccio as a staging port for landing-craft proceeding to the assault from Italy. All these arrangements now bore fruit. Under the Commander-in-Chief, Admiral Sir John Cunningham, the naval attack was entrusted to Vice-Admiral Hewitt, U.S.N., who had had much experience in similar operations in the Mediterranean. Lieut.-General Eaker, U.S.A.A.F., commanded the air forces, with Air Marshal Slessor as his Deputy.

Landing-craft restricted the first seaborne landing to three divisions, and the more experienced Americans led the van. Shore defences all along the coast were strong, but the enemy were weak in numbers and some were of poor quality. In June there had been fourteen German divisions in Southern France, but four of these were drawn away to the fighting in Normandy and no more then ten remained to guard the 200 miles of coastline. Only three of these lay near the beaches on which we landed. The enemy were also short of aircraft. Against our total of 5,000 in the Mediterranean, of which 2,000 were based in Corsica and Sardinia, they could muster a bare two hundred, and these were mauled in the days before the invasion. In the midst of the Germans in Southern France over 25,000 armed men of the Resistance were ready to revolt. We had sent them their weapons, and, as in so many other parts of France, they had been organised by some of that devoted band of men and women trained in Britain for the purpose during the past three years.

The strength of the enemy's defences demanded a heavy preliminary bombardment, which was provided from the air for the previous fortnight all along the coast, and, jointly with the Allied Navies, on the landing beaches immediately before our descent. No fewer than six battleships, twenty-one cruisers, and a hundred destroyers took part. The three U.S. divisions, with American and French Commandos on their left, landed early on August 15 between Cannes and Hyères. Thanks to the bombardment, successful deception plans, continuous fighter cover, and good staff work, our casualties were relatively few. During the previous night the airborne division had dropped around Le Muy, and soon joined hands with the seaborne attack.

By noon on the 16th the three American divisions were ashore.

One of them moved northwards to Sisteron, and the other tw
struck north-west towards Avignon. The IInd French Corp
landed immediately behind them and made for Toulon an
Marseilles. Both places were strongly defended, and althoug
the French were built up to a force of five divisions the por
were not fully occupied till the end of the month. The insta
lations were severely damaged, but Port de Bouc had bee
captured intact with the aid of the Resistance, and supplies soo
began to flow. This was a valuable contribution by the Frenc
forces under General de Lattre de Tassigny. In the meantime th
Americans had been moving fast, and on August 28 were be
yond Valence and Grenoble. The enemy made no serious a
tempt to stop the advance, except for a stiff fight at Montélima
by a Panzer division. The Allied Tactical Air Force was treatin
them roughly and destroying their transport. Eisenhower's pu
suit from Normandy was cutting in behind them, having reache
the Seine at Fontainebleau on August 20, and five days later
was well past Troyes. No wonder the surviving elements of th
German Nineteenth Army, amounting to a nominal five division
were in full retreat, leaving 50,000 prisoners in our hands. Lyor
was taken on September 3, Besançon on the 8th, and Dijon wa
liberated by the Resistance Movement on the 11th. On that da
'Dragoon' and 'Overlord' joined hands at Sombernon. In th
triangle of South-West France, trapped by these concentr
thrusts, were the isolated remnants of the German First Arm
over 20,000 strong, who freely gave themselves up.

*   *   *

To sum up the 'Anvil'-'Dragoon' story, the original pro
posal at Teheran in November 1943 was for a descent in th
south of France to help take the weight off 'Overlord'. Th
timing was to be either in the week before or the week afte
D-Day. All this was changed by what happened in the interva
The latent threat from the Mediterranean sufficed in itself
keep ten German divisions on the Riviera. Anzio alone ha
meant that the equivalent of four enemy divisions was lost t
other fronts. When, with the help of Anzio, our whole battle lir
advanced, captured Rome and threatened the Gothic Line, th
Germans hurried a further eight divisions to Italy. Delay in th
capture of Rome and the dispatch of landing-craft from th
Mediterranean to help 'Overlord' caused the postponement
'Anvil'-'Dragoon' till mid-August, or two months later than ha

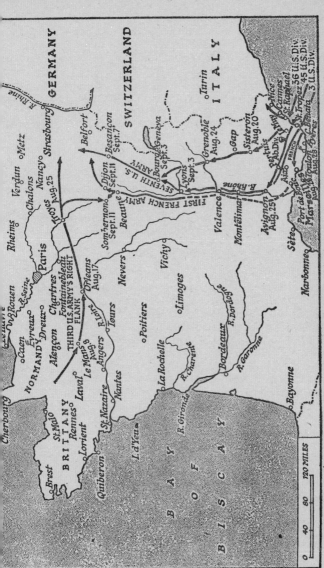

'Anvil'

been proposed. It therefore did not in any way affect 'Overlord
When it was belatedly launched it drew no enemy down from
the Normandy battle theatre. Therefore none of the reasor
present in our minds at Teheran had any relation to what wa
done and 'Dragoon' caused no diversion from the forces oppo
ing General Eisenhower. In fact, instead of helping him, h
helped it by threatening the rear of the Germans retiring up th
Rhone valley. This is not to deny that the operation as carrie
out eventually brought important assistance to General Eiser
hower by the arrival of another army on his right flank and th
opening of another line of communications thither. For this
heavy price was paid. The army of Italy was deprived of it
opportunity to strike a most formidable blow at the German
and very possibly to reach Vienna before the Russians, with a
that might have followed therefrom. But once the final decisio
was reached I of course gave 'Dragoon' my full support thoug
I had done my best to constrain or deflect it.

*　　　*　　　*

At this time I received some pregnant messages from Smut
now back at the Cape. He had always agreed wholeheartedl
with my views on 'Dragoon', 'but,' he now wrote (August 30
'please do not let strategy absorb all your attention to th
damage of the greater issue now looming up.

*'From now on it would be wise to keep a very close eye on a
matters bearing on the future settlement of Europe. This is th
crucial issue on which the future of the world for generation
will depend. In its solution your vision, experience, and gre
influence may prove a main factor.'**

I have been taxed in the years since the war with pressin
after Teheran, and particularly during these weeks under re
view, for a large-scale Allied invasion of the Balkans in defianc
of American thinking on the grand strategy of the war. Th
essence of my oft-repeated view is contained in the followin
reply to these messages from Smuts:

Prime Minister to Field-Marshal Smuts　　　　31 Aug 4
　Local success of 'Dragoon' has quite delighted Americans
who intend to use this route to thrust in every reinforcemen
Of course 45,000 prisoners have been taken, and there will b
many more. The idea now, from which nothing will turn them

* My italics.—W.S.C.

is to work in a whole Army Group through the captured
ports instead of using the much easier ports on the Atlantic.

'My object now,' I said, 'is to keep what we have got in Italy,
which should be sufficient since the enemy has withdrawn four
of his best divisions. With this I hope to turn and break the
Gothic Line, break into the Po valley, and ultimately advance
by Trieste and the Ljubljana Gap to Vienna. Even if the war
came to an end at an early date I have told Alexander to be
ready for a dash with armoured cars.'

CHAPTER 7

Rome. The Greek Problem

Alexander Prepares to Attack the Gothic Line – Field-Marshal Smuts Surveys the Situation, August 12 – I Visit the Front August 17 – Two Days at Siena – The Weakening of the Fifteenth Army Group – A Visit to General Mark Clark – Sombre Reflections – I Fly to Rome, August 21 – Preparations to Liberate Greece – My Telegram to the President, August 17 – His Reply – A Meeting with M. Papandreou – The Future of the Greek Monarchy – I Report to Mr. Eden, August 22 – I Meet Some Italian Politicians – Audience with Pope Pius XII – The Crown Prince Umberto, Lieutenant of the Realm.

During the early weeks of August Alexander was planning and regrouping his depleted forces to attack the main Gothic Line with whose outpost positions he was already in close contact. Skilfully sited to make full use of the natural difficulties of the country, the main defences firmly barred all likely lines of approach from the south, leaving enticingly weak only those sectors which were almost inaccessible.

The difficulties of launching the attack directly through the mountains from Florence to Bologna were obvious, and Alexander decided that the Eighth Army should make the first major stroke on the Adriatic side, where the succession of river valleys, difficult though they would be, offered less unfavourable ground provided heavy rain held off. Kesselring could not afford to have his eastern flank turned and Bologna captured behind his main front, so it was certain that if our attack made good progress he would have to reinforce the flank by troops from the centre. Alexander therefore planned to have ready a second attack, to be carried out by Mark Clark's Fifth Army towards Bologna and Imola, which would be launched when enemy reserves had been committed and their centre weakened.

The preparatory troop and air movements, carried out in great secrecy during the third week of August, were skilfully accomplished. Leaving the XIIIth British Corps east of Florence to come under Fifth Army command, two whole corps

of the Eighth Army were transferred eastwards and concentrated near Pergola on the left of the Polish Corps. When all
was completed Alexander held ready for battle the equivalent
of twenty-three divisions, of which rather more than half were
with the Eighth Army. Opposing him Kesselring had twenty-six
German divisions, in good shape, and two reconstituted Italian
divisions ; nineteen of them were disposed for the defence of his
main positions.

*　　*　　*

Smuts fully realised what was at stake as the following telegram shows.

Field-Marshal Smuts to Prime Minister　　　　12 Aug 44
　　Knowing how deeply occupied you are, I have refrained
from worrying you unduly with correspondence. I myself have
also been fully engaged with difficult local problems. I am
glad to hear you are once more in Italy, in close contact with
that important section of our war front, and wish you a very
successful and happy trip, as well as health and strength for
the exacting tasks still awaiting you.
　　2. I assumed that one of the objects of your present visit
will be to strengthen Alexander's hands by combing our
Mediterranean theatre as drastically as possible. Considerable
forces must still be in reserve there for contingencies now no
longer important. The end can best be hastened by the concentration of our forces in the few decisive theatres, of which
Alexander's is one. With Turkey now lost to the enemy and
Bulgaria more and more shaky, we can afford to ignore the
theatres for which large forces have been kept in the Middle
East and assemble whatever we have to strengthen Alexander's
move, which may lead to very great results both in the Balkans
and in Hitler's European fortress. I would cut off the frills
elsewhere in order to improve the alluring chances before
this move. A front extending along North Italy, the Adriatic,
and the route through Trieste to Vienna is one worthy of our
concentrated effort and of one of the ablest generals this war
has produced. I am sure both Wilson and Paget agree that this
is the correct strategy for us to follow in order to complete
our task and gather the mature fruits of our great Mediterranean campaigns. Any further assistance I could still give
from here is in the air, and I have already offered to man a
number of additional squadrons from personnel released from
the air training schools now being closed down in the Union.
Already I am manning some R.A.F. squadrons with South
Africans, and by this means could probably man six more for

Alexander's operations. As we are now scraping the bottom in our recruiting campaign, and owing to the dispersal of our man-power in many other directions, I am unable to do more for the infantry than keep up the strength of the 6th South African Division. The additional air help would only be possible if the Air Ministry accept my offer already made to them. They have the details.

A decisive stage has now been reached in the war, and an all-out offensive on all three main fronts against Germany must lead to the grand finale this summer. If the present tremendous successful offensive can only be maintained the end cannot be long deferred, especially in view of what we now know of conditions inside the German Army.

I shall be glad to see the 'Dragoon' correspondence, disheartening as it may be. The way things are going now Southern France has ceased to be a theatre of real military significance, and our large forces and resources detached for it will have small bearing on the tremendous decisions elsewhere. I even doubt whether the enemy will trouble to reinforce it.

*   *   *

On the morning of August 17 I set out by motor to meet General Alexander. I was delighted to see him for the first time since his victory and entry into Rome. He drove me all along the old Cassino front, showing me how the battle had gone and where the main struggles had occurred. The monastery towered up a dominating ruin. Anyone could see the tactical significance of this stately crag and building which for so many weeks played its part in stopping our advance. When we had finished it was time for lunch, and a picnic table had been prepared in an agreeable grove. Here I met General Clark and eight or ten of the leading British officers of the Fifteenth Army Group. Alexander then took me in his own plane, with which I was familiar, by a short flight to Siena, the beautiful and famous city, which I had visited in bygone peaceful days. Thence we visited our battle-front on the Arno. We had the south bank of the river and the Germans the north. Considerable efforts were made by both sides to destroy as little as possible, and the historic bridge at Florence was at any rate preserved. We were lodged in a beautiful but dismantled château a few miles to the west of Siena, and here I passed a couple of days, mostly working in bed, reading, and dictating telegrams. Of course in all these journeys I kept close to me the nucleus of my Private Office and the necessary ciphering staff, which enabled me to receive and to answer all messages from hour to hour.

Alexander brought his chief officers to dinner, and explained to me fully his difficulties and plans. The Fifteenth Group of Armies had indeed been skinned and starved. The far-reaching projects we had cherished must now be abandoned. It was still our duty to hold the Germans in the largest numbers on our front. If this purpose was to be achieved an offensive was imperative; but the well-integrated German armies were almost as strong as ours, composed of so many different contingents and races. It was proposed to attack along the whole front early on the 26th. Our right hand would be upon the Adriatic, and our immediate objective Rimini. To the westward, under Alexander's command, lay the Fifth American Army. This had been stripped and mutilated for the sake of 'Anvil', but would nevertheless advance with vigour.

On August 19 I set off to visit General Mark Clark at Leghorn. This was a long drive and everywhere we stopped to visit brigades and divisions. Mark Clark received me at his headquarters. We lunched in the open air by the sea. In our friendly and confidential talks I realised how painful the tearing to pieces of this fine army had been to those who controlled it. I toured the harbour, which had often played a part in our naval affairs, in a motor torpedo-boat. Then we went to the American batteries. A pair of new 9-inch guns had just been mounted and I was asked to fire the first shot. Everyone stood clear—I tugged a lanyard—there was a loud bang and a great recoil, and the observation post reported that the shell had hit its mark. I claim no credit for the aim. Later I was asked to inspect and address a parade of the Brazilian Brigade, the forerunners of the Brazilian Division, which had just arrived and made an imposing spectacle, together with Negro and Japanese-American units.

All the time amid these diversions I talked with Mark Clark. The General seemed embittered that his army had been robbed of what he thought—and I could not disagree—was a great opportunity. Still, he would drive forward to his utmost on the British left and keep the whole front blazing. It was late and I was thoroughly tired out when I got back to the château at Siena, where Alexander came again to dine.

When one writes things on paper to decide or explain large questions affecting action there is mental stress. But all this bites much deeper when you see and feel it on the spot. Here was this splendid army, equivalent to twenty-five divisions, of which a quarter were American, reduced till it was just not strong enough to produce decisive results against the immense power of the defensive. A very little more, half what had been taken from us, and we could have broken into the valley of the Po, with all the gleaming possibilities and prizes which lay open towards Vienna. As it was our forces, about a million strong, could play a mere secondary part in any commanding strategic conception. They could keep the enemy on their front busy at the cost and risk of a hard offensive. They could at least do their duty. Alexander maintained his soldierly cheerfulness, but it was in a sombre mood that I went to bed. In these great matters failing to gain one's way is no escape from the responsibility for an inferior solution.

* * *

As Alexander's offensive could not start till the 26th I flew to Rome on the morning of the 21st. Here another set of problems and a portentous array of new personages to meet awaited me. Brooke had arrived, and also 'Peter' Portal. Walter Moyne, so soon to die from an assassin's bullet, had come from Cairo, and Mr. Leeper was also present.* Again the issue was in most cases not what ought to be done—that would have been too easy— but what was likely to be agreed to not only at home but between Allies.

First I had to deal with the impending Greek crisis, which had been one of the chief reasons for my Italian visit. On July 7 the King of Greece had telegraphed from Cairo that after two months of 'cunning and futile arguments' the E.A.M. extremists had repudiated the Lebanon agreement which their leaders had signed in May.† He begged us to declare once again that we would support the Government of M. Papandreou, because it represented most of the Greek nation except the extremists and was the only body which could stop civil war and unite the country against the Germans. He also asked us to denounce E.L.A.S. and withdraw the military missions which we had sent to help them fight against Hitler. The British Government agreed to support M. Papandreou, but after a long talk on July 15 with

* The Chief of the Imperial General Staff, the Chief of the Air Staff, and our Ambassadors to Egypt and Greece.
† See Book 10, Chapter 13.

Colonel Woodhouse, a British officer who was serving with the missions in Greece, I consented to let them remain for the time being. He argued that they were a valuable restraint on E.A.M. and that it might be difficult and dangerous to get them out, but I feared that one day they would be taken as hostages and I asked for them to be reduced.

Rumours of the German evacuation of Greece raised intense excitement and discord in M. Papandreou's Cabinet, and revealed the frail and false foundation upon which common action stood. This made it all the more necessary for me to see Papandreou and those he trusted.

Before I left London the following telegrams had passed:

Prime Minister to Foreign Secretary   6 Aug 44
Surely we should tell M. Papandreou he should continue as Prime Minister and defy them all. The behaviour of E.A.M. is absolutely intolerable. Obviously they are seeking nothing but the Communisation of Greece during the confusion of the war, without allowing the people to decide in any manner understood by democracy.

2. We cannot take a man up as we have done Papandreou and let him be thrown to the wolves at the first snarlings of the miserable Greek [Communist] banditti. Difficult as the world is now, we shall not make our course easier by abandoning people whom we have encouraged to take on serious jobs by promises of support. . . .

4. Should matters go downhill and E.A.M. become master we should have to reconsider keeping any of our missions there and put the Greek people bluntly up against Bolshevism. The case seems to me to have reached the following point: either we support Papandreou, if necessary with force as we have agreed, or we disinterest ourselves utterly in Greece.

I also warned our Chiefs of Staff.

Prime Minister to C.I.G.S.   6 Aug 44
It may be that within a month or so we shall have to put 10,000 or 12,000 men into Athens, with a few tanks, guns, and armoured cars. You have a division in England which has above 13,000 troops. Such a force could be embarked now, and would probably be in time for the political crisis, which is of major consequence to the policy of His Majesty's Government. Such a force could be supported by troops from the airfields of the Delta, and by scrapings and combings from the 200,000 tail we have in Egypt.

2. I repeat there is no question of trying to dominate

Greece or going outside the immediate curtilage of Athens, but this is the centre of government, and, with the approaches to it, must be made secure. Bren gun carriers would be very useful. If you have a better plan let me know it.

3. It is to be presumed that the Germans have gone or are streaking away to the north, and the force landed at the Piræus would be welcomed by the great majority of the population of Athens, including all notables. The utmost secrecy must enwrap this project. The whole matter will be debated in a Staff conference, with Ministers present, on Tuesday or Wednesday.

4. You should note that time is more important than numbers, and that 5,000 men in five days is better than 7,000 men in seven days. The force is not of course expected to be mobile. Pray speak to me at the first opportunity.

Matters were arranged accordingly.

* * *

After reaching Naples I began to make the necessary arrangements.

Prime Minister (Italy) to Foreign Secretary   16 Aug 44

I am not aware of, and certainly never consciously agreed to, any British Cabinet decision that the King of Greece should be advised not to return to Greece until after the plebiscite has taken place, but to come to London. It would be much better to see how events develop, particularly as it may not be possible for a plebiscite to be held under orderly conditions for many months. Perhaps Papandreou's new Government, once safely installed in Athens, may be prepared to invite the King, who would not of course start for Greece at once, but would stay behind in Cairo awaiting developments. I can meet Papandreou in Rome on 21st, when Mr. Leeper should be present.

Regarding our expedition to Greece, General Wilson and his staff are already taking action on the Chiefs of Staff telegram, which I have read. . . . I have strongly emphasised that the operation must be regarded as one of reinforced diplomacy and policy rather than an actual campaign, and that it is to be confined to Athens, with possibly a detachment at Salonika.

As soon as the landing-ground has been secured by the 1,500 British parachutists the Greek Government would follow almost immediately, and within a very few hours should be functioning in Athens, where the people would probably receive the British parachutists with rapture. The arrival of the parachutists in the neighbourhood of Athens could be effected with complete surprise, and might well be effected before E.A.M. had taken any steps to seize the capital. It might be possible to rely on the two Greek aviation squadrons as part of the air force mentioned, but this can be settled at a later date.

Our small expedition, not exceeding 10,000 men, should start from Alexandria or from the heel of Italy, at about the same time that the parachute landing took place, and after entering the Piræus when the mines were out of the way, relieve the parachutists, who will be needed elsewhere. Most careful consideration will need to be given to the date. We should however be there first, and another unopposed landing might thus be ensured.

Providing the minesweepers were available, and especially if there was a friendly Government installed in Athens, the considerable process of sweeping the mined approaches to the Piræus, on which the C.-in-C. Mediterranean dwelt a great deal, could no doubt be effected in a few days. The C.-in-C. would like about a month's notice to carry out all the necessary preparations.

It is of course necessary in an integrated Anglo-American Staff that the Americans should share in planning such a movement. They have up to now shared fully in post-war planning for Greece in common with the rest of the Mediterranean. American carrying aircraft will be needed for the operation, and we shall have to detach a portion of the minesweepers from 'Dragoon'. With the large naval resources available this should not be difficult.

I had also telegraphed to the President.

Prime Minister to President Roosevelt   17 Aug 44

We have always marched together in complete agreement about Greek policy, and I refer to you on every important point. The War Cabinet and Foreign Secretary are much concerned about what will happen in Athens, and indeed in Greece, when the Germans crack or when their divisions try to evacuate the country. If there is a long hiatus after German authorities have gone from the city before organised government can be set up it seems very likely that E.A.M. and Communist extremists will attempt to seize the city and crush all other forms of Greek expression but their own.

2. You and I have always agreed that the destinies of Greece are in the hands of the Greek people, and that they will have the fullest opportunity of deciding between monarchy or republic as soon as tranquillity has been restored, but I do not expect you will relish more than I do the prospect either

of chaos and street-fighting or of a tyrannical Communist Government being set up. This could only serve to delay and hamper all the plans which are being made by U.N.R.R.A. for the distribution of relief to the sorely tried Greek people. I therefore think that we should make preparations through the Allied Staff in the Mediterranean to have in readiness a British force, not exceeding 10,000 men, which could be sent by the most expeditious means into the capital when the time is ripe. The force would include parachute troops, for which the help of your Air Force would be needed. I do not myself expect that anything will happen for a month, and it may be longer, but it is always well to be prepared. As far as I can see there will be no insuperable difficulty. I hope therefore you will agree that we may make these preparations by the Staffs out here in the usual way. If so, the British Chiefs of Staff will submit to the Combined Chiefs of Staff draft instructions to General Wilson.

His reply, which arrived more than a week later, was decisive.

President Roosevelt to Prime Minister   26 Aug 44
   I have no objection to your making preparations to have in readiness a sufficient British force to preserve order in Greece when the German forces evacuate that country. There is also no objection to the use by General Wilson of American transport aeroplanes that are available to him at that time and that can be spared from his other operations.

*   *   *

I met M. Papandreou in Rome on the evening of August 21. He said that E.A.M. had joined his Government because the British had been firm towards them, but the Greek State itself still had no arms and no police. He asked for our help to unite Greek resistance against the Germans. At present only the wrong people had arms, and they were a minority. I told him we could make no promise and enter into no obligations about sending British forces into Greece, and that even the possibility should not be talked about in public; but I advised him to transfer his Government at once from Cairo, with its atmosphere of intrigue, to somewhere in Italy near the headquarters of the Supreme Allied Commander. This he agreed to do.

At this point Lord Moyne joined us, and conversation turned to the position of the Greek King. I said there was no need for him to make any new declarations, because he had already said he would follow his Government's advice about going back to his country. The British nation felt friendly and chivalrous towards him for his conduct at a difficult moment in both our histories. We had no intention of interfering with the solemn right of the Greek people to choose between monarchy and a republic. But it must be for the Greek people as a whole, and not a handful of doctrinaires, to decide so grave an issue. Although I personally gave my loyalty to the constitutional monarchy which had taken shape in England, His Majesty's Government were quite indifferent as to which way the matter was settled for Greece provided there was a fair plebiscite.

I observed that now that E.A.M. had stopped demanding his withdrawal and were asking to join him M. Papandreou was head of a truly national Government. But I warned him against subversive influences. We agreed that the Greek mutineers ought not to be released from custody at this climax of the war, and that we should wait and see how they and their representatives behaved before sending any more arms to E.L.A.S. We should try instead to form a National Army for Greece.

M. Papandreou also complained that the Bulgarians were still occupying Greek soil. I said we would order them back to their own frontiers as soon as we were able to make sure they would obey us, but that Greek claims against them here and in the Dodecanese must wait till after the war. In the meantime we would do all we could for the relief and reconstruction of his country, which had suffered much and deserved the best possible treatment. They too must pull their weight, and the best thing he could do was to establish a Greek Government in Greece. Frontier questions must wait for the peace settlement.

* * *

I told Mr. Eden about all this.

Prime Minister (Rome) to Foreign Secretary 22 Aug 44
For reasons which will presently become apparent, I shall be returning to Alexander's army on the night of the 22nd–23rd and hope to be at Chequers in time for Matins next Sunday.

2. We hope to effect some simplifications in the military commands here, and the C.I.G.S. is working in collaboration with Alexander and later with Wilson to secure to the maximum extent the unique position held by Alexander in Italy.

3. As to the King of Greece, they none of them want him to make a fresh declaration now. Regarding his proposal to

return to London, I have advised him to wait till he sees M
Papandreou when he gets back, and then come on home. At a
later date a visit to Italy might be considered, and he could
then revisit the purged and penitent Greek Brigade here
preferably when they are in the line.

4. I like Papandreou, and there are great advantages in the
removal of the Greek Government from the Cairo atmo
sphere. I think it will do good to save an alert in Greece both
of foes and friends such as will be produced by its movement
But while the military affairs are being planned and sorted
out here under my direction in accordance with the wishes
you expressed a date cannot be fixed ; it must be fitted in with
other needs, unless the situation itself takes charge. I canno
be ready to act for a month, but thereafter we may be able to
pounce when the going is good. Moyne is working with General
Wilson this morning, subdividing the departments which re
main and those which came forward to Italy. Of course the
heavy international organisations and dumps will remain
where they are.

I am very glad you had a tour in France in these thrilling and
decisive days.

*　　*　　*

I stayed while in Rome at the Embassy, and our Ambassador
Sir Noel Charles, and his wife devoted themselves to my
business and comfort. Guided by his advice, I met most of the
principal figures in the *débris* of Italian politics produced by
twenty years of dictatorship, a disastrous war, revolution, invasion, occupation, Allied control, and other evils. I had talks
with, among others, Signor Bonomi and General Badoglio, also
with Comrade Togliatti, who had returned to Italy at the beginning of the year after a long sojourn in Russia. The leaders of al
the Italian parties were invited to meet me. None had any elec-
toral mandate, and their party names, revived from the past, had
been chosen with an eye to the future. 'What is your party?' I
asked one group. 'We are the Christian Communists,' their chief
replied. I could not help saying, 'It must be very inspiring to
your party, having the Catacombs so handy.' They did not seem
to see the point, and, looking back, I am afraid their minds must
have turned to the cruel mass executions which the Germans
had so recently perpetrated in these ancient sepulchres. One
may however be pardoned for making historical references in
Rome. The Eternal City, rising on every side, majestic and
apparently invulnerable, with its monuments and palaces, and

with its splendour of ruins not produced by bombing, seemed to contrast markedly with the tiny and transient beings who flitted within its bounds.

On August 23 I was received in audience by the Pope. I had visited his predecessor when I came to Rome as Chancellor of the Exchequer with Randolph, then very young, in 1926, and I preserved most agreeable memories of the kindness with which we have been received. Those were the days of Mussolini. Now I was received by Pope Pius XII with the highest ceremony. Not only did the Papal Guard in all their stately array line the long series of ante-rooms and galleries through which we passed, but the Noble Guards, formed of representatives of the highest and most ancient families of Rome, with a magnificent mediæval uniform I had never seen before, were present. The Pope received me in his study with the dignity and informality which he can so happily combine. We had no lack of topics for conversation. The one that bulked the largest at this audience, as it had done with his predecessor eighteen years before, was the danger of Communism. I have always had the greatest dislike of it ; and should I ever have the honour of another audience with the Supreme Pontiff I should not hesitate to recur to the subject.

Our Minister to the Vatican, Sir D'Arcy Osborne, drove me back to the Embassy. Here I met for the first time the Crown Prince Umberto, who, as Lieutenant of the Realm, was commanding the Italian forces on our front. His powerful and engaging personality, his grasp of the whole situation, military and political, were refreshing, and gave one a more lively feeling of confidence than I had experienced in my talks with the politicians. I certainly hoped he would play his part in building up a constitutional monarchy in a free, strong, united Italy. However, this was none of my business. I had enough on hand as it was. The Warsaw rising had now been in progress for nearly a month. The insurgents were in desperate straits, and I was engaged in a tense correspondence with Stalin and the President which will be set forth in another chapter.

CHAPTER 8

Alexander's Summer Offensive

Early on August 24, after my short visit to Rome, I returned by
air to Alexander's headquarters at Siena, living in the château a
few miles away. The offensive was now fixed for the 26th. I took
the opportunity of visiting the New Zealand Division. The last
time I had inspected them was at Tripoli in February 1943. I
did not wish to have another formal parade, and instead the
soldiers gathered along the route and gave me an informal,
enthusiastic welcome. I was delighted to see Freyberg and his
officers again. To Mr. Fraser I telegraphed:

Prime Minister to Prime Minister of New Zealand 25 Aug 44
   It was with great pleasure that I saw about 15,000 men of
   your really magnificent division in the best of spirits. The
   division is sorely needed in the forthcoming operation. I had
   lunch with General Freyberg and his officers yesterday. I told
   them a good many things they had not heard, and would not
   hear in the ordinary course. Freyberg sends his respects and
   good wishes, and so do I.

We were to fly to General Leese's battle headquarters of the
Eighth Army, on the Adriatic side, on the afternoon of the 25th.
Before starting I spent some hours with Alexander in his headquarters camp. While I was there General Devers and another
high American general arrived unexpectedly. The much-dis-
puted operation 'Anvil', now called 'Dragoon', was at present
under General Patch, but Devers as Deputy to General Wilson
had for many weeks been drawing units and key men ruthlessly
from the Fifteenth Army Group, and particularly from the
Fifth Army under Mark Clark. It was known that the troops of

'Dragoon' were likely to be raised to an Army Group Command, and that Devers would be designated as its chief. Naturally he sought to gather all the forces he could for the great enterprise to be entrusted to him, and to magnify it in every way. I saw very soon, although no serious topic was broached, that there was a coolness between him and Alexander. Gay, smiling, debonair, Alexander excused himself after the first few minutes, and left me in the mess tent with our two American visitors. As General Devers did not seem to have anything particular to say to me, and I did not wish to enter upon thorny ground, I also confined myself to civilities and generalities. I expected Alexander to return, but he did not, and after about twenty minutes Devers took his leave. There was of course no public business to be done. I wished him all good luck in his operation, and his courtesy call came to an end. I was conscious however of the tension between these high officers beneath an impeccable surface of politeness.

Presently Alexander came to tell me that we should now drive to the airfield. We took off in his plane and flew north-eastwards for half an hour to Loreto, whence we drove to Leese's camp behind Monte Maggiore. Here we had tents overlooking a magnificent panorama to the northward. The Adriatic, though but twenty miles away, was hidden by the mass of Monte Maggiore. General Leese told us that the barrage to cover the advance of his troops would begin at midnight. We were well placed to watch the long line of distant gun-flashes. The rapid, ceaseless thudding of the cannonade reminded me of the First World War. Artillery was certainly being used on a great scale. After an hour of this I was glad to go to bed, for Alexander had planned an early start and a long day on the front. He had also promised to take me wherever I wanted to go.

* * *

Before going to sleep I dictated the following message to Smuts, with whom my correspondence was continuous:

Prime Minister to Field-Marshal Smuts   26 Aug 44

A very considerable battle starts this morning and afternoon, and will reach its full power to-morrow. Hence my presence here for a couple of days. I must then return to England, visit France, and thereafter go on to Canada, for conferences starting about the middle of September. I tried to see the South Africans yesterday, but they were on the march.

So far 'Anvil' has had the opposite effects for which its designers intended it. Firstly, it has attracted no troops away from General Eisenhower at all. On the contrary, two and a half to three divisions of German rearguard troops will certainly reach the main battle-front before the Allied landed troops. Secondly, a stage of stagnation has been enforced here by the breaking in full career of these two great armies, the Fifth and the Eighth, and by the milking out of the key personnel in them. The consequence of this has been the withdrawal from the Italian front of three German divisions, including one very strong Panzer having an active strength of 12,500. These have proceeded direct to the Chalons area. Thus about five divisions have been deployed against Eisenhower, which would not have happened had we continued our advance here in the direction of the Po and ultimately on the great city [Vienna]. I still hope that we may achieve this. Even if the war comes to an end suddenly, I can see no reason why our armour should not slip through and reach it, as we can.

* * *

Alexander and I started together at about nine o'clock. His aide-de-camp and Tommy came in a second car. We were thus a conveniently small party. The advance had now been in progress for six hours, and was said to be making headway. But no definite impressions could yet be formed. We first climbed by motor up a high outstanding rock pinnacle, upon the top of which a church and village were perched. The inhabitants, men and women, came out to greet us from the cellars in which they had been sheltering. It was at once plain that the place had just been bombarded. Masonry and wreckage littered the single street. 'When did this stop?' Alexander asked the small crowd who gathered round us, grinning rather wryly. 'About a quarter of an hour ago,' they said. There was certainly a magnificent view from the ramparts of bygone centuries. The whole front of the Eighth Army offensive was visible. But apart from the smoke puffs of shells bursting seven or eight thousand yards away in a scattered fashion there was nothing to see. Presently Alexander said that we had better not stay any longer, as the enemy would naturally be firing at observation posts like this and might begin again. So we motored two or three miles to the westward, and had a picnic lunch on the broad slope of a hillside, which gave almost as good a view as the peak and was not likely to attract attention.

News was now received that our troops had pushed on a mile

or two beyond the river Metauro. Here Hasdrubal's defeat had sealed the fate of Carthage, so I suggested that we should go across too. We got into our cars accordingly, and in half an hour were across the river, where the road ran into undulating groves of olives, brightly patched with sunshine. Having got an officer guide from one of the battalions engaged, we pushed on through these glades till the sounds of rifle and machine-gun fire showed we were getting near to the front line. Presently warning hands brought us to a standstill. It appeared there was a minefield, and it was only safe to go where other vehicles had already gone without mishap. Alexander and his aide-de-camp now went off to reconnoitre towards a grey stone building which our troops were holding, which was said to give a good close-up view. It was evident to me that only very loose fighting was in progress. In a few minutes the aide-de-camp came back and brought me to his chief, who had found a very good place in the stone building, which was in fact an old château overlooking a rather sharp declivity. Here one certainly could see all that was possible. The Germans were firing with rifles and machine-guns from thick scrub on the farther side of the valley, about five hundred yards away. Our front line was beneath us. The firing was desultory and intermittent. But this was the nearest I got to the enemy and the time I heard most bullets in the Second World War. After about half an hour we went back to our motor-cars and made our way to the river, keeping very carefully to our own wheel tracks or those of other vehicles. At the river we met the supporting columns of infantry, marching up to lend weight to our thin skirmish line, and by five o'clock we were home again at General Leese's headquarters, where the news from the whole of the Army front was marked punctually on the maps. On the whole the Eighth Army had advanced since daybreak about seven thousand yards on a ten- or twelve-mile front, and the losses had not been at all heavy. This was an encouraging beginning.

*   *   *

The next morning plenty of work arrived, both by telegram and pouch. It appeared that General Eisenhower was worried by the approach of the German divisions I had mentioned to Smuts as having been withdrawn from Italy. I was glad that our offensive, prepared under depressing conditions, had begun. I drafted a telegram to the President explaining the position as I had learned it from the generals on the spot and from my own knowledge. I wished to convey in an uncontroversial form our sense of frustration, and at the same time to indicate my hopes and ideas for the future. If only I could revive the President's interest in this sphere we might still keep alive our design of an ultimate advance to Vienna.

Prime Minister to President Roosevelt   28 Aug 44
General Alexander received a telegram from S.H.A.E.F. asking for efforts to be made to prevent the withdrawal of more [German] divisions from the Italian front. This of course was the consequence of the great weakening of our armies in Italy, and has taken place entirely since the attack on the Riviera. In all, four divisions have left, including a very strong Panzer *en route* for Chalons. However, in spite of the weakening process Alexander began about three weeks ago to plan with Clark to turn or pierce the Apennines. For this purpose the British XIIIth Corps of four divisions has been placed under General Clark's orders, and we have been able to supply him with the necessary artillery, of which his army had been deprived. This army of eight divisions—four American and four British—is now grouped around Florence on a northerly axis.

2. By skinning the whole front and holding long stretches with nothing but anti-aircraft gunners converted to a kind of artillery-infantry and supported by a few armoured brigades, Alexander has also been able to concentrate ten British or British-controlled divisions representative of the whole British Empire on the Adriatic flank. The leading elements of these attacked before midnight on the 25th, and a general barrage opened and an advance began at dawn on the 26th. An advance of about nine miles was made over a large area, but the main position, the Gothic Line, has still to be encountered. I had the good fortune to go forward with this advance, and was consequently able to form a much clearer impression of the modern battlefield than is possible from the kinds of pinnacles and perches to which I have hitherto been confined.

3. The plan is that the Eighth Army of ten divisions, very heavily weighted in depth, will endeavour to pierce the Gothic Line and turn the whole enemy's position, entering the Po valley on the level of Rimini; but at the right moment, depending on the reactions of the enemy, Mark Clark will strike with his eight divisions and elements of both armies should converge to Bologna. If all goes well I hope that the advance will be much more rapid after that and that the continued

heavy fighting will prevent further harm being done to Eisenhower by the withdrawal of divisions from Italy.

4. I have never forgotten your talks to me at Teheran about Istria, and I am sure that the arrival of a powerful army in Trieste and Istria in four or five weeks would have an effect far outside purely military values. Tito's people will be awaiting us in Istria. What the condition of Hungary will be then I cannot imagine, but we shall at any rate be in a position to take full advantage of any great new situation.

I did not send this message off till I reached Naples, whither I flew on the 28th, nor did I receive the answer till three days after I got home.

President Roosevelt to Prime Minister   31 Aug 44

I was very glad to receive your account of the way in which General Wilson has concentrated his forces in Italy and has now renewed the offensive. My Chiefs of Staff feel that a vigorous attack, using all the forces available, should force the enemy into the Po valley. The enemy may then choose to withdraw entirely from Northern Italy. Since such action on his part might enable the enemy to release divisions for other fronts, we must do our best to destroy his forces while we have them in our grasp. I am confident that General Wilson has this as his objective. With an offensive under way and being pressed full strength in Italy, I am sure that General Eisenhower will be satisfied that everything possible is being done in the Mediterranean to assist him by mauling German divisions which might otherwise be moved against his forces in the near future. I understand all available British resources in the Mediterranean are being put into Italy. We are pressing into France all reinforcements and resources we can in order to guarantee that General Eisenhower will be able to maintain the impetus of the joint victories our forces have already won. With the smashing success of our invasion of Southern France and the Russians now crumbling the enemy flank in the Balkans, I have great hopes that complete and final victory will not be long delayed.

It is my thought that we should press the German Army in Italy vigorously with every facility we have available, and suspend decision of the future use of General Wilson's armies until the results of his campaign are better known and we have better information as to what the Germans may do.

We can renew our Teheran talk about Trieste and Istria at 'Octagon' [Quebec].

I was struck by the emphasis which this message laid upon General Wilson.

Prime Minister to President Roosevelt   31 Aug 44

All operations in Italy are conceived and executed by General Alexander in accordance with his general directives from the Supreme Commander. You will see that he is now in contact for twenty miles on the Adriatic flank with the Gothic Line, and a severe battle will be fought by the Eighth Army. Also General Clark with the Fifth Army has made an advance from the direction of Florence. I have impressed most strongly upon General Alexander the importance of pressing with his utmost strength to destroy the enemy's armed forces as well as turn his line. It will not be easy for the Germans to effect a general retreat from the Gothic Line over the Alps, especially if we can arrive in the neighbourhood of Bologna. The western passes and tunnels into France are already blocked by your advance into the Rhone valley. Only the direct route to Germany is open. We shall do our utmost to engage, harry, and destroy the enemy. The decisive battle has yet however to be fought.

2. In view of the fact that the enemy on the Italian front has been weakened by four of his best divisions, we no longer ask for further American reinforcements beyond the 92nd Division, which I understand will shortly reach us. On the other hand, I take it for granted that no more will be withdrawn from Italy—*i.e.*, that the four divisions of Clark's army and the elements remaining with them will continue there, and that General Alexander should make his plans on that basis. So much for the present.

3. As to the future, continuous employment against the enemy will have to be found for the Eighth and Fifth Armies once the German armies in Italy have been destroyed or unluckily have made their escape. This employment can only take the form of a movement first to Istria and Trieste and ultimately upon Vienna. Should the war come to an end in a few months, as may well be possible, none of these questions will arise. Anyhow, we can talk this over fully at Quebec.

4. I congratulate you upon the brilliant success of the landings in Southern France. I earnestly hope the retreating Germans may be nipped at Valence or Lyons and rounded up. Another mob of about 90,000 is apparently streaming back from the south via Poitiers.

Roosevelt sent me another telegram on September 4.

President Roosevelt to Prime Minister   4 Sept 44

I share your confidence that the Allied divisions we have in Italy are sufficient to do the task before them and that the battle commander will press the battle unrelentingly with the objective of shattering the enemy forces. After breaking the German forces on the Gothic Line we must go on to use our divisions in the way which best aids General Eisenhower's decisive drive into the enemy homeland.

As to the exact employment of our forces in Italy in the future, this is a matter we can discuss at Quebec. It seems to me that American forces should be used to the westward, but I am completely open-minded on this, and in any event this depends on the progress of the present battle in Italy, and also in France, where I strongly feel that we must not stint in any way the forces needed to break quickly through the western defences of Germany.

The credit for the great Allied success in Southern France must go impartially to the combined Allied force, and the perfection of execution of the operation from its beginning to the present belong to General Wilson and his Allied staff and to Patch and his subordinate commanders. With the present chaotic conditions of the Germans in Southern France, I hope that a junction of the north and south forces may be obtained at a much earlier date than was first anticipated.

We shall see that both these hopes proved vain. The army which we had landed on the Riviera at such painful cost to our operations in Italy arrived too late to help Eisenhower's first main struggle in the north, while Alexander's offensive failed, by the barest of margins, to achieve the success it deserved and we so badly needed. Italy was not to be wholly free for another eight months; the right-handed drive to Vienna was denied to us; and, except in Greece, our military power to influence the liberation of South-Eastern Europe was gone.

On August 28 I flew home from Naples. Before leaving Italy I set myself to composing a short message of encouragement and hope for the Italian people, for whom I have always had, except when we were actually fighting, a great regard. I had been deeply touched by the kindness with which I was welcomed in all the villages and small towns through which I had driven in traversing the entire front. In return I offered a few words of counsel.

28 Aug 44

... It has been said that the price of freedom is eternal vigilance. The question arises, What is freedom? There are one or two quite simple, practical tests by which it can be known in the modern world in peace conditions, namely:

Is there the right to free expression of opinion and of opposition and criticism of the Government of the day?

Have the people the right to turn out a Government of which they disapprove, and are constitutional means provided by which they can make their will apparent?

Are their courts of justice free from violence by the Executive and from threats of mob violence, and free of all association with particular political parties?

Will these courts administer open and well-established làws which are associated in the human mind with the broad principles of decency and justice?

Will there be fair play for poor as well as for rich, for private persons as well as Government officials?

Will the rights of the individual, subject to his duties to the State, be maintained and asserted and exalted?

Is the ordinary peasant or workman who is earning a living by daily toil and striving to bring up a family free from the fear that some grim police organisation under the control of a single party, like the Gestapo, started by the Nazi and Fascist parties, will tap him on the shoulder and pack him off without fair or open trial to bondage or ill-treatment?

These simple, practical tests are some of the title-deeds on which a new Italy could be founded. . . .

This does not seem to require any alteration to-day.

CHAPTER 9

The Martyrdom of Warsaw

*The Russians Cross the Vistula – Germany's Collapse on the
Eastern Front – The Broadcast from Moscow, July 29, Calling
for a General Rising in Warsaw – The Insurrection Begins,
August 1 – My Telegram to Stalin of August 4 – A Grim Reply
– The German Counter-Attack – A Distressing Message from
Warsaw – My Telegram to Eden, August 14 – Vyshinsky's
Astonishing Statement, and Stalin's Telegram of August 16 – The
President and I Send a Joint Appeal, August 20 – Stalin's
Answer – The Agony of Warsaw Reaches its Height – Mr.
Roosevelt's Message to Me of August 24 – Our Need of Soviet
Airfields – The President is Adverse – Anger of the British War
Cabinet – Their Telegram to Moscow, September 4 – Mr.
Roosevelt's Message of September 5 – Apparent Change in
Soviet Tactics – Our Heavy Bombers Drop Supplies on War-
saw, September 18 – End of the Tragedy.*

The Russian summer offensive brought their armies in late July
to the river Vistula. All reports indicated that in the very near
future Poland would be in Russian hands. The leaders of the
Polish Underground Army, which owed allegiance to the London Government, had now to decide when to raise a general
insurrection against the Germans, in order to speed the liberation of their country and prevent them fighting a series of bitter
defensive actions on Polish territory, and particularly in Warsaw
itself. The Polish commander, General Bor-Komorowski, and
his civilian adviser were authorised by the Polish Government
in London to proclaim a general insurrection whenever they
deemed fit. The moment indeed seemed opportune. On July 20
came the news of the plot against Hitler, followed swiftly by the
Allied break-out from the Normandy beach-head. About July
22 the Poles intercepted wireless messages from the German
Fourth Panzer Army ordering a general withdrawal to the west
of the Vistula. The Russians crossed the river on the same day,
and their patrols pushed forward in the direction of Warsaw.
There seemed little doubt that a general collapse was at hand.

In the Nuremberg trials General Guderian described the situation in these terms:

On July 21, 1944, I received a new appointment as Chief of Staff of the German forces on the Eastern Front. After my appointment the whole front—if it can be called a front—was hardly more than an agglomeration of the remains of our armies which were endeavouring to withdraw to the line of the Vistula ; twenty-five divisions were completely annihilated.

General Bor therefore decided to stage a major rising and liberate the city. He had about forty thousand men, with reserves of food and ammunition for seven to ten days' fighting. The sound of Russian guns across the Vistula could now be heard. The Soviet Air Force began bombing the Germans in Warsaw from recently captured airfields near the capital, of which the closest was only twenty minutes' flight away. At the same time a Communist Committee of National Liberation had been formed in Eastern Poland, and the Russians announced that liberated territory would be placed under their control. Soviet broadcasting stations had for a considerable time been urging the Polish population to drop all caution and start a general revolt against the Germans. On July 29, three days before the rising began, the Moscow radio station broadcast an appeal from the Polish Communists to the people of Warsaw, saying that the guns of liberation were now within hearing, and calling upon them as in 1939 to join battle with the Germans, this time for decisive action. 'For Warsaw, which did not yield but fought on, the hour of action has already arrived.' After pointing out that the German plan to set up defence points would result in the gradual destruction of the city, the broadcast ended by reminding the inhabitants that 'all is lost that is not saved by active effort', and that 'by direct active struggle in the street, houses, etc., of Warsaw the moment of final liberation will be hastened and the lives of our brethren saved'.

On the evening of July 31 the Underground command in Warsaw got news that Soviet tanks had broken into the German defences east of the city. The German military wireless announced, 'To-day the Russians started a general attack on Warsaw from the south-east.' Russian troops were now at points less then ten miles away. In the capital itself the Polish Underground command ordered a general insurrection at 5 p.m.

on the following day. General Bor has himself described what happened:

At exactly five o'clock thousands of windows flashed as they were flung open. From all sides a hail of bullets struck passing Germans, riddling their buildings and their marching formations. In the twinkling of an eye the remaining civilians disappeared from the streets. From the entrances of houses our men streamed out and rushed to the attack. In fifteen minutes an entire city of a million inhabitants was engulfed in the fight. Every kind of traffic ceased. As a big communications centre where roads from north, south, east, and west converged, in the immediate rear of the German front, Warsaw ceased to exist. The battle for the city was on.

The news reached London next day, and we anxiously waited for more. The Soviet radio was silent and Russian air activity ceased. On August 4 the Germans started to attack from strongpoints which they held throughout the city and suburbs. The Polish Government in London told us of the agonising urgency of sending in supplies by air. The insurgents were now opposed by five hastily concentrated German divisions. The Hermann Goering Division had also been brought from Italy, and two more S.S. divisions arrived soon afterwards.

I accordingly telegraphed to Stalin:

Prime Minister to Marshal Stalin   4 Aug 44
At urgent request of Polish Underground Army we are dropping, subject to weather, about sixty tons of equipment and ammunition into the south-west quarter of Warsaw, where it is said a Polish revolt against the Germans is in fierce struggle. They also say that they appeal for Russian aid, which seems to be very near. They are being attacked by one and a half German divisions. This may be of help to your operation.

The reply was prompt and grim.

Marshal Stalin to Prime Minister   5 Aug 44
I have received your message about Warsaw.
I think that the information which has been communicated to you by the Poles is greatly exaggerated and does not inspire confidence. One could reach that conclusion even from the fact that the Polish emigrants have already claimed for themselves that they all but captured Vilna with a few stray units of the Home Army, and even announced that on the radio. But that of course does not in any way correspond with

the facts. The Home Army of the Poles consists of a few detachments, which they incorrectly call divisions. They have neither artillery nor aircraft nor tanks. I cannot imagine how such detachments can capture Warsaw, for the defence of which the Germans have produced four tank divisions, among them the Hermann Goering Division.

Meanwhile the battle went on street by street against the German 'Tiger' tanks, and by August 9 the Germans had driven a wedge right across the city through to the Vistula, breaking up the Polish-held districts into isolated sectors. The gallant attempts of the R.A.F., with Polish, British, and Dominion crews, to fly to the aid of Warsaw from Italian bases were both forlorn and inadequate. Two planes appeared on the night of August 4, and three four nights later.

*   *   *

The Polish Prime Minister, Mikolajczyk, had been in Moscow since July 30 trying to establish some kind of terms with the Soviet Government, which had recognised the Polish Communist Committee of National Liberation as the future administrators of the country. These negotiations were carried on throughout the early days of the Warsaw rising. Messages from General Bor were reaching Mikolajczyk daily, begging for ammunition and anti-tank weapons and for help from the Red Army. Meanwhile the Russians pressed for agreement upon the post-war frontiers of Poland and the setting up of a joint Government. A last fruitless talk took place with Stalin on August 9.

On August 12 I telegraphed to him:

Prime Minister to Marshal Stalin   12 Aug 44
I have had the following distressing message from the Poles in Warsaw, who after ten days are still fighting against considerable German forces, who have cut the city into three:

[*Begins.*] 'To the President of the Republic, the Government, and the Commander-in-Chief, from the Vice-Premier:

'Tenth day. We are conducting a bloody fight. The town is cut by three routes. ... All these routes are strongly held by German tanks and their crossing is extremely difficult (all the buildings along them are burnt out). Two armoured trains on the railway line from Gdansk Station to West Station and artillery from Praga fire continuously on the town, and are supported by air forces.

'In these conditions the fight continues. We receive from you only once a small drop. On the German-Russian front silence since the 3rd. We are therefore without any material or moral support, as, with the exception of a short speech by the [Polish] Vice-Prime Minister (from London), which took place on the eighth day, we have not had from you even an acknowledgment of our action. The soldiers and the population of the capital look hopelessly at the skies, expecting help from the Allies. On the background of smoke they see only German aircraft. They are surprised, feel deeply depressed, and begin to revile.

'We have practically no news from you, no information with regard to the political situation, no advice and no instructions. Have you discussed in Moscow help for Warsaw? I repeat emphatically that without immediate support, consisting of drops of arms and ammunition, bombing of objectives held by the enemy, and air landing, our fight will collapse in a few days.

'With the above-mentioned help the fight will continue.

'I expect from you the greatest effort in this respect.' [*Ends*.]

They implore machine-guns and ammunition. Can you not give them some further help, as the distance from Italy is so very great?

* * *

On the 14th I telegraphed to Mr. Eden from Italy, whither I had gone to see General Alexander's army:

It will cause the Russians much annoyance if the suggestion that the Polish patriots in Warsaw were deserted gets afoot, but they can easily prevent it by operations well within their power. It certainly is very curious that at the moment when the Underground Army has revolted the Russian armies should have halted their offensive against Warsaw and withdrawn some distance. For them to send in all the quantities of machine-guns and ammunition required by the Poles for their heroic fight would involve only a flight of 100 miles. I have been talking to [Air Marshal] Slessor, trying to send all possible assistance from here. But what have the Russians done? I think it would be better if you sent a message to Stalin through Molotov referring to the implications that are afoot in many quarters and requesting that the Russians should send all the help they can. This course would be more impersonal than that I should do it through Stalin. Last night twenty-eight aircraft did the 700 miles flight from Italy. Three were lost. This was the fourth flight made from here under these quite exceptional conditions.

On the night of August 16 Vyshinsky asked the United States Ambassador in Moscow to call, and, explaining that he wished to avoid the possibility of misunderstanding, read out the following astonishing statement:

The Soviet Government cannot of course object to English or American aircraft dropping arms in the region of Warsaw, since this is an American and British affair. But they decidedly object to American or British aircraft, after dropping arms in the region of Warsaw, landing on Soviet territory, since the Soviet Government do not wish to associate themselves either directly or indirectly with the adventure in Warsaw.

On the same day I received the following message couched in softer terms from Stalin:

Marshal Stalin to Prime Minister   16 Aug 44
After the conversation with M. Mikolajczyk I gave orders that the command of the Red Army should drop arms intensively in the Warsaw sector. A parachutist liaison officer was also dropped, who, according to the report of the command, did not reach his objective as he was killed by the Germans.
Further, having familiarised myself more closely with the Warsaw affair, I am convinced that the Warsaw action represents a reckless and terrible adventure which is costing the population large sacrifices. This would not have been if the Soviet command had been informed before the beginning of the Warsaw action and if the Poles had maintained contact with it.
In the situation which has arisen the Soviet command has come to the conclusion that it must dissociate itself from the Warsaw adventure, as it cannot take either direct or indirect responsibility for the Warsaw action.

According to Mikolajczyk's account, the first paragraph of this telegram is quite untrue. Two officers arrived safely in Warsaw and were received by the Polish command. A Soviet colonel had also been there for some days, and sent messages to Moscow via London urging support for the insurgents.

*   *   *

On the 18th I telegraphed again to Mr. Eden.

Prime Minister to Foreign Secretary   18 Aug 44
I have seen the extremely lukewarm telegram of August 15 from the American Joint Chiefs of Staff to General Eisen-

hower, which was received after I had sent you my last message.

The air authorities out here assured me that the Americans wished help sent from England to Warsaw, and that the operation was quite practicable, providing of course the Russians gave their consent. It seems hardly credible to me that the request for landing facilities would have been submitted to the Russians unless the practicability of the operation had been examined by General Doolittle. It is most important that you should find out whether it is practicable or not.

Before the President or I, or both, make any personal or joint appeals to Stalin it is of course necessary that the military difficulties should be resolved.

At the same time I appealed to the President.

Prime Minister (Italy) to President Roosevelt   18 Aug 44
An episode of profound and far-reaching gravity is created by the Russian refusal to permit American aircraft to bring succour to the heroic insurgents in Warsaw, aggravated by their own complete neglect to provide supplies by air when only a few score of miles away. If, as is almost certain, a wholesale massacre follows the German triumph in that capital no measure can be put upon the full consequences that will arise.

2. I am prepared to send a personal message to Stalin if you think this wise, and if you will yourself send a separate similar message. Better far than two separate messages would be a joint message signed by us both.

3. The glorious and gigantic victories being achieved in France by the United States and British forces are vastly changing the situation in Europe, and it may well be that the victory gained by our armies in Normandy will eclipse in magnitude anything that the Russians have achieved on any particular occasion. I feel therefore that they will have some respect for what we say so long as it is expressed plainly and simply. We are nations serving high causes, and must give true counsels towards world peace even at the risk of Stalin resenting it. Quite possibly he wouldn't.

Two days later we sent the following joint appeal, which the the President had drafted:

*Prime Minister (Italy) and President Roosevelt to
Marshal Stalin*   20 Aug 44
We are thinking of world opinion if the anti-Nazis in Warsaw are in effect abandoned. We believe that all three of us

should do the utmost to save as many of the patriots there as possible. We hope that you will drop immediate supplies and munitions to the patriot Poles in Warsaw, or will you agree to help our planes in doing it very quickly? We hope you will approve. The time element is of extreme importance.

This was the reply we got:

Marshal Stalin to Prime Minister and
President Roosevelt   22 Aug 44

I have received the message from you and Mr. Roosevelt about Warsaw. I wish to express my opinions.

2. Sooner or later the truth about the group of criminals who have embarked on the Warsaw adventure in order to seize power will become known to everybody. These people have exploited the good faith of the inhabitants of Warsaw, throwing many almost unarmed people against the German guns, tanks, and aircraft. A situation has arisen in which each new day serves, not the Poles for the liberation of Warsaw, but the Hitlerites who are inhumanly shooting down the inhabitants of Warsaw.

3. From the military point of view, the situation which has arisen, by increasingly directing the attention of the Germans to Warsaw, is just as unprofitable for the Red Army as for the Poles. Meanwhile the Soviet troops, which have recently encountered new and notable efforts by the Germans to go over to the counter-attack, are doing everything possible to smash these counter-attacks of the Hitlerites and to go over to a new wide-scale attack in the region of Warsaw. There can be no doubt that the Red Army is not sparing its efforts to break the Germans round Warsaw and to free Warsaw for the Poles. That will be the best and most effective help for the Poles who are anti-Nazis.

*   *   *

Meanwhile the agony of Warsaw reached its height.

Prime Minister to President Roosevelt   24 Aug 44

The following is an eye-witness account of the Warsaw rising. A copy has already been given to the Soviet Ambassador in London.

1. August 11.

The Germans are continuing, despite all efforts of A.K.,* their ruthless terror methods. In many cases they have burnt whole streets of houses and shot all the men belonging to them and turned the women and children out on to the street,

* The Polish Underground Army.

where battles are taking place, to find their way to safety. On Krolewska Street many private houses have been bombed out. One house was hit by four separate bombs. In one house, where lived old retired professors of Polish universities, the S.S. troops forced an entrance and killed many of them. Some succeeded in escaping through the cellars to the other houses. The morale of A.K. and the civilian population is of the highest standard. The watchword is 'Death to the Germans'.

2. August 11.

The German tank forces during last night made determined efforts to relieve some of their strong-points in the city. This is no light task however, as on the corner of every street are built huge barricades, mostly constructed of concrete pavement slabs torn up from the streets especially for this purpose. In most cases the attempts failed, so the tank crews vented their disappointment by setting fire to several houses and shelling others from a distance. In many cases they also set fire to the dead, who litter the streets in many places. ... The German Tank Corps have begun to have a great respect for the Polish barricade, for they know that behind each one wait determined troops of A.K. with petrol bottles. These petrol bottles have caused great destruction to many of their comrades.

3. August 13.

The German forces have brutally murdered wounded and sick people, both men and women, who were lying in the SS. Lazarus and Karol and Marsa hospitals.

When the Germans were bringing supplies by tanks to one of their outposts they drove before them 500 women and children to prevent the troops of A.K. from taking action against them. Many of them were killed and wounded. The same kind of action has been reported from many other parts of the city.

Despite lack of weapons, the Polish forces continue to hold the initiative in the battle for Warsaw. In some places they have broken into German strongholds and captured much-needed arms and ammunition. On August 12 11,600 rounds of rifle ammunition, five machine-guns, 8,500 [rounds of] small arms ammunition, twenty pistols, thirty anti-tank mines, and transports were captured. The German forces are fighting desperately. When A.K. set fire to a building which the Germans were holding as a fortress two German soldiers tried to escape to the Polish lines with a white flag, but an S.S. officer saw them and shot them dead. During the night of August 12–13 A.K. received some weapons from Allied aircraft.

4. August 15.

The dead are buried in backyards and squares. The food

situation is continually deteriorating, but as yet there is no
starvation. To-day there is no water at all in the pipes. It is
being drawn from the infrequent wells and house supplies.
All quarters of the town are under shell fire, and there are
many fires. The dropping of supplies has intensified the morale.
Everyone wants to fight and will fight, but the uncertainty
of a speedy conclusion is depressing.

5. August 16.

Fighting continues to be very bitter in Warsaw. The Germans fight for every inch of ground. It is reported that in
some places whole districts have been burnt and the inhabitants either shot or taken to Germany. The inhabitants continue to repeat, 'When we get weapons we will pay them back.'

Fighting for the electric power station began on August 1
at 5.10 p.m. Twenty-three soldiers of the Polish Home Army
were stationed in the works before that hour, because they
were employed in the normal course of things, expecting the
outbreak of the rising. The Germans had on the day before
raised the strength of the garrison to 150 militarised police,
stationed in concrete pill-boxes and block-houses, also in all the
works buildings. The signal for action was the explosion of a
mine under one of the buildings. After nineteen hours of fighting the electric power station was fully in Polish hands. The
Polish losses were seventeen killed and twenty-seven wounded.
The German losses were twenty killed and twenty-two
wounded, with fifty-six taken as prisoners of war. The detachment which captured the station consisted solely of manual
and metal workers of the works. In spite of the fact that the
buildings of the station are daily bombarded with 75-mm.
shells by the Germans, the personnel has succeeded in maintaining the supply of current to the civil population without
the slightest interruption.

The battle also raged literally underground. The only means
of communication between the different sectors held by the
Poles lay through the sewers. The Germans threw hand
grenades and gas bombs down the manholes. Battles developed
in pitch-darkness between men waist-deep in excrement, fighting
hand to hand at times with knives or drowning their opponents
in the slime. Above ground German artillery and fighters set
alight large areas of the city.

I thought that some of this tale of villainy and horror should
reach the world.

Prime Minister (Italy) to Minister of Information   23 Aug 44
    Is there any stop on the publicity for the facts about the

agony of Warsaw, which seem, from the papers, to have been practically suppressed? It is not for us to cast reproaches on the Soviet Government, but surely the facts should be allowed to speak for themselves? There is no need to mention the strange and sinister behaviour of the Russians, but is there any reason why the consequences of such behaviour should not be made public?

*   *   *

The President now replied to my telegram.

President Roosevelt to Prime Minister   24 Aug 44
Thanks for your telegram describing the inhuman behaviour of the Nazis and the dreadful situation of the Poles in Warsaw.
Stalin's reply to our joint proposal for assisting the Warsaw Poles is far from encouraging.
The supply by us of the Warsaw Poles is, I am informed, impossible unless we are permitted to land and take off from Soviet airfields. Their use for the relief of Warsaw is at present prohibited by the Russian authorities.
I do not see what further steps we can take at the present time that promise results.

I replied next day:

Prime Minister to President Roosevelt   25 Aug 44
As Stalin's reply evades the definite questions asked and adds nothing to our knowledge, I propose a reply on the following lines:
[*Begins.*] 'We earnestly desire to send U.S. aircraft from England. Is there any reason why the refuelling ground assigned to us behind the Russian lines should not be used by them to land on without inquiry as to their activities on the way? In this way your Government could preserve the principle of dissociation from this particular episode. We feel confident that if disabled British or American aircraft come down behind the lines of your armies your usual consideration will ensure their being succoured. Our sympathies are aroused for these "almost unarmed people" whose special faith has led them to attack German tanks, guns, and planes, but we are not concerned to form a judgment about the persons who instigated the rising, which was certainly called for repeatedly by Moscow Radio. We cannot think that Hitler's atrocities will end with their resistance, but rather that that is the moment when they will probably begin with full ferocity. The Warsaw massacre will certainly be a matter fraught with trouble for us when we all meet at the end of the war. We therefore propose to send the aircraft unless you directly forbid it.' [*Ends.*]

In the event of his failing to reply to this my feeling is that we ought to send the planes and see what happens. I cannot believe that they would be ill-treated or detained. Since this was signed I have seen that the Russians are even endeavouring to take away your airfields which are located at Poltava and elsewhere behind their lines.

The reply was adverse.

President Roosevelt to Prime Minister   26 Aug 44
I do not consider it would prove advantageous to the long-range general war prospect for me to join with you in the proposed message to Stalin, but I have no objection to your sending such a message if you consider it advisable to do so. In arriving at this conclusion I have taken into consideration Uncle J.'s present attitude towards the relief of the Underground forces in Warsaw, as indicated in his message to you and to me, his definite refusal to allow the use by us of Russian airfields for that purpose, and the current American conversations on the subject of the subsequent use of other Russian bases.

*   *   *

I had hoped that the Americans would support us in drastic action. On September 1 I received the Polish Premier, Mikolajczyk, on his return from Moscow. I had little comfort to offer. He told me that he was prepared to propose a political settlement with the Lublin Committee, offering them fourteen seats in a combined Government. These proposals were debated under fire by the representatives of the Polish Underground in Warsaw itself. The suggestion was accepted unanimously. Most of those who took part in these decisions were tried a year later for 'treason' before a Soviet court in Moscow.

When the Cabinet met on the night of September 4 I thought the issue so important that though I had a touch of fever I went from my bed to our underground room. We had met together on many unpleasant affairs. I do not remember any occasion when such deep anger was shown by all our members, Tory, Labour, Liberal alike. I should have liked to say, 'We are sending our aeroplanes to land in your territory, after delivering supplies to Warsaw. If you do not treat them properly all convoys will be stopped from this moment by us.' But the reader of these pages in after-years must realise that everyone always has to keep in mind the fortunes of millions of men fighting in a world-wide struggle, and that terrible and even humbling submissions must at times be made to the general aim. I did not therefore propose this drastic step. It might have been effective, because we were dealing with men in the Kremlin who were governed by calculation and not by emotion. They did not mean to let the spirit of Poland rise again at Warsaw. Their plans were based on the Lublin Committee. That was the only Poland they cared about. The cutting off of the convoys at this critical moment in their great advance would perhaps have bulked in their minds as much as considerations of honour, humanity, decent commonplace good faith, usually count with ordinary people. The telegrams which follow show the best that we thought it wise to do.

Prime Minister (London) to President Roosevelt   4 Sept 44
    The War Cabinet are deeply disturbed at the position in Warsaw and at the far-reaching effects on future relations with Russia of Stalin's refusal of airfield facilities.

2. Moreover, as you know, Mikolajczyk has sent his proposals to the Polish Committee of Liberation for a political settlement. I am afraid that the fall of Warsaw will not only destroy any hope of progress, but will fatally undermine the position of Mikolajczyk himself.

3. My immediately following telegrams contain the text of a telegram which the War Cabinet in their collective capacity have sent to our Ambassador in Moscow, and also of a message which the women of Warsaw have communicated to the Pope and which has been handed by the Vatican to our Minister.

4. The only way of bringing material help quickly to the Poles fighting in Warsaw would be for United States aircraft to drop supplies, using Russian airfields for the purpose. Seeing how much is in jeopardy, we beg that you will again consider the big stakes involved. Could you not authorise your air forces to carry out this operation, landing, if necessary, on Russian airfields without their formal consent? In view of our great successes in the West, I cannot think that the Russians could reject this *fait accompli*. They might even welcome it as getting them out of an awkward situation. We would of course share full responsibility with you for any action taken by your Air Force.

Prime Minister to President Roosevelt   4 Sept 44
    Following is text of telegram sent to Moscow this evening, mentioned in my immediately preceding telegram:
    'The War Cabinet at their meeting to-day considered the latest reports of the situation in Warsaw, which show that the

Poles fighting against the Germans there are in desperate straits.

'The War Cabinet wish the Soviet Government to know that public opinion in this country is deeply moved by the events in Warsaw and by the terrible sufferings of the Poles there. Whatever the rights and wrongs about the beginnings of the Warsaw rising, the people of Warsaw themselves cannot be held responsible for the decision taken. Our people cannot understand why no material help has been sent from outside to the Poles in Warsaw. The fact that such help could not be sent on account of your Government's refusal to allow United States aircraft to land on aerodromes in Russian hands is now becoming publicly known. If on top of all this the Poles in Warsaw should now be overwhelmed by the Germans, as we are told they must be within two or three days, the shock to public opinion here will be incalculable. The War Cabinet themselves find it hard to understand your Government's refusal to take account of the obligations of the British and American Governments to help the Poles in Warsaw. Your Government's action in preventing this help being sent seems to us at variance with the spirit of Allied co-operation to which you and we attach so much importance both for the present and the future.

'Out of regard for Marshal Stalin and for the Soviet peoples, with whom it is our earnest desire to work in future years, the War Cabinet have asked me to make this further appeal to the Soviet Government to give whatever help may be in their power, and above all to provide facilities for United States aircraft to land on your airfields for this purpose.'

Prime Minister to President Roosevelt   4 Sept 44

Following is text of message from women of Warsaw referred to in my earlier telegram:

'Most Holy Father, we Polish women in Warsaw are inspired with sentiments of profound patriotism and devotion for our country. For three weeks, while defending our fortress, we have lacked food and medicine. Warsaw is in ruins. The Germans are killing the wounded in hospitals. They are making women and children march in front of them in order to protect their tanks. There is no exaggeration in reports of children who are fighting and destroying tanks with bottles of petrol. We mothers see our sons dying for freedom and the Fatherland. Our husbands, our sons, and our brothers are not considered by the enemy to be combatants. Holy Father, no one is helping us. The Russian armies which have been for three weeks at the gates of Warsaw have not advanced a step. The aid coming to us from Great Britain is insufficient. The world is ignorant of our fight. God alone is with us. Holy Father, Vicar of Christ, if you can hear us, bless us Polish women who are fighting for the Church and for freedom.'

President Roosevelt to Prime Minister   5 Sept 44
Replying to your telegrams, I am informed by my Office of Military Intelligence that the fighting Poles have departed from Warsaw and that the Germans are now in full control.

The problem of relief for the Poles in Warsaw has therefore unfortunately been solved by delay and by German action, and there now appears to be nothing we can do to assist them.

I have long been deeply distressed by our inability to give adequate assistance to the heroic defenders of Warsaw, and I hope that we may together still be able to help Poland to be among the victors in this war with the Nazis.

*   *   *

On September 10, after six weeks of Polish torment, the Kremlin appeared to change their tactics. That afternoon shells from the Soviet artillery began to fall upon the eastern outskirts of Warsaw, and Soviet planes appeared again over the city. Polish Communist forces, under Soviet orders, fought their way into the fringe of the capital. From September 14 onwards the Soviet Air Force dropped supplies; but few of the parachutes opened and many of the containers were smashed and useless. The following day the Russians occupied the Praga suburb, but went no farther. They wished to have the non-Communist Poles destroyed to the full, but also to keep alive the idea that they were going to their rescue. Meanwhile, house by house, the Germans proceeded with their liquidation of Polish centres of resistance throughout the city. A fearful fate befell the population. Many were deported by the Germans. General Bor's appeals to the Soviet commander, Marshal Rokossovsky, were unanswered. Famine reigned.

My efforts to get American aid led to one isolated but large-scale operation. On September 18 a hundred and four heavy bombers flew over the capital, dropping supplies. It was too late. On the evening of October 2 Premier Mikolajczyk came to tell me that the Polish forces in Warsaw were about to surrender to the Germans. One of the last broadcasts from the heroic city was picked up in London.

This is the stark truth. We were treated worse than Hitler's satellites, worse than Italy, Roumania, Finland. May God, Who is just, pass judgment on the terrible injustice suffered by the Polish nation, and may He punish accordingly all those who are guilty.

Your heroes are the soldiers whose only weapons against tanks, planes, and guns were their revolvers and bottles filled with petrol. Your heroes are the women who tended the wounded and carried messages under fire, who cooked in bombed and ruined cellars to feed children and adults, and who soothed and comforted the dying. Your heroes are the children who went on quietly playing among the smouldering ruins. These are the people of Warsaw.

Immortal is the nation that can muster such universal heroism. For those who have died have conquered, and those who live on will fight on, will conquer and again bear witness that Poland lives when the Poles live.

These words are indelible. The struggle in Warsaw had lasted more than sixty days. Of the 40,000 men and women of the Polish Underground Army about 15,000 fell. Out of a population of a million nearly 200,000 had been stricken. The suppression of the revolt cost the German Army 10,000 killed, 7,000 missing, and 9,000 wounded. The proportions attest the hand-to-hand character of the fighting.

When the Russians entered the city three months later they found little but shattered streets and the unburied dead. Such was their liberation of Poland, where they now rule. But this cannot be the end of the story.

The Second Quebec Conference

On Tuesday, September 5, we sailed once again from the Clyde in the *Queen Mary*. All the Chiefs of Staff came with me, and met daily, and sometimes twice a day, during our six days' voyage. I wanted, before meeting our American friends, to harmonise and grip the many plans and projects which were now before us. In Europe, 'Overlord' was not only launched, but triumphant. How, when, and where could we strike at Japan, and assure for Britain an honourable share in the final victory there? We had lost as much, if not more, than the United States. Over 160,000 British prisoners and civilian internees were in Japanese hands. Singapore must be redeemed and Malaya freed. For nearly three years we had persisted in the strategy of 'Germany First'. The time had now come for the liberation of Asia, and I was determined that we should play our full and equal part in it. What I feared most at this stage of the war was that the United States would say in after-years, 'We came to your help in Europe and you left us alone to finish off Japan.' We had to regain on the field of battle our rightful possessions in the Far East, and not have them handed back to us at the peace table.

Our main contribution must obviously be on the sea and in

the air. Most of our Fleet was now free to move eastwards, and I resolved that our first demand on our American Allies should be for its full participation in the main assault on Japan. The Royal Air Force should follow as soon as possible after Germany was defeated.

The military operations were much more complicated. Things were going badly in China, and Admiral Mountbatten was being pressed both to hurry on the opening of the Burma Road by advancing into Central Burma—an operation called 'Capital'—and to increase the supplies which were being flown over the Himalayas. Another project which promised more immediate results was an amphibious expedition to sail across the Bay of Bengal, capture Rangoon, move a few miles inland, and cut off the Japanese troops from their bases and lines of communication in Siam. This was known as Operation 'Dracula'. At the same time our troops in Central Burma would sweep down and join the force which was to land at Rangoon. It was hoped that this would clear the country and enable us to make an amphibious assault on Sumatra.

But all these tasks called for men and material, and there were not enough in South-East Asia. The only place they could come from was Europe. The landing-craft would have to be taken either from the Mediterranean or from 'Overlord', and the troops from Italy and elsewhere, and they would have to leave soon. It was now September. Rangoon lies forty miles up a winding estuary, complicated with backwaters and mud-banks. The monsoon starts in early May, and we should therefore have to attack by April 1945 at the latest. Was it yet safe to start weakening our effort in Europe?

I was by no means certain that Germany would be defeated in 1944. It was true that we had had nearly seven weeks of unbroken military success. Paris was liberated and large areas of France had been cleared of the enemy. Our advance in Italy continued. The Soviet offensive, though temporarily halted, might at any moment surge forward again. Greece would soon be free. Hitler's 'secret weapons' were almost mastered, and there was no evidence that he had learned how to make the atomic bomb. All these and many other factors induced a belief in our military circle that the Nazis would soon collapse. But I was not convinced. I remembered the German onslaught in March 1918. At a meeting of the Chiefs of Staff over which I presided on September 8 I accordingly warned them against

op: Supply vehicles litter the Normandy beaches after **D-Day.** *Bottom:*
*liders, here seen landing on an improvised landing strip, were also used
to supply the advancing Allied forces

Top: The little Normandy town of St. Lô was almost completely des
troyed during the American 3rd Division's tremendous battle there
Bottom: Mr. Churchill and Field-Marshal Montgomery inspect
'Mulberry' harbour near Arromanches, from a 'Dukw'

Top: Hidden collaborators shoot at civilians on their way to the Notre-Dame to attend a service to commemorate the liberation of Paris—August 26, 1944. *Bottom:* Churchill with General de Gaulle at the head of a procession which walked down the Champs-Elysées to the Place de la Concorde and then on to the Notre-Dame

Warsaw after the sixty-day agony of the rising by the courageous Polish
Underground Force—destroyed buildings and unburied dead

Japanese *kamikaze* suicide aircraft shot down before it could reach its
target

American trucks on their way from the Chinese front via a vertiginous mountain track in the interior of Burma

Top: British transport moves over the bridge at Nijmegen which fell *in*tact into British hands on September 20, 1944. *Bottom:* The last phase *in* the mopping up of the Scheldt estuary—41 Royal Marine Commando landing at Westkapelle on Walcheren Island, November 1, 1944.

British troops, surrounded and outnumbered, fighting the E.L.A.S. (the Greek 'People's National Army of Liberation') in Athens

basing their plans on an imminent German collapse. I pointed out that resistance in the West had stiffened and the Americans had been sharply checked at Nancy. German garrisons, I said, were offering stout resistance at most of the ports ; the Americans had not taken St. Nazaire ; and the enemy showed every intention of fighting hard on the shores of the estuary of the Scheldt leading to Antwerp, which we so badly needed.

Another matter lay heavy on my mind. I was very anxious to forestall the Russians in certain areas of Central Europe. The Hungarians, for instance, had expressed their intention of resisting the Soviet advance, but would surrender to a British force if it could arrive in time. If the Germans either evacuated Italy or retired to the Alps I much desired that Alexander should be enabled to make his amphibious thrust across the Adriatic, seize and occupy the Istrian peninsula, and try to reach Vienna before the Russians. It seemed much too early to start sending his troops to South-East Asia. The C.I.G.S. agreed that there should be no question of withdrawing any of Alexander's troops until Kesselring had been driven across the Piave. Our front would then be considerably less than half its present width. For the time being only the first of the Indian divisions needed for the assault on Rangoon would be taken from Alexander. I was discontented even at this prospect. As for landing in the Istrian peninsula, I was told that we should either have to borrow American landing-craft which were due to leave for the Pacific or weaken the campaign in France. The rest of our craft were needed for taking Rangoon. This must be done before the May monsoon, and if we used these vessels in the Adriatic they would not get there in time.

As a result of our lengthy talks on the voyage we reached agreement about what we should say to our great Ally.

*   *   *

We landed at Halifax on September 10, and reached Quebec the following morning. The President and Mrs. Roosevelt, who were our guests, had arrived just before us, and the President waited at the station to greet me. Once again the Citadel was our home, while the staffs again monopolised the Château Frontenac.

On the morning of Wednesday, September 13, we held our first plenary meeting. With me were Brooke, Portal, Cunningham, Dill, Ismay, and Major-General Laycock, who had succeeded Mountbatten as Chief of Combined Operations. The

President had with him Leahy, Marshall, King, and Arnold. But this time, alas, there was no Harry Hopkins. He had sent me a telegram just before I left England: 'Although I am now feeling much better, I still must take things easy, and I therefore feel that I should not run the risk of a setback in health by attempting to fight the Battle of Quebec on the Plains of Abraham, where better men than I have been killed.' I was not then aware of the change in the character of his relationship with the President, but I was sure that he would be sorely missed.

Mr. Roosevelt asked me to open the discussion. I thereupon made a general survey of the war which I had prepared on the voyage. Since our meeting in Cairo the affairs of the United Nations had taken a revolutionary turn for the better. Everything we had touched had turned to gold, and during the last seven weeks there had been an unbroken run of military success. The manner in which the situation had developed since the Teheran Conference gave the impression of remarkable design and precision of execution. First there had been the Anzio landing, and then on the day before the launching of 'Overlord' we had captured Rome. This seemed the most perfect timing. I congratulated the United States Chiefs of Staff on the gratifying results of 'Dragoon'. It seemed that eighty or ninety thousand prisoners had already been captured, and the south and western parts of France were being systematically cleared of the enemy. Future historians would surely say that since Teheran our Allied war machine had worked with extraordinary efficiency.

I was also glad to record that although the British Empire had now entered the sixth year of the war it was still keeping its position, with a total population, including the Dominions and Colonies, of only seventy million white people. Our effort in Europe, measured by divisions in the field, was about equal to that of the United States. This was as it should be, and I was proud that we could claim equal partnership with our great Ally. Our strength had now reached its peak, whereas our Ally's was ever increasing. There was complete confidence in General Eisenhower, and his relations with General Montgomery were of the best, as were those between General Montgomery and General Bradley. The part played by General Bedell Smith in directing and cementing the staffs was of the highest order. An efficient integrated American-British Staff machine had been built up, and the battle was being brilliantly exploited.

In Italy General Alexander had resumed the offensive at the end of August. Since then the Eighth Army had suffered about 8,000 casualties and the Fifth Army about 1,000. The Fifth Army had hitherto not been so heavily engaged, but they were expected to attack that very day. In this theatre there was the most representative British Empire army there had ever been. There were in all sixteen British Empire divisions, namely, eight British, two Canadian, one New Zealand, one South African, and four British-Indian. I explained that I had been anxious lest General Alexander might be short of certain essentials for the vigorous prosecution of his campaign, but I now understood that the Combined Chiefs of Staff had agreed to withdraw nothing from his army until either Kesselring's troops had been destroyed or were on the run out of Italy.

General Marshall confirmed this undertaking, and I accordingly emphasised that in that case we should have to look for fresh woods and pastures new. It would never do for our armies to remain idle. I said I had always been attracted by a right-handed movement to give Germany a stab in the Adriatic armpit. Our objective should be Vienna. If German resistance collapsed we should of course be able to reach the city more quickly and more easily. If not I had given considerable thought to aiding this movement by capturing Istria and occupying Trieste and Fiume. I had been relieved to learn that the United States Chiefs of Staff were willing to leave in the Mediterranean certain landing-craft now engaged in the attack on the south of France to provide an amphibious lift for such an operation, if this was found desirable and necessary. Another reason for this right-handed movement was the rapid encroachment of the Russians into the Balkan peninsula and the dangerous spread of Soviet influence there.

*   *   *

I then reviewed the campaign in Burma. This had been on a considerable scale. 250,000 men had been engaged, and the fighting for Imphal and Kohima had been extremely bitter. General Stilwell was to be congratulated on his brilliant capture of Myitkyina. We had suffered 40,000 battle casualties and 288,000 sick. Of the sick, happily, the greater proportion recovered and returned to duty. As a result of this campaign the air line to China had been kept open and India made safe from attack. It was estimated that the Japanese had lost 100,000 men.

The Burma campaign was the largest land engagement of Japanese forces so far attained.

In spite of these successes it was, I continued, most undesirable that the fighting in the Burmese jungles should go on indefinitely. For this reason the British Chiefs of Staff had proposed Operation 'Dracula', the capture of Rangoon. Difficulties were being experienced in gathering the necessary forces and transporting them to South-East Asia in time to take Rangoon before the monsoon of 1945. The present situation in Europe, favourable as it was, did not permit a decision being taken now to withdraw forces. What we wanted was to keep an option open for as long as possible, and every effort was being directed to this end.

Certain trouble-makers had said that we would take no share in the war against Japan once Germany had been defeated. Far from shirking this task, the British Empire was eager to play the greatest possible part in it. We had every reason for doing so. Japan was as much the bitter enemy of the British Empire as of the United States. British territory had been captured in battle and grievous losses had been suffered. The offer I now made was for the British main fleet to take part in the major operations against Japan under United States Supreme Command. We should have available a powerful and well-balanced force. We hoped that by the end of 1945 this would include our newest battleships. A fleet train of adequate proportions would be built up, making the warships independent of shore-based resources for considerable periods.

The President intervened to say that the British Fleet was no sooner offered than accepted. In this, though the fact was not mentioned, he overruled Admiral King's opinion.

I continued that placing a British fleet in the Central Pacific would not prevent us sending a detachment to General Mac-Arthur in the South-West Pacific if this was desired. We had of course no intention of interfering in any way with his command. As a further contribution to the defeat of the enemy, the Royal Air Force would like to take part in the heavy bombardment of Japan. A bomber force of no mean size could be made available, and would feel honoured to share with their American colleagues the dangers of striking at the heart of the enemy. As for land forces, when Germany had been beaten we should probably be able to send six divisions from Europe to the East, and perhaps six more later on. In South-East Asia we had sixteen divisions, which might ultimately be drawn upon. I had always advocated an advance across the Bay of Bengal and operations to recover Singapore, the loss of which had been a grievous and shameful blow to British prestige and must be avenged. There was nothing cast-iron in these ideas. First we should capture Rangoon and then survey the situation. If a better plan could be evolved it should certainly not be ruled out in advance. The key-note should be to engage the largest number of our own forces against the largest number of the enemy at the earliest possible moment.

* * *

The President thanked me for this review, and said it was a matter of profound satisfaction that at each succeeding Conference between the Americans and the British there had been ever-increasing solidarity of outlook and identity of basic thought. Added to this there had always been an atmosphere of cordiality and friendship. Our fortunes had prospered, but it was still not quite possible to forecast when the war with Germany would end. It was clear that the Germans were withdrawing from the Balkans, and it seemed likely that in Italy they would retire to the Alps. The Russians were on the edge of Hungary. The Germans had shown themselves good at staging withdrawals, and had been able to save many men, although they had lost much material. If Alexander's battle went well we should reach the Piave reasonably soon. All forces in Italy should be engaged to the maximum intensity. In the West it seemed probable that the Germans would retire behind the Rhine. Its right bank would be the western rampart of their defence and would present a formidable obstacle. We should have to attack them either from the east or from the west, and our plans must therefore be flexible. The Germans could not yet be counted out. One more big battle would have to be fought, and our operations against Japan would to some extent depend on what happened in Europe.

The President agreed that we should not remain in Burma any longer than was necessary to clean up the Japanese in that theatre. The American plan was to regain the Philippines and to dominate the mainland of Japan from there or Formosa, and from bridgeheads which would be seized in China. If forces could be established on the mainland of China, China could be saved. American experience had been that the 'end run' method paid a handsome dividend. Rabaul was an example of this by-passing technique which had brought considerable success at small cost of life. Would it not be possible, he asked, to by-pass Singapore by seizing an area to the north or east of it, such as Bangkok? He said that he had not hitherto been greatly attracted to the Sumatra plan, but now the operation had acquired greater merit.

I said that all these projects were being examined and would be put in order. No decision could be reached until after we had taken Rangoon. It should not be overlooked that Stalin had volunteered a solemn undertaking at Teheran that Russia would enter the war against Japan the day that Hitler was beaten. There was no reason to doubt that Stalin would be as good as his word. The Russians undoubtedly had great ambitions in the East. If Hitler was beaten by, say, January, and Japan was confronted with the three most powerful nations in the world, she would undoubtedly think twice about continuing the fight.

I then cast back to make sure where we stood, and asked for a definite undertaking about employing the British Fleet in the main operations against Japan.

'I should like,' said the President, 'to see the British Fleet wherever and whenever possible.'

Admiral King said that a paper had been prepared for the Combined Chiefs of Staff, and the question was being actively studied.

'The offer of the British Fleet has been made,' I repeated. 'Is it accepted?'

'Yes,' said Mr. Roosevelt.

'Will you also let the British Air Force take part in the main operations?'

Here it was much more difficult to get a direct answer. Marshall said that General Arnold and he were trying to see how to use the greatest number of aircraft they could. 'Not so long ago,' he explained, 'we were crying out for planes. Now we have a glut. If you are going to be heavily engaged in South-East Asia and Malaya won't you need most of your Air Force? Or is Portal's plan to bomb Japan something quite separate?'

'Quite separate,' answered Portal. 'If our Lancaster bombers are refuelled in the air they can go nearly as far as your B.29s.'

I said that for the sake of good relations, on which so much depended in the future, it was of vital importance that the British should be given their fair share in the main operations

against Japan. The United States had given us the most handsome assistance in the fight against Germany. It was only to be
expected that the British Empire in return should wish to give
the United States all the help in their power towards defeating
Japan.

* * *

After the meeting I telegraphed home.

Prime Minister to Deputy Prime Minister and　　13 Sept 44
War Cabinet
The Conference has opened in a blaze of friendship. The
Staffs are in almost complete agreement already. There is to
be no weakening of Alexander's army till Kesselring has bolted
beyond the Alps or been destroyed. We are to have all the
landing-craft in the Mediterranean to work up in the Northern
Adriatic in any amphibious plan which can be made for Istria,
Trieste, etc.
2. The idea of our going to Vienna, if the war lasts long
enough and if other people do not get there first, is fully
accepted here.
3. After their work in the Adriatic the landing-craft will of
course be free to go on to the Bay of Bengal, or farther, as
circumstances may require.

I was also able to reassure our commanders in the Mediterranean.

Prime Minister to General Wilson and　　13 Sept 44
General Alexander
Everything has opened here very well so far as your affairs
are concerned. There is to be no weakening of Alexander's
army till after Kesselring is disposed of, which our Intelligence
indicates as probable.
2. Moreover, Admiral King is not making any claims on the
landing-craft in the Mediterranean, and the Americans are
quite ready to agree that as many as necessary of these should
be used for any amphibious work in the Northern Adriatic
that may be found practicable.
3. Pray therefore address yourselves to this greatly improved situation in a spirit of audacious enterprise. The
Americans talk without any hesitation of our pushing on to
Vienna, if the war lasts long enough. I am greatly relieved at

the reception all our ideas have met here. We must turn these
advantages to the best account.

*   *   *

During the days which followed I had a number of conversations with the President and his advisers. I had been surprised to
find when I arrived at Quebec that the President was accompanied by Mr. Morgenthau, the Secretary of the United States
Treasury, though neither the Secretary of State nor Harry Hopkins was present. But I was glad to see Morgenthau, as we were
anxious to discuss financial arrangements between our two
countries for the period between the conquest of Germany and
the defeat of the Japanese. The President and his Secretary of
the Treasury were however much more concerned about the
treatment of Germany after the war. They felt very strongly that
military strength rested on industrial strength. We had seen
during the nineteen-thirties how easy it was for a highly indus-
trialised Germany to arm herself and threaten her neighbours
and they asserted that there was no need for so much manufacturing in a country as large as Germany, who could to all
intents and purposes feed herself. The United Kingdom had lost
so many overseas investments that she could only pay her way
when peace came by greatly increasing her exports, so that for
economic as well as military reasons we ought to restrict German industry and encourage German agriculture. At first I
violently opposed this idea. But the President, with Mr. Morgenthau—from whom we had much to ask—was so insistent that
in the end we agreed to consider it.

The so-called Morgenthau Plan, which I had not time to
examine in detail, seems to have carried these ideas to an ultra-
logical conclusion. Even if it had been practicable I do not think
it would have been right to depress Germany's standard of
life in such a way; but at that time, when German militarism
based on German industry had done such appalling damage to
Europe, it did not seem unfair to agree that her manufacturing
capacity need not be revived beyond what was required to give
her the same standards of life as her neighbours. All this was of
course subject to the full consideration of the War Cabinet, and
in the event, with my full accord, the idea of 'pastoralising'
Germany did not survive.

*   *   *

We held our last meeting at midday on Saturday, September 16. The Combined Chiefs of Staff had now completed their final report to the President and myself, and at Mr. Roosevelt's request Admiral Leahy read it out to us paragraph by paragraph. The principal passages were as follows:

9. The Supreme Commander's broad intention is to press on with all speed to destroy the German armed forces and occupy the heart of Germany. He considers his best opportunity of defeating the enemy in the West lies in striking at the Ruhr and Saar, since he is convinced that the enemy will concentrate the remainder of his available forces in the defence of these essential areas. The first operation will be to break the Siegfried Line and seize crossings over the Rhine. In doing this his main effort will be on the left. He will then prepare logistically and otherwise for a deep thrust into Germany.

10. We have approved General Eisenhower's proposals and drawn his attention

(a) to the advantages of the northern line of approach into Germany, as opposed to the southern, and

(b) to the necessity for the opening up of the north-west ports, particularly Antwerp and Rotterdam, before bad weather sets in.

I had no quarrel with these broad intentions, but the reader will remember the doubts which I had voiced to the British Chiefs of Staff during our voyage across the Atlantic about the imminence of Germany's defeat. I had also written a paper in this sense which will be printed in a later chapter. Rundstedt's counter-stroke was still to come, and the crossing of the Rhine was not to be achieved for more than another six months.

*　　　*　　　*

The military recommendations about Italy were as follows:

11. We have examined a report by General Wilson on operations within his theatre. In so far as the battle in Italy is concerned, he considers that operations will develop in one of two ways:

(a) Either Kesselring's forces will be routed, in which case it should be possible to undertake a rapid regrouping and a pursuit towards the Ljubljana Gap (and across the Alps through the Brenner Pass), leaving a small force to clear up North-West Italy ; or

(b) Kesselring's army will succeed in effecting an orderly withdrawal, in which event it does not seem possible that we can do more than clear the Lombardy plains this year. Difficult terrain and severe weather in the Alps during winter would prevent another major offensive until the spring of 1945.

The report continued as follows:

12. We have agreed:

(a) That no major units should be withdrawn from Italy until the outcome of General Alexander's present offensive is known.

(b) That the desirability of withdrawing formations of the United States Fifth Army should be reconsidered in the light of the results of General Alexander's present offensive and of a German withdrawal in Northern Italy, and in the light of the views of General Eisenhower.

(c) To inform General Wilson that if he wishes to retain for use in the Istrian peninsula the amphibious lift at present in the Mediterranean he should submit his plan to the Combined Chiefs of Staff as soon as possible, and not later than October 10. We have instructed the Supreme Allied Commander accordingly.

Here I had to beware of bargains. No major units to be withdrawn until we knew the result of Alexander's offensive ; so far, so good. But how far was the offensive to be pushed? If he was only to be allowed to go to the Rimini line, for instance, then the proposal was quite unacceptable. I accordingly said I presumed he would be allowed to invade and dominate the valley of the Po, and I was much relieved when Marshall and Leahy agreed that this was what they meant.

I then thanked Admiral King for promising to lend us his landing-craft for an attack on the Istrian peninsula. The Admiral stressed that they would also be wanted for the assault on Rangoon, and we must therefore make up our minds about invading Istria by October 15.

*   *   *

The next paragraph of the report set forth our joint proposals about operations in the Balkan peninsula. It read as follows:

13. General Wilson considers that a situation can be anticipated in which the bulk of the German forces south of a line Trieste–Ljubljana–Zagreb and the Danube will be immobilised, and will so remain until their supplies are exhausted, in which case they would be ready to surrender to us or will be

liquidated by Partisans or the Russian forces. We have noted that as long as the battle in Italy continues there will be no forces available in the Mediterranean to employ in the Balkans except:

(a) the small force of two British brigades from Egypt which is being held ready to occupy the Athens area and so pave the way for commencement of relief and establishment of law and order and the Greek Government ;

(b) the small land forces in the Adriatic which are being actively used primarily for Commando type operations.

This was accepted by all of us without amendment or discussion.

* * *

The proposals for war in the Pacific dwelt on the importance of flexibility and short-cuts. The Allied superiority of naval and air power should enable us to avoid, wherever possible, costly land campaigns. In South-East Asia it was agreed that the land advance into Burma from the north should be combined with the amphibian capture of Rangoon. I said that while I accepted the British obligation to secure the air route and attain overland communication with China, any tendency to overdo it would rule out our assault on Rangoon, which both the Chiefs of Staff and I wanted to capture before the monsoon of 1945.

The rest of the report was approved with little or no discussion. The planning date for the end of the war against Japan was set for the time being at eighteen months after the defeat of Germany.

The following passage requires verbatim statement.

33. Upon the collapse of organised resistance by the German Army the following subdivision of that part of Germany not allocated to the Soviet Government for disarmament, policing, and the preservation of order is acceptable from a military point of view by the Combined Chiefs of Staff.

34. For disarmament, policing, and preservation of order:

(a) The British forces, under a British commander, will occupy Germany west of the Rhine and east of the Rhine north of the line from Koblenz, following the northern border of Hesse and Nassau to the border of the area allocated to the Soviet Government.

(b) The forces of the United States, under a United States commander, will occupy Germany east of the line, south of the line Koblenz-northern border of Hesse-Nassau and west of the area allocated to the Soviet Government.

(c) Control of the ports Bremen and Bremerhaven, and the necessary staging areas in that immediate vicinity, will be vested in the commander of the American Zone.

(d) American area to have in addition access through the western and north-western seaports and passage through the British-controlled area.

(e) Accurate delineation of the above outlined British and American areas of control can be made at a later date.

* * *

On Sunday, September 17, I left Quebec by train with my wife and daughter Mary to pay a farewell visit to the President at Hyde Park.

I lunched there on September 19. Harry Hopkins was present. He was obviously invited to please me. He explained to me his altered position. He had declined in the favour of the President. There was a curious incident at luncheon, when he arrived a few minutes late and the President did not even greet him. It was remarkable how definitely my contacts with the President improved and our affairs moved quicker as Hopkins appeared to regain his influence. In two days it seemed to be like old times. He said to me, 'You must know I am not what I was.' He had tried too much at once. Even his fullness of spirit broke under his variegated activities.

After dinner I left for New York, and boarded the *Queen Mary* the following morning. The voyage home was without incident. We arrived in the Clyde on September 25, and left immediately by train for London.

CHAPTER 11

Advance in Burma

The Relief of Imphal, June 1944 – Ruinous Japanese Losses – The Advance of the Fourteenth Army – The Fight Against the Monsoon – General Stilwell Captures Myitkyina, August – His 'Mars Brigade' – Mountbatten Visits London to Explain His Plans – My Minute of September 12 About the Operations – German Resistance Compels Us to Postpone the Assault on Rangoon – Hard Tidings for Mountbatten, October 5 – The Advance Continues – Changes in the American High Command – Crisis in China – The President's Telegram of December 1 – Withdrawal of Two Chinese Divisions and of the Transport Squadrons – The Advance on Mandalay – Reopening of the Burma Road, January 1945 – My Telegram to Mountbatten of January 23 – Winter Fighting in the Arakan – The Capture of Akyab.

The swaying battle in Burma has already been described up to the point when the initiative was about to pass into our hands.* Japan's invasion of India collapsed on the mountain plateau of Imphal at the end of June 1944, when relieving troops from the north met the outward thrust of General Scoones' garrison. The road to Dimapur was open and the convoys flowed in. But the three Japanese divisions had still to be thrust back to and beyond the river Chindwin, whence they had come. Their losses had been ruinous. Over thirteen thousand dead were counted on the battlefields, and, allowing for those who died of wounds, disease, or hunger, the total amounted on a Japanese estimate to 65,000 men. The monsoon, now at its height, had in previous years brought active operations to a standstill, and the Japanese doubtless counted on a pause during which they could extricate and rebuild their shattered Fifteenth Army. They were given no such respite.

The British-Indian Fourteenth Army, under the able and forceful leadership of General Slim, took the offensive. Their XXXIIIrd Corps first cleared up around Ukhrul, while the IVth recaptured the southern part of the Imphal plain. By the

* Book 10, Chapter 14, 'Burma and Beyond'.

end of July Japanese resistance was broken and the XXXIIIr
took up a general pursuit to the Chindwin. All along the moun
tain tracks they found evidence of disaster—quantities of abar
doned guns, transport, and equipment ; thousands of the enem
lay dead or dying. The 5th Indian Division, thrusting south to
wards Tiddim, had at first a harder task. The Japanese 33r
Division, which opposed them, had not been handled s
roughly as the others and had been reinforced. The road twiste
its narrow way through mountainous country and was easy t
defend. One by one the Japanese positions were overcome, th
221 Group R.A.F., under Air Marshal Vincent, providing vic
lent bombardments immediately before the infantry assault
Here, as everywhere in Burma at this time, progress, measure
in miles a day, was very slow. But our men were fighting i
tropical rainfall, soaked to the skin by day and night. The so
called roads were mostly fair-weather dust-tracks, which wer
now churned into deep mud, through which guns and vehicle
had often to be manhandled. It is not the slowness of advanc
but the fact that any advance was made at all that should caus
surprise.

In the Arakan our troops were held on an active defensiv
In that tangle of jungle-covered hills, with its narrow coast:
strip of ricefields and mangrove swamps, the monsoon rainfa
which sometimes reached twenty inches a week,* stoppe
serious operations. On the northern front General Stilwell
forces made steady progress. The capture of Myitkyina o
August 3 gave him a forward base for future land operation
and, even more important, provided a staging post for th
American air-lift to China. The famous 'Hump' traffic n
longer had to make the direct and often dangerous flight fro
Northern Assam over the great mountains to Kunming. Wor
was progressing on the long road from Northern Assam, destine
later to link up with the former road from Burma to China. Th
strain on rearward communications in Assam was relieved by
new oil pipe-line 750 miles long laid from Calcutta, a greate
span than the famous desert pipe-line from Iraq to Haifa.

For his southward advance Stilwell reorganised his fiv
Chinese divisions into two 'Armies', one directed from Myi
kyina on Bhamo and Namkhan, the other on Shwegu and Katha
The latter advance was led by the British 36th Division, whic
had been placed under Stilwell's orders. It replaced the Chind

* The average *yearly* rainfall in London is about twenty-four inches.

rigades,* under General Lentaigne, when, after nearly six
months of arduous and exacting operations, in which they had
fought and overcome at least eleven enemy battalions, they were
withdrawn for long-needed rest and recoupment. As a reserve
in his own hands Stilwell retained his 'Mars Brigade', a mobile,
lightly equipped force of about ten thousand men, whose principal component was an American regiment. With these forces he
began his advance in early August to cross the river Irrawaddy,
and, on his eastern flank, to get touch with the Chinese 'Yunnan'
armies, about 100,000 strong, which were advancing from the
river Salween towards Namkhan.

*   *   *

The policy for future operations in South-East Asia was
again under review at this time, and, after consultation with his
Commanders-in-Chief, Admiral Somerville, General Giffard,
and Air Chief Marshal Peirse, Mountbatten came to London to
explain his plans. He was already committed to a land advance
into Central Burma, which was to continue until the Fourteenth
Army was across the Chindwin and had joined hands with
Stilwell's forces coming from the north. But with his ever-
lengthening line of communications and the limited number of
supply aircraft on which he so greatly depended it was doubtful
whether he could advance from Mandalay as far as Rangoon.
He therefore proposed to carry out the large-scale amphibious
attack on Rangoon mentioned in the previous chapter and given
the code name 'Dracula'. Once firmly established there, his
troops could thrust northwards and meet the Fourteenth Army.
This was an excellent idea, but it demanded many more troops
and much more shipping than Mountbatten possessed. They
could only be found from North-West Europe.

My views on this and its variants are given in a minute written
at Quebec.

Prime Minister to General Ismay,   12 Sept 44
for C.O.S. Committee
THE WAR AGAINST JAPAN

The British share in this war may take the form either of
direct participation in particular United States enterprises in
the Far East or of British diversionary enterprises on a major
scale calculated to wear down the enemy forces by land and

---
* The late General Wingate's Long-Range Penetration Force.

air, and also to regain British possessions conquered by th
Japanese. Of the two I favour the latter, because:

(a) It is nearly always a sound war policy to engage th
largest number of the enemy as closely and continuousl
as possible, at the earliest moment and for the longest tim

(b) This can best be achieved by a direct thrust acros
the short-haul of the Bay of Bengal, aimed at 'Dracula
[Rangoon], 'Culverin' [Sumatra], or other attainable pre
liminary objectives.

(c) A great diminution of the forces engaged with th
enemy results from lengthening the communications. A gus
has to be poured into the pipe-line at one end to produc
only a trickle at the other, so great is the leakage as th
route lengthens.

2. It follows, for the above reasons, that I am opposed t
sending any British troops to join the Australians and Ne
Zealanders under General MacArthur. The contribution woul
be both petty and tardy. On the other hand, I do not object t
supporting General MacArthur with a British Naval Tas
Force, including carriers, or with R.A.F. squadrons, provide
that the detachment of these does not weaken our majo
operations across the Bay of Bengal.

3. Admiral Leahy informed me yesterday that it had bee
decided to accept the British offer to send our Fleet to partic
pate in the main operations against Japan. It would not b
inconsistent with this policy to make a detachment from it fo
the purpose of sustaining General MacArthur's operations.

4. To sum up, our policy should be to give naval assistanc
on the largest scale to the main American operations, but t
keep our own thrust for Rangoon as a preliminary operatio
or one of the preliminary operations, to a major attack upo
Singapore. Here is the supreme British objective in the who
of the Indian and Far Eastern theatres. It is the only prize tha
will restore British prestige in this region, and in pursuing
we render the maximum aid to the United States operation
by engaging the largest numbers of the enemy in the mos
intense degree possible and at the earliest moment.

In our discussions at Quebec we had carried the American
with us on the Rangoon plan. This promised many advantages
Six months' fighting in the hills and jungles of Burma and on th
frontier of India was estimated to have cost the British an
Imperial forces 288,000 losses from sickness alone, but a sea
borne stroke against Rangoon and a northward advance woul
cut the enemy's communications and divide his forces. Th
destruction of the Japanese in Burma would liberate a con

siderable army, which could immediately attack such targets across the Bay of Bengal as might be considered to be most beneficial to the common cause, the wearing down of Japanese troops, and above all air forces. For this purpose we had resolved to strain every nerve to attack Rangoon by March 15, 1945. It was thought that five or six divisions would be needed for such an operation, but Mountbatten could only supply two or three and not more than one could be spared from the United Kingdom. Failure meant not only needless sacrifices through prolonging in Burma operations ravaged by disease, but the setback of our whole further deployment against the Malay peninsula and beyond until 1946.

Thus the solution, I had suggested, was to send one or two United States divisions to Burma instead of to Europe. This was better than taking two divisions from Montgomery's army which were actually fighting, and would bring more troops rapidly into action against Japan without withdrawing any of those who were engaged against Germany. I explained at Quebec that I did not want a decision there and then, but only that the United States Chiefs of Staff should examine my suggestions. This General Marshall agreed to do, but for various reasons my proposals were not adopted. The sanguine hopes, which I had not shared, that Germany would collapse before the end of the year failed. At the end of September it was obvious that German resistance would continue into and beyond the winter, and Mountbatten was instructed, not for the first time, that he must do what he could with what he had got. I telegraphed accordingly:

Prime Minister to Admiral Mountbatten   5 Oct 44
The Defence Committee have been forced to the conclusion that March 'Dracula' is off, and Chiefs of Staff have made this proposal to United States Chiefs of Staff. You will receive official instructions in due course. Meanwhile you should know that the postponement of the operation is due to the working of far larger forces in the Western theatre rather than to any attitude which you or S.E.A.C. have adopted. You have now to address yourself to the problem of bringing 'Dracula' on in November [1945]. I am very sorry indeed that we have not been able to carry out this operation, on which I had set my heart, but the German resistance both in France and Italy has turned out to be far more formidable than we had hoped. We must clean them out first.

*   *   *

All this time our Fourteenth and Stilwell's Armies had been forging slowly ahead. The 5th Indian Division captured Tiddin on October 18, and with the help of concentrated pin-point bombing soon cleared the enemy from the dominating 8,000-feet Kennedy Peak. Thence they fought on towards Kalemyo. The XXXIIIrd Corps, after taking Tamu, sent an East African brigade eastwards. It established a valuable bridgehead across the river Chindwin at Sittaung. The rest of the 11th East African Division went south along the Kabaw valley towards Kalemyo which they entered hand-in-hand with the 5th Indian Division on November 14. This was a remarkable march against great physical difficulties through an area notorious for malaria and scrub-typhus. The good hygiene discipline now practised by all our units in Burma, the use of the new drug mepacrine, and constant spraying with D.D.T. insecticide kept the sick rate admirably low. But the Japanese were not versed in these precautions and died in hundreds. From Kalemyo the East Africans pushed on to Kalewa and crossed the Chindwin. Here the engineers built a bridge nearly four hundred yards long in twenty-eight working hours, not the least of their many achievements throughout the campaign. Thus on the central front in early December General Slim's Fourteenth Army, with two bridge-heads across the Chindwin, was poised for his main advance into the central plain of Burma.

Changes among the senior United States officers took place in November. General Stilwell was recalled by Washington. His widespread, multifarious duties were taken over by three others. General Wedemeyer succeeded him as military adviser to Chiang Kai-shek, General Wheeler became Deputy to Mountbatten, and General Sultan took over the northern front. Here the Allied forces slowly threw back the two divisions of the Japanese Thirty-third Army. By mid-November Bhamo was closely invested, but held out stubbornly for a further month. The 36th British Division took Indaw on December 10. Six days later they made contact there with the 19th Indian Division, which had crossed the Chindwin at the Sittaung bridgehead and thrust eastwards. So at last, after more than a year of hard endeavour, marked by many ups and downs, the two Allied armies joined hands.

*   *   *

But formidable administrative problems lay ahead. Far away

in South-East China, some months before, the Japanese had begun an advance on Chungking, the Generalissimo's capital, and Kunming, the delivery point of the American supply air-lift. In November General Wedemeyer took a serious view of this situation. Already the forward bases of the U.S. Air Force in China, which had been operating against enemy coastwise shipping, were being overrun. The Chinese troops gave little promise, and Wedemeyer appealed for two of the Chinese divisions in North Burma, and also for more American air squadrons, in particular for three transport squadrons.

The President addressed me.

President Roosevelt to Prime Minister   1 Dec 44
A telegram has been received from General Wedemeyer outlining the gravity of the situation in China and stating that he concurs in the decision of the Generalissimo to transfer the two best trained divisions of Chinese troops from Burma to the Kunming area. You have undoubtedly seen this message, which went to Mountbatten and has been furnished to your mission here in Washington, so I shall not repeat it.

We have General Wedemeyer's view on the ground as to the gravity of the situation, along with his knowledge of the situation and the plans for operations in Burma. I feel that he is better informed as to the general situation and requirements than any other individual at this moment. Furthermore, we are faced by the fact that the Generalissimo, in a grave crisis which threatens the existence of China, has decided that he must recall these two divisions in order to check the Japanese drive on Kunming. It would avail us nothing to open a land-line to China if the Japanese seized the Kunming terminal for air and ground. Under the circumstances I therefore am of the opinion that we are not in a position to bring pressure on the Generalissimo to alter his decision.

These were hard tidings, but we had no choice but to accept.

Prime Minister to General Hollis,   2 Dec 44
for C.O.S. Committee
There can be no dispute about the right of the Generalissimo to withdraw any division he requires to defend himself against the Japanese attack upon his vitals. I have little doubt he will first wish to bring home the two divisions [trained by the Americans]. We cannot make a fight about this. If he claims them he must have them. What happens [afterwards] in Burma demands urgent but subsequent study. Pray let me have a telegram drafted agreeing with the Americans about the with-drawal of the divisions.

The loss of two good Chinese divisions was not so grave an inconvenience to the Burma operations as that of the transport squadrons. The Army was four hundred miles beyond its railhead and General Slim relied on air supply to help the tenuous road link. Mountbatten's general plans depended on his transport aircraft. The squadrons needed for China had to go, and although they were later replaced, mostly from British sources, their absence at a critical time caused severe delay to the campaign.

In spite of all this the Fourteenth Army broke out of the hills into the plain north-west of Mandalay. While the leading division of General Messervy's IVth Corps drove south in secret to establish a bridgehead over the Irrawaddy south of its junction with the Chindwin, General Stopford's XXXIIIrd Corps, supported by the 221 Group R.A.F., occupied the north bank of the Irrawaddy upstream from that junction. The 19th Indian Division was already across the river in two places forty miles north of Mandalay. By the end of January General Sultan's forces had reached Namkhan, on the old Burma–China road, and made contact with the Yunnan force farther east. The land route to China, closed by the Japanese invasion of Burma in the spring of 1942, was open again. The first road convoy from Assam reached the Chinese frontier on January 28.

Prime Minister to Admiral Mountbatten   23 Jan 45
(South-East Asia)

On behalf of His Majesty's Government I send you our warmest congratulations on having reopened the land route to China in fulfilment of the first part of the directive given to you at Quebec. It reflects the greatest credit on yourself, all your field commanders, and above all upon the well-tried troops of the Fourteenth Army, that this should have been achieved despite your many disappointments in the delay of promised reinforcements.

His Majesty's Government warmly and gratefully recognise, as you have done throughout, the ready assistance given in all possible ways by the forces of the United States and also by those of China.

*   *   *

Later developments in Central Burma fall to another chapter, but the winter fighting in the Arakan, subsidiary but important, must be recorded here. Its importance lay in two spheres. The air-lift to the Fourteenth Army in the Mandalay plain had

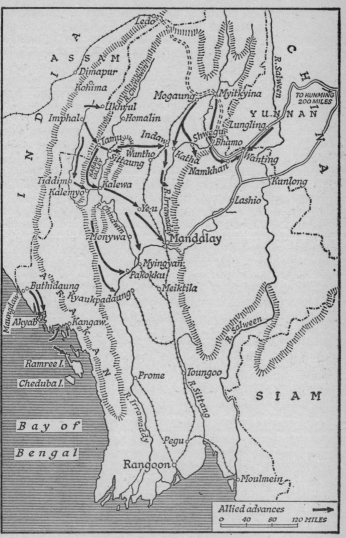

Burma, July 1944–January 1945

nearly reached the limit of the Dakota aircraft. Moreover, al
the stores thus carried forward had to be brought to the dis
patching airfields by the hard-worked Assam railway. I
General Christison's XVth Corps could establish airfields south
of Akyab, aircraft operating from there, and replenished by sea
direct from India, could supply the Fourteenth Army in a
southern thrust from Mandalay to Rangoon. Secondly, if the
single Japanese division facing our superior forces in the Arakar
was quickly defeated and dispersed two or three of our division:
and their supporting 224 Group R.A.F., under Air Commodore
the Earl of Bandon, could be taken for operations elsewhere.

The Arakan offensive opened on December 12, and made
good headway. By the end of the month our troops had reached
the inlet which separates Akyab Island from the mainland and
were preparing to assault. On January 2 an officer in an artillery
observation aircraft saw no sign of the enemy. He landed on
Akyab airfield, and was told by inhabitants that the Japanese
had left. Most of the garrison had been drawn into the fight
ing farther north ; the remaining battalion had been withdrawn
two days before. This was a strange anticlimax to the long story
of Akyab, which for nearly three years had caused us much
tribulation and many disappointments. Soon afterwards the
XVth Corps occupied Ramree Island, developing air-strip
there, and on the mainland occupied Kangaw after a sharp fight
At the end of January the XVth Corps, like those farther north
had reached its primary objectives, and was ready for further
advances.

CHAPTER 12

The Battle of Leyte Gulf

Ocean war against Japan now reached its climax. From the Bay of Bengal to the Central Pacific Allied maritime power was in the ascendant. By April 1944 three British capital ships, two carriers, and some light forces were assembled in Ceylon. These were augmented by the American carrier *Saratoga*, the French battleship *Richelieu*, and a Dutch contingent. A strong flotilla of British submarines also arrived in February and at once began to take toll of enemy shipping in the Malacca Strait. As the year advanced two more British carriers arrived, and the *Saratoga* returned to the Pacific. With these forces Admiral Somerville could do much more. In April his carriers struck at Sabang, at the northern end of Sumatra, and in May at the oil refinery and engineering works at Sourabaya, in Java. This operation lasted twenty-two days, and the fleet steamed seven thousand miles. In the following months the Japanese sea route to Rangoon was severed by British submarines and aircraft.

In August Admiral Somerville, who had commanded the Eastern Fleet through all the troubled times since March 1942, was relieved by Admiral Sir Bruce Fraser, and soon afterwards succeeded Admiral Noble at the head of our Naval Delegation at Washington. A month later the progress of the war in Europe enabled us to reduce the Home Fleet to no more than a single battleship, with supporting forces. The move to the Far East was hastened, and two modern battleships, the *Howe* and *King George V*, joined Admiral Fraser. On November 22, 1944, the British Pacific Fleet came officially into existence, and subsequently took part in a series of operations which fall to a later chapter.

* * *

In the Pacific the organisation and production of the United States were in full stride, and had attained astonishing proportions. A single example may suffice to illustrate the size and success of the American effort. In the autumn of 1942, at the peak of the struggle for Guadalcanal, only three American aircraft-carriers were afloat; a year later there were fifty; by the end of the war there were more than a hundred. This achievement had been matched by an increase in aircraft production which was no less remarkable. The advance of these great forces was animated by an aggressive strategy and an elaborate, novel, and effective tactic. The task which confronted them was formidable.

A chain of island-groups, nearly two thousand miles long, stretches southward across the Pacific from Japan to the Marianas and the Carolines. Many of these islands had been fortified by the enemy and equipped with good airfields, and at the southernmost end of the chain was the Japanese naval base of Truk. Behind this shield of archipelagos lay Formosa, the Philippines, and China, and in its shelter ran the supply routes for the more advanced enemy positions. It was thus impossible to invade or bomb Japan itself. The chain must be broken first. It would take too long to conquer and subdue every fortified island, and the Americans had accordingly advanced leapfrog fashion. They seized only the more important islands and by-passed the rest; but their maritime strength was now so great and was growing so fast that they were able to establish their own lines of communication and break the enemy's, leaving the defenders of the by-passed islands immobile and powerless. Their method of assault was equally successful. First came softening attacks by planes from the aircraft-carriers, then heavy and sometimes prolonged bombardment from the sea, and finally amphibious landing and the struggle ashore. When an island had been won and garrisoned land-based planes moved in and beat off counter-attacks. At the same time they helped in the next onward surge. The fleets worked in echelons. While one group waged battle another prepared for a new leap. This needed very large resources, not only for the fighting, but also for developing bases along the line of advance. The Americans took it all in their stride.

*   *   *

Earlier Books have described the two-pronged American attack across the Pacific, and when this narrative opens in June 1944 it was well advanced. In the south-west General Mac-Arthur had nearly completed his conquest of New Guinea, and in the centre Admiral Nimitz was pressing deep into the chain of fortified islands. Both were converging on the Philippines, and the struggle for this region was soon to bring about the destruction of the Japanese Fleet. The Fleet had already been much weakened and was very short of carriers, but Japan's only hope of survival lay in victory at sea. To conserve her strength for this perilous but vital hazard her main fleet had withdrawn from Truk and was now divided between the East Indies and her home waters; but events soon brought it to battle. At the beginning of June Admiral Spruance struck with his carriers at the Marianas, and on the 15th he landed on the fortified island of Saipan. If he captured Saipan and the adjacent islands of Tinian and Guam the enemy's defence perimeter would be broken. The threat was formidable, and the Japanese Fleet resolved to intervene. That day five of their battleships and nine carriers were sighted near the Philippines, heading east. Spruance had ample time to make his dispositions. His main purpose was to protect the landing at Saipan. This he did. He then gathered his ships, fifteen of which were carriers, and waited for the enemy to the west of the island. On June 19 Japanese carrier-borne aircraft attacked the American carrier fleet from all directions, and air-fighting continued throughout the day. The Americans suffered little damage, and so shattered the Japanese air squadrons that their carriers had to withdraw.

That night Spruance searched in vain for the vanished enemy. Late in the afternoon of the 20th he found them about 250 miles away. Attacking just before sunset, the American airmen sank one carrier and damaged four others, besides a battleship and a heavy cruiser. The previous day American submarines had sunk two other large carriers. No further attack was possible, and remnants of the enemy fleet managed to escape, but its departure sealed the fate of Saipan. Though the garrison fought hard the landings continued, the build-up progressed, and by July 9 all organised resistance came to an end. The neighbouring islands of Guam and Tinian were overcome, and by the first days of August the American grip on the Marianas was complete.

The fall of Saipan was a great shock to the Japanese High Command, and led indirectly to the dismissal of General Tojo's Government. The enemy's concern was well founded. The fortress was little more than 1,300 miles from Tokyo. They had believed it was impregnable; now it was gone. Their southern defence regions were cut off and the American heavy bombers had gained a first-class base for attacking the very homeland of Japan. For a long time United States submarines had been sinking Japanese merchantmen along the China coast, and now the way was open for other warships to join in the onslaught. Japan's oil and raw materials would be cut off if the Americans advanced any farther. The Japanese Fleet was still powerful, but unbalanced, and so weak in destroyers, carriers, and air-crews that it could no longer fight effectively without land-based planes. Fuel was scarce, and not only hampered training, but made it impossible to keep the ships concentrated in one place, so that in the late summer most of the heavy vessels and cruisers lay near Singapore and the oil supplies of the Dutch East Indies, while the few surviving carriers remained in home waters, where their new air groups were completing their training.

The plight of the Japanese Army was little better. Though still strong in numbers, it sprawled over China and South-East Asia or languished in remote islands beyond reach of support. The more sober-minded of the enemy leaders began to look for some way of ending the war; but their military machine was too strong for them. The High Command brought reinforcements from Manchuria and ordered a fight to the finish both in Formosa and the Philippines. Here and in the homeland the troops would die where they stood. The Japanese Admiralty were no less resolute. If they lost the impending battle for the islands the oil from the East Indies would be cut off. There was no purpose, they argued, in preserving ships without fuel. Steeled for sacrifice but hopeful of victory, they decided in August to send the entire Fleet into battle.

*   *   *

On September 15 the Americans made another advance. General MacArthur seized Morotai Island, midway between the western tip of New Guinea and the Philippines, and Admiral Halsey, who had now assumed command of the United States naval forces, captured an advanced base for his fleet in the Palau group. These simultaneous moves were of high importance. At the same time Halsey continually probed the enemy's defences with his whole force. Thus he hoped to provoke a general action at sea which would enable him to destroy the Japanese Fleet, particularly its surviving carriers. The next leap would be at the Philippines themselves, and there now occurred a dramatic change in the American plan. Till then our Allies had purposed to invade the southernmost portion of the Philippines, the island of Mindanao, and planes from Halsey's carriers had already attacked the Japanese airfields both there and in the large northern island of Luzon. They destroyed large numbers of enemy aircraft, and discovered in the clash of combat that the Japanese garrison at Leyte was unexpectedly weak. This small but now famous island, lying between the two larger but strategically less important land masses of Mindanao and Luzon, became the obvious point for the American descent. On September 13, while the Allies were still in conference at Quebec, Admiral Nimitz, at Halsey's suggestion, urged its immediate invasion. MacArthur agreed, and within two days the American Chiefs of Staff resolved to attack on October 20, two months earlier than had been planned. Such was the genesis of the Battle of Leyte Gulf.

The Americans opened the campaign on October 10 with raids on airfields between Japan and the Philippines. Devastating and repeated attacks on Formosa provoked the most violent resistance, and from the 12th to the 16th there followed a heavy and sustained air battle between ship-borne and land-based aircraft. The Americans inflicted grievous losses both in the air and on the ground, but suffered little themselves, and their carrier fleet withstood powerful land-based air attack. The result was decisive. The enemy's Air Force was broken before the battle for Leyte was joined. Many Japanese naval aircraft destined for the fleet carriers were improvidently sent to Formosa as reinforcements and there destroyed. Thus in the supreme naval battle which now impended the Japanese carriers were manned by little more than a hundred partially trained pilots.

*   *   *

To comprehend the engagements which followed a study of the accompanying maps is necessary. The two large islands of the Philippines, Luzon in the north and Mindanao in the south, are separated by a group of smaller islands of which Leyte is the key and centre. This central group is pierced by two navigable straits, both destined to dominate this famous battle. The northerly strait is San Bernardino, and about 200 miles south of it, leading directly to Leyte, is the strait of Surigao. The Americans, as we have seen, intended to seize Leyte, and the Japanese were resolved to stop them and to destroy their fleet. The plan was simple and desperate. Four divisions under General MacArthur would land on Leyte, protected by the guns and planes of the American fleet—so much they knew or guessed. Draw off this fleet, entice it far to the north, and engage it in a secondary battle—such was the first step. But this would be only a preliminary. As soon as the main fleet was lured away two strong columns of warships would sail through the straits, one through San Bernardino and the other through Surigao, and converge on the landings. All eyes would be on the shores of Leyte, all guns trained on the beaches, and the heavy ships and the big aircraft-carriers which alone could withstand the assault would be chasing the decoy force in the far north. The plan very nearly succeeded.

On October 17 the Japanese Commander-in-Chief ordered his fleet to set sail. The decoy force, under Admiral Ozawa, the Supreme Commander, sailing direct from Japan, steered for Luzon. It was a composite force, including carriers, battleships, cruisers, and destroyers. Ozawa's task was to appear on the eastern coast of Luzon, engage the American fleet, and draw it away from the landings in Leyte Gulf. The carriers were short of both planes and pilots, but no matter. They were only bait, and bait is made to be eaten. Meanwhile the main Japanese striking forces made for the straits. The larger, or what may be termed the Centre Force, coming from Singapore, and consisting of five battleships, twelve cruisers, and fifteen destroyers, under Admiral Kurita, headed for San Bernardino to curl round Sumar Island to Leyte; the smaller, or Southern Force, in two independent groups, comprising in all two battleships, four cruisers, and eight destroyers, sailed through Surigao.

On October 20 the Americans landed on Leyte. At first all went well. Resistance on shore was weak, a bridgehead was quickly formed, and General MacArthur's troops began their advance. They were supported by Admiral Kinkaid's Seventh United States Fleet, which was under MacArthur's command, and whose older battleships and small aircraft-carriers were well suited to amphibious operations. Farther away to the northward lay Admiral Halsey's main fleet, shielding them from attack by sea.

I was on my way home from Moscow at the time, but Field-Marshal Brooke and I recognised the importance of what had happened and we sent the following telegram:

Prime Minister and C.I.G.S. to General   22 Oct 44
MacArthur
    Hearty congratulations on your brilliant stroke in the Philippines.
    All good wishes.

The crisis however was still to come. On October 23 American submarines sighted the Japanese Centre Force (Admiral Kurita) off the coast of Borneo and sank two of its heavy cruisers, one of which was Kurita's flagship, and damaged a third. Next day, October 24, planes from Admiral Halsey's carriers joined in the attack. The giant battleship *Musashi*, mounting nine eighteen-inch guns, was sunk, other vessels were damaged, and Kurita turned back. The American airmen brought back optimistic and perhaps misleading reports, and Halsey concluded, not without reason, that the battle was won, or at any rate this part of it. He knew that the second or Southern enemy force was approaching the Surigao Strait, but he judged, and rightly, that it could be repelled by Kinkaid's Seventh Fleet.

But one thing disturbed him. During the day he had been attacked by Japanese naval planes. Many of them were shot down, but the carrier *Princeton* was damaged and had later to be abandoned. The planes, he reasoned, probably came from carriers. It was most unlikely that the enemy had sailed without them, yet none had been found. The main Japanese fleet, under Kurita, had been located, and was apparently in retreat, but Kurita had no carriers, neither were there any in the Southern

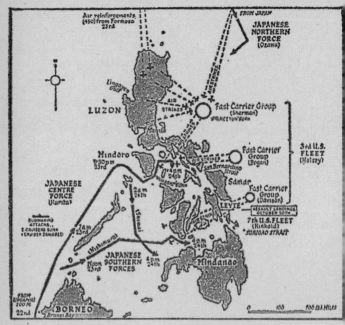

Battle of Leyte Gulf, Philippines: Approach and Contact, October 22–24, 1944

Force. Surely there must be a carrier force, and it was imperative to find it. He accordingly ordered a search to the north, and late in the afternoon of October 24 his flyers came upon Admiral Ozawa's decoy force, far to the north-east of Luzon and steering south. Four carriers, two battleships equipped with flying decks, three cruisers, and ten destroyers! Here, he concluded, was the source of the trouble and the real target. If he could now destroy these carriers, he and his Chief of Staff, Admiral Carney, rightly considered that the power of the Japanese fleet to intervene in future operations would be broken irretrievably. This was a dominating factor in his mind, and would be of particular advantage when MacArthur came later to attack Luzon. Halsey could not know how frail was their power, nor that most of the attacks he had endured came not from carriers at all but from airfields in Luzon itself. Kurita's

Centre Force was in retreat. Kinkaid could cope with the Southern Force and protect the landings at Leyte, the way was clear for a final blow, and Halsey ordered his whole fleet to steam northward and destroy Admiral Ozawa next day. Thus he fell into the trap. That same afternoon, October 24, Kurita again turned east, and sailed once more for the San Bernardino Strait. This time there was nothing to stop him.

*   *   *

Meanwhile the Southern Japanese Force was nearing Surigao Strait, and that night they entered it in two groups. A fierce battle followed, in which all types of vessel, from battleships to light coastal craft, were closely engaged.* The first group was annihilated by Kinkaid's fleet, concentrated at the northern exit under the distinguished command of Admiral Oldendorf; the second tried to break through but was driven back. All seemed to be going well, but the Americans had still to reckon with Admiral Kurita. While Kinkaid was fighting in the Surigao Strait and Halsey was in hard pursuit of the decoy force far to the north Kurita had passed unchallenged in the darkness through the Strait of San Bernardino, and in the early morning of October 25 he fell upon a group of escort carriers who were supporting General MacArthur's landings. Taken by surprise and too slow-moving to escape, the carriers could not at once rearm their planes to repel the onslaught from the sea. For about two and a half hours the small American ships fought a valiant retreat under cover of smoke. Two of their carriers, three destroyers, and over a hundred planes were lost, one of the carriers by suicide bomber attack; but they succeeded in sinking three enemy cruisers and damaging others.† Help was far away. Kinkaid's heavy ships were well south of Leyte, having routed the Southern Force, and were short of ammunition and fuel. Halsey, with ten carriers and all his fast battleships, was yet more distant, and although another of his carrier groups had been detached to refuel and was now recalled it could not arrive for some hours. Victory seemed to be in Kurita's hands. There was nothing to stop him steaming into Leyte Gulf and destroying MacArthur's amphibious fleet.

---

* Among them were two Australian warships, the cruiser *Shropshire* and the destroyer *Arunta*.
† Suicide bombers made their first appearance in the Leyte operations. The Australian cruiser *Australia*, operating with Kinkaid's fleet, had been hit by one a few days before and had suffered casualties but no serious damage.

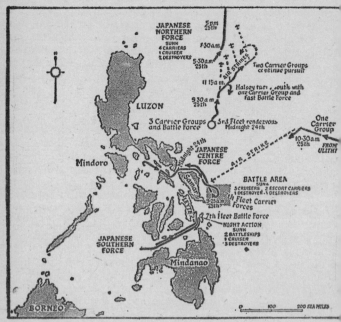

JAPANESE
NORTHERN
FORCE
SUNK
4 CARRIERS
1 CRUISER
2 DESTROYERS

5 a.m.
25th

7.30 a.m.

5.30 a.m.
25th

AIR STRIKES

Two Carrier Groups
continue pursuit

11.15 a.m.

Halsey turns south with
one Carrier Group and
fast Battle Force

9.30 a.m.
25th

LUZON

3 Carrier Groups
and Battle Force

3rd Fleet rendezvous
Midnight 24th

One
Carrier
Group

10.30 a.m.
25th
FROM
ULITHI

Midnight 24th

JAPANESE
CENTRE
FORCE

AIR STRIKE

Mindoro

BATTLE AREA
SUNK
3 CRUISERS   2 ESCORT CARRIERS
1 DESTROYER   3 DESTROYERS

Samar

11.25 a.m.
25th

Fleet Carrier
Forces

LEYTE

7th Fleet Battle Force

NIGHT ACTION
SUNK
2 BATTLESHIPS
1 CRUISER
3 DESTROYERS

JAPANESE
SOUTHERN
FORCE

Mindanao

0   100   200 SEA MILES

BORNEO

Battle of Leyte Gulf: The Decisive Phase, October 25, 1944

But once again Kurita turned back. His reasons are obscure.
Many of his ships had been bombed and scattered by Kinkaid's
light escort carriers, and he now knew that the Southern Force
had met with disaster. He had no information about the fortunes
of the decoys in the north and was uncertain of the whereabouts
of the American fleets. Intercepted signals made him think that
Kinkaid and Halsey were converging on him in overwhelming
strength and that MacArthur's transports had already managed
to escape. Alone and unsupported, he now abandoned the desperate venture for which so much had been sacrificed and which
was about to gain its prize, and, without attempting to enter
Leyte Gulf, he turned about and steered once more for the San
Bernardino Strait. He hoped to fight a last battle on the way
with Halsey's fleet, but even this was denied him. In response to
Kinkaid's repeated calls for support Halsey had indeed at last

turned back with his battleships, leaving two carrier groups to continue the pursuit to the north. During the day these destroyed all four of Ozawa's carriers. But Halsey himself got back to San Bernardino too late. The fleets did not meet. Kurita escaped. Next day Halsey's and MacArthur's planes pursued the Japanese admiral and sank another cruiser and two more destroyers. This was the end of the battle. It may well be that Kurita's mind had become confused by the pressure of events. He had been under constant attack for three days, he had suffered heavy losses, and his flagship had been sunk soon after starting from Borneo. Those who have endured a similar ordeal may judge him.

*   *   *

The Battle of Leyte Gulf was decisive. At a cost to themselves of three carriers, three destroyers, and a submarine the Americans had conquered the Japanese Fleet. The struggle had lasted from October 22 to October 27. Three battleships, four carriers, and twenty other enemy warships had been sunk, and the suicide bomber was henceforward the only effective naval weapon left to the foe. As an instrument of despair it was still deadly, but it carried no hope of victory.

This time there was no doubt about the result, and we hastened to send our congratulations.

Prime Minister to President Roosevelt   27 Oct 44
    Pray accept my most sincere congratulations, which I tender on behalf of His Majesty's Government, on the brilliant and massive victory gained by the sea and air forces of the United States over the Japanese in the recent heavy battles.
    We are very glad to know that one of His Majesty's Australian cruiser squadrons had the honour of sharing in this memorable event.

The scale of the battle may be judged from the following table:

TOTAL LOSSES

Japanese	United States
Three battleships.	One light fleet carrier.
One fleet carrier.	Two escort carriers.
Three light carriers.	Three destroyers.
Six heavy cruisers	One submarine.
Four light cruisers.	
Nine destroyers.	
One submarine.	

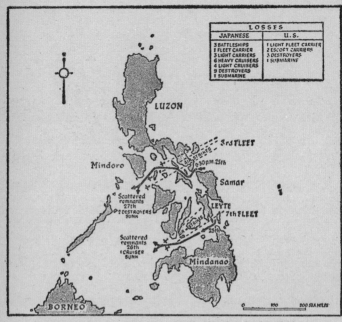

LOSSES	
JAPANESE	U.S.
3 BATTLESHIPS 1 FLEET CARRIER 3 LIGHT CARRIERS 6 HEAVY CRUISERS 4 LIGHT CRUISERS 9 DESTROYERS 1 SUBMARINE	1 LIGHT FLEET CARRIER 2 ESCORT CARRIERS 3 DESTROYERS 1 SUBMARINE

Battle of Leyte Gulf: The Pursuit, October 26–27, 1944

Long should this victory be treasured in American history. Apart from valour, skill, and daring, it shed a light on the future more vivid and far-reaching than any we had seen. It shows a battle fought less with guns than by predominance in the air. I have told the tale fully because at the time it was almost unknown to the harassed European world. Perhaps the most important single conclusion to be derived from study of these events is the vital need for unity of command in conjoint operations of this kind in place of the concept of control by co-operation such as existed between MacArthur and Halsey at this time. The Americans learnt this lesson, and in the final operations planned against the homeland of Japan they intended that supreme command should be exercised by either Admiral Nimitz or General MacArthur, as might be advisable at any given moment.

*　　　*　　　*

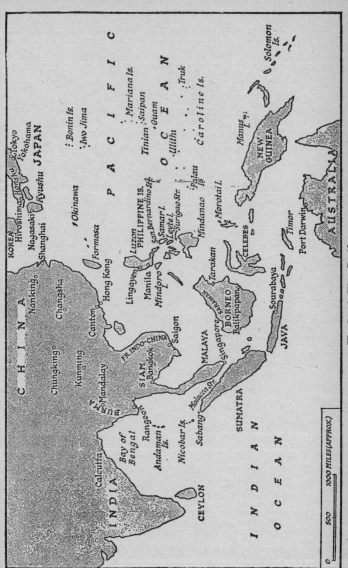

The South-West Pacific

In the following weeks the fight for the Philippines spread and grew. By the end of November nearly a quarter of a million Americans had landed in Leyte, and by mid-December Japanese resistance was broken. MacArthur pressed on with his main advance, and soon landed without opposition on Mindoro Island, little more than a hundred miles from Manila itself. On January 9, 1945, a new phase opened with the landing of four divisions in Lingayen Gulf, north of Manila, which had been the scene of the major Japanese invasion three years before. Elaborate deception measures kept the enemy guessing where the blow would fall. It came as a surprise and was only lightly opposed. As the Americans thrust towards Manila resistance stiffened, but they made two more landings on the west coast and surrounded the city. A desperate defence held out until early March, when the last survivors were killed. Sixteen thousand Japanese dead were counted in the ruins. Attacks by suicide aircraft were now inflicting considerable losses, sixteen ships being hit in a single day. The cruiser *Australia* was again unlucky, being hit five times in four days, but stayed in action. This desperate expedient however caused no check to the fleets. In mid-January Admiral Halsey's carriers broke unmolested into the South China Sea, ranging widely along the coast and attacking airfields and shipping as far west as Saigon. At Hong Kong on January 16 widespread damage was inflicted, and great oil fires were started at Canton.

Although fighting in the islands continued for several months, command of the South China seas had already passed to the victor, and with it control of the oil and other supplies on which Japan depended.

CHAPTER 13

The Liberation of Western Europe

General Eisenhower Takes Command, September 1 – The Plight of the German Army – The Allied Thrusts – Montgomery's Counter-Proposals – The Forward Leap – The Liberation of Brussels, September 3 – Advance of the Canadian Army – Surrender of Havre, September 12 – Capture of Dieppe, Boulogne, and Calais – Bruges and Ghent Taken – The American Pursuit – Fall of Charleroi, Mons, Liége, and Luxembourg – 'Overlord' and 'Dragoon' Join Hands – The Report on 'German Capacity to Resist' – The Race for the Lower Rhine – The Descent on Arnhem, September 17 – The Struggle for the Nijmegen Bridge – Montgomery Orders the 1st Airborne to Retire, September 25 – My Telegram to Smuts, October 9 – Clearing the Scheldt Estuary – The Fall of Breskens 'Island' – The Battle for Walcheren – Commandos Triumphant – the First Convoy Reaches Antwerp, November 28 – The Onslaught of Our Strategic Air Forces – Speer Foresees a Production Catastrophe in Germany.

General Eisenhower, in accordance with previous and agreed arrangements, assumed direct command of the land forces in Northern France on September 1. These comprised the British Twenty-first Army Group, under Field-Marshal Montgomery, and the American Twelfth Army Group, under General Omar Bradley, whose operations Montgomery had hitherto controlled. Eisenhower disposed of five armies in all. In Montgomery's Twenty-first Army Group were the First Canadian Army, under General Crerar, and the Second British Army, under General Dempsey ; a total of fourteen divisions and seven armoured brigades. On their right, under the Twelfth U.S. Army Group, were the First Army, under General Hodges, the Third Army, under General Patton, and the Ninth Army, not yet operational, under General Simpson. Eisenhower thus wielded more than thirty-seven divisions, or over half a million fighting men. Each Army Group had its own tactical air force, the whole being under the control of Air Chief Marshal Leigh-Mallory.

This great array was driving before it the remnants of the

German armies in the West, who were harassed day and night by our dominating air forces. The enemy were still about seventeen divisions strong, but until they could re-form and were reinforced from the homeland there was little fight left in most of them. General Speidel, Rommel's former Chief of Staff, has described their plight:

> An orderly retreat became impossible. The Allied motorised armies surrounded the slow and exhausted German foot divisions in separate groups and smashed them up. . . . There were no German ground forces of any importance that could be thrown in, and next to nothing in the air.*

Eisenhower planned to thrust north-eastwards in the greatest possible strength and to the utmost limit of his supplies. The main effort was to be made by the British Twenty-first Army Group, whose drive along the Channel coast would not only overrun the launching sites of the flying bomb, but also take Antwerp. Without the vast harbour of this city no advance across the lower Rhine and into the plains of Northern Germany was possible. The Twelfth U.S. Army Group was also to pursue the enemy, its First Army keeping abreast of the British, while the remainder, bearing eastwards towards Verdun and the upper Meuse, would prepare to strike towards the Saar.

Montgomery made two counter-proposals, one in late August that his Army Group and the Twelfth U.S. Army Group should strike north together with a solid mass of nearly forty divisions, and the second on September 4, that only one thrust should be made, either towards the Ruhr or the Saar. Whichever was chosen the forces should be given all the resources and maintenance they needed. He urged that the rest of the front should be restrained for the benefit of the major thrust, which should be placed under one commander, himself or Bradley as the case might be. He believed it would probably reach Berlin, and considered that the Ruhr was better than the Saar.

But Eisenhower held to his plan. Germany still had reserves in the homeland, and he believed that if a relatively small force were thrust far ahead across the Rhine it would play into the enemy's hands. He thought it was better for the Twenty-first Army Group to make every effort to get a bridgehead over the Rhine, while the Twelfth advanced as far as they could against the Siegfried Line.

---

* *We Defended Normandy*, Speidel, pp. 152–153.

Strategists may long debate these issues.

Their discussion caused no check in the pursuit. The number of divisions that could be sustained, and the speed and range of their advance, depended however entirely on harbours, transport, and supplies. Relatively little ammunition was being used, but food, and above all petrol, governed every movement. Cherbourg and the 'Mulberry' harbour at Arromanches were the only ports we had, and these were daily being left farther behind. The front line was still sustained from Normandy, and each day about 20,000 tons of supplies had to be carried over ever-increasing distances, together with much material for mending roads and bridges and building airfields. The Brittany ports, when captured, would be even more remote, but the Channel ports from Havre northwards, and especially Antwerp, if we could capture it before it was too seriously damaged, were prizes of vital consequence.

Antwerp was thus the immediate aim of Montgomery's Army Group, which now had its first chance to show its mobility. The Second Army led the advance north of the Seine towards Belgium, grounding one corps and using its transport to sustain the others. The XXXth Corps was in the van. Its 11th Armoured Division captured the commander of the Seventh German Army at his breakfast in Amiens on August 31. The frontier towns so well known to the British Expeditionary Force of 1940, and, at least by name, to their predecessors a quarter of a century before—Arras, Douai, Lille, and many others—were soon reached. Brussels, hastily evacuated by the Germans, was entered by the Guards Armoured Division on September 3, and, as everywhere in Belgium, our troops had a splendid welcome and were much helped by the well-organised Resistance. Thence the Guards turned east for Louvain, and the 11th Armoured entered Antwerp on September 4, where, to our surprise and joy, they found the harbour almost intact. So swift had been the advance—over 200 miles in under four days—that the enemy had been run off their legs and given no time for their usual and thorough demolition. Farther to the west the XIIth Corps met more resistance, but reached their principal objective, Ghent, on September 5.

Of course this pace could not last. The forward leap was over and the check was evident before we sailed to Quebec. The enemy managed to destroy the crossings over the Albert Canal between Antwerp and Hasselt, and XXXth Corps found it defended by about ten battalions, some of them quite fresh. The Guards forced a crossing west of Hasselt on September 6, but they had a hard fight and it was not till four days later that they reached the Meuse–Scheldt canal and took a bridge which was still intact.

*   *   *

Meanwhile the First Canadian Army had the heavy and responsible task of clearing the western flank. Their commander, General Crerar, had under him the Ist British Corps and the IInd Canadian Corps, which included the Polish Armoured Division. Their main task was to clear the Channel ports from Havre to the north, occupy the flying bomb sites, and establish themselves on the south shore of the Scheldt. Although Antwerp was in our hands our ships could only reach it through the winding, difficult estuary of the Scheldt, and the Germans held both banks. These hard and costly operations were to fall principally on this Canadian Army, and much depended on their success.

The Ist British Corps crossed the Seine near Rouen, swung left-handed, and on September 2 the 51st Highland Division occupied St. Valery, the scene of the tragedy to its parent unit in June of 1940. The left of the corps turned and advanced on Havre, where a garrison of over 11,000 resisted fiercely. In spite of bombardment from the sea by 15-inch guns, and more than 10,000 tons of bombs from the air, the Germans did not surrender Havre till September 12. Meanwhile the Canadian Corps, on their right, had moved swiftly. Dieppe, where they repaid their old scores of 1942, fell to them on September 1. Boulogne and Calais were invested by September 6, then Dunkirk. By the 9th the Canadian Army had cleared all the Pas de Calais, with its flying-bomb launching sites, and reached Bruges. Ghent was taken by the Polish Armoured Division. Boulogne, with nearly 10,000 prisoners, fell on September 22, and Calais on the 30th. Dunkirk, with its garrison of 12,000, was only masked, as the advance to the Scheldt was far more urgent. Here for the moment we must leave the Canadians to follow the fortunes of the American Army Group.

Their advance beyond Paris had also been conducted with all the thrustful impulse of Bradley and his ardent officers. After crossing the Seine on the right of the British the First U.S. Army made for Namur and Liége. They reached Charleroi and Mons by September 3, cutting off and capturing a large pocket of

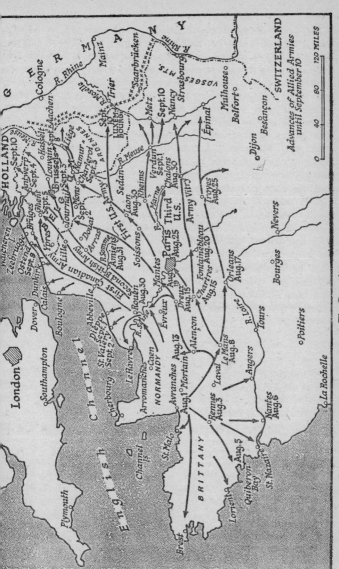

The Pursuit

30,000 Germans south-east of Mons; then, wheeling to the east, they liberated Liége on September 8 and the city of Luxembourg two days later. Resistance was increasing, but on the 12th they closed up to the German frontier on a sixty-mile front and pierced the Siegfried Line south of Aachen. In a fortnight they had freed all Luxembourg and Southern Belgium. The Third Army captured Verdun on August 31 and crossed the Meuse. A week later they had enough petrol to advance to the Moselle. The enemy had scraped up sufficient strength to defend the river, and Metz held a substantial and determined garrison. However, by September 16 bridgeheads were won at Nancy and just south of Metz. As already related, the Seventh U.S. Army and the First French Army, now formed into the Sixth Army Group under General Devers, coming up from their landing in Southern France, had met patrols from Patton's army west of Dijon on September 11. Swinging to the east, they drew level with the general advance on a line from Épinal southwards to the Swiss frontier. This was the end of the great pursuit. For the next few months we could only advance after very hard fighting. Everywhere enemy resistance was stiffening, and our supplies had been stretched to the limit. These had to be restored, and the forward troops reinforced and replenished for the coming autumn battles.

*   *   *

During our voyage to Quebec our Joint Intelligence Committee had furnished a report on 'German Capacity to Resist', which I deemed somewhat optimistic, and I had minuted to the Chiefs of Staff as follows:

Prime Minister to General Ismay,   8 Sept 44
for C.O.S. Committee

I have now read this report, and have not noticed any facts in it of which I was not already aware. Generally speaking, I consider it errs on the side of optimism. At the present time we are at a virtual standstill and progress will be very slow. I trust the assumption of a decisive Russian offensive on the Eastern Front will be realised; but it is at present only an assumption.

2. On the other side there are factors to be noted. Apart from Cherbourg and Arromanches, we have not yet obtained any large harbours. The Germans intend to defend the mouth of the Scheldt, and are still resisting in the northern suburbs

of Antwerp. Brest has not been taken in spite of very heavy fighting, and at least six weeks will be needed after it is taken before it is available. Lorient still holds out. No attempt has been made to take and clear the port of St. Nazaire, which is about twice as good as Brest and twice as easy to take. No attempt has been made to get hold of Bordeaux. Unless the situation changes remarkably the Allies will still be short of port accommodation when the equinoctial gales are due.

3. One can already foresee the probability of a lull in the magnificent advances we have made. General Patton's army is heavily engaged on the line Metz–Nancy. Field-Marshal Montgomery has explained his misgivings as to General Eisenhower's future plan. It is difficult to see how the Twenty-first Army Group can advance in force to the German frontier until it has cleared up the stubborn resistance at the Channel ports and dealt with the Germans at Walcheren and to the north of Antwerp. . . .

6. No one can tell what the future may bring forth. Will the Allies be able to advance in strength through the Siegfried Line into Germany during September, or will their forces be so limited by supply conditions and the lack of ports as to enable the Germans to consolidate on the Siegfried Line? Will the Germans withdraw from Italy?—in which case they will greatly strengthen their internal position. Will they be able to draw on their forces, at one time estimated at between twenty-five and thirty-five divisions, in the Baltic States? The fortifying and consolidating effect of a stand on the frontier of the native soil should not be underrated. *It is at least as likely that Hitler will be fighting on January* 1 *as that he will collapse before then*.* If he does collapse before then, the reason will be political rather than purely military.

My view was unhappily to be justified.

*　　　*　　　*

But there was still the chance of crossing the lower Rhine. Eisenhower thought this prize so valuable that he gave it priority over clearing the shores of the Scheldt estuary and opening the port of Antwerp. To renew Montgomery's effort Eisenhower gave him additional American transport and air supply. The First Airborne Army, under the American General Brereton, composed of the 1st and 6th British Airborne Divisions, three U.S. divisions, and a Polish brigade, with a

---

* Author's subsequent italics.

great complement of British and American aircraft, stood ready to strike from England. Montgomery resolved to seize a bridgehead at Arnhem by the combined action of airborne troops and the XXXth Corps, who were fighting in a bridgehead across the Meuse–Scheldt canal on the Dutch border. He planned to drop the 1st British Airborne Division, supported later by the Polish Brigade, on the north bank of the lower Rhine to seize the Arnhem bridge. The 82nd U.S. Division was to capture the bridges at Nijmegen and Grave, while the 101st U.S. Division secured the road from Grave to Eindhoven. The XXXth Corps, led by the Guards Armoured Division, would force their way up the road to Eindhoven and thence to Arnhem along the 'carpet' of airborne troops, hoping to find the bridges over the three major water obstacles already safely in their hands.

The preparations for this daring stroke, by far the greatest operation of its kind yet attempted, were complicated and urgent, because the enemy were growing stronger every day. It is remarkable that they were completed by the set date, September 17. There were not sufficient aircraft to carry the whole airborne force simultaneously, and the movement had to be spread over three days. However, on the 17th the leading elements of the three divisions were well and truly taken to their destinations by the fine work of the Allied air forces. The 101st U.S. Division accomplished most of their task, but a canal bridge on the road to Eindhoven was blown and they did not capture the town till the 18th. The 82nd U.S. Division also did well, but could not seize the main bridge at Nijmegen.

From Arnhem the news was scarce, but it seemed that some of our Parachute Regiment had established themselves at the north end of the bridge. The Guards Armoured Division of the XXXth Corps began to advance in the afternoon up the Eindhoven road, preceded by an artillery barrage and rocket-firing planes. The VIIIth Corps on the right and the XIIth on the left protected the flanks of the XXXth. The road was obstinately defended, and the Guards did not reach the Americans till the afternoon of the 18th. German attacks against the narrow Eindhoven–Nijmegen salient began next day and grew in strength. The 101st Division had great difficulty in keeping the road open. At times traffic had to be stopped until the enemy were beaten off. By now the news from Arnhem was bad. Our parachutists still held the northern end of the bridge, but the enemy remained in the town, and the rest of the 1st Airborne

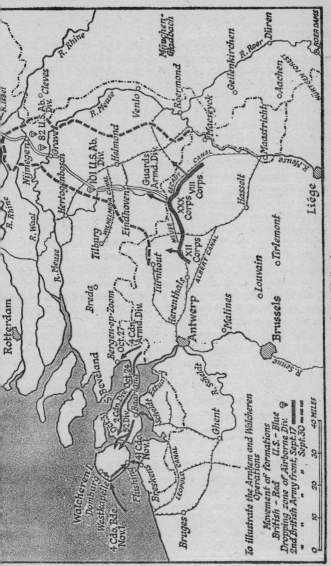

South Holland

To illustrate the Arnhem and Walcheren Operations

Movement of formations
British – Red   U.S. – Blue
Dropping zone of Airborne Div. Sept.17
2nd British Army front. Sept.30

0   10   20   30   40 MILES

Division, which had landed to the west, failed to break in an
reinforce them.

The canal was bridged on the 18th, and early next mornin
the Guards had a clear run to Grave, where they found th
82nd U.S. Division. By nightfall they were close to the strongl
defended Nijmegen bridge, and on the 20th there was a tre
mendous struggle for it. The Americans crossed the river wes
of the town, swung right, and seized the far end of the railwa
bridge. The Guards charged across the road bridge. The de
fenders were overwhelmed and both bridges were taken intac

There remained the last lap to Arnhem, where bad weathe
had hampered the fly-in of reinforcements, food, and ammu
nition, and the 1st Airborne were in desperate straits. Unable t
reach their bridge, the rest of the division was confined to
small perimeter on the northern bank and endured violen
assaults. Every possible effort was made from the southern ban
to rescue them, but the enemy were too strong. The Guards, th
43rd Division, the Polish Parachute Brigade, dropped near th
road, all failed in their gallant attempts at rescue. For four mor
days the struggle went on, in vain. On the 25th Montgomer
ordered the survivors of the gallant 1st Airborne back. They ha
to cross the fast-flowing river at night in small craft and unde
close-range fire. By daybreak about 2,400 men out of the origin
10,000 were safely on our bank.

Even after all was over at Arnhem there was hard fighting fc
a fortnight to hold our gains. The Germans conceived that ou
salient imperilled the whole western bank of the lower Rhin
and later events proved they were right. They made many heav
counter-attacks to regain Nijmegen. The bridge was bombe
from the air, and damaged, though not destroyed, by swim
mers with demolition charges. Gradually the three corps of th
Second Army expanded the fifty-mile salient until it was twent
miles wide. It was still too narrow, but for the moment
sufficed.

Heavy risks were taken in the Battle of Arnhem, but they wer
justified by the great prize so nearly in our grasp. Had we bee
more fortunate in the weather, which turned against us a
critical moments and restricted our mastery in the air, it i
probable that we should have succeeded. No risks daunted th
brave men, including the Dutch Resistance, who fought fo
Arnhem.

*   *   *

It was not till I returned from Canada, where the glorious
eports had flowed in, that I was able to understand all that had
appened. General Smuts was grieved at what seemed to be a
ailure, and I telegraphed:

Prime Minister to Field-Marshal Smuts   9 Oct 44
   I like the situation on the Western Front, especially as
enormous American reinforcements are pouring in and we
hope to take Antwerp before long. As regards Arnhem, I
think you have got the position a little out of focus. The battle
was a decided victory, but the leading division, asking, quite
rightly, for more, was given a chop. I have not been afflicted by
any feeling of disappointment over this and am glad our commanders are capable of running this kind of risk.

*   *   *

Clearing the Scheldt estuary and opening the port of Antwerp
ad been delayed for the sake of the Arnhem thrust. Thereafter
was given first priority. During the last fortnight of September
number of preliminary actions had set the stage. The IInd
'anadian Corps had forced the enemy back from the line
ntwerp–Ghent–Bruges into the restricted Breskens 'island',
ounded on the south by the Leopold Canal. East of Antwerp
ae Ist Corps, also under the Canadian Army command, had
ached and crossed the Antwerp–Turnhout canal.
   The problem was threefold: the capture of the Breskens
sland'; the occupation of the peninsula of South Beveland;
nally, the capture of Walcheren Island by attacks from east,
)uth, and west. The first two proceeded simultaneously. Bres-
ens 'island', defended by an experienced German division,
roved tough, and there was hard fighting to cross the Leopold
'anal. The scales were turned by a Canadian brigade, which
nbarked upstream, landed at the eastern extremity of the
sland', and forced a way along the shore towards Breskens,
hich fell on October 22. Meanwhile the 1st Corps had steadily
dvanced north-west from the Antwerp–Turnhout canal, meet-
ıg increased opposition as they went. The South Beveland
thmus was sealed off, and plans could be made for continuing
ae operations westwards towards Walcheren.
   This hard task was undertaken by the 2nd Canadian Division,
hich forced its way westwards through large areas of flooding,
ıeir men often waist-deep in water. They were helped by the
eater part of the 52nd Division, who were ferried across the

Scheldt and landed on the south shore at Baarland. By the en
of the month, after great exertions, the whole isthmus wa
captured. Meantime the last pockets of enemy on Bresken
'island' were being eliminated and all was set for the Walchere
attack. The Canadian Army's success was an essential prelim
inary to more spectacular operations. In four weeks of har
fighting, during which the 2nd Tactical Air Force, under Ai
Marshal Coningham, gave them conspicuous support, they too
no fewer than 12,500 German prisoners, who were anythin
but ready to surrender.

*   *   *

The island of Walcheren is shaped like a saucer and rimme
by sand-dunes which stop the sea from flooding the centra
plain. At the western edge, near Westkapelle, is a gap in th
dunes where the sea is held by a great dyke, thirty feet hig
and over a hundred yards wide at the base. The garrison o
nearly 10,000 men was installed in strong artificial defences, an
supported by about thirty batteries of artillery, some of larg
calibre in concrete emplacements. Anti-tank obstacles, mine
and wire abounded, for the enemy had had four years in whic
to fortify the gateway to Antwerp.

Early in October the Royal Air Force struck the first blow. I
a series of brilliant attacks they blew a great gap, nearly fou
hundred yards across, in the Westkapelle dyke. Through i
poured the sea, flooding all the centre of the saucer and drown
ing such defences and batteries as lay within. But the mos
formidable emplacements and obstacles were on the saucer'
rim, and their capture, already admirably described,* can b
told here only in outline. The attack was concentric. In the eas
the 2nd Canadian Division tried to advance from South Beve
land over the connecting causeway, and finally seized a bridge
head with the help of a brigade of the 52nd Division. In th
centre, on November 1, No. 4 Commando was ferried acros
from Breskens, and boldly landed on the sea-front of Flushin
This first move was followed rapidly by troops of the 52n
Division, who battled their way into the town. The main attac
was from the west, launched by three Marine Commando
under Brigadier Leicester. Embarking at Ostend, they sailed fo
Westkapelle, and at 7 a.m. on November 1 they sighted th
lighthouse tower. As they approached the naval bombardin

* *The Green Beret*, by H. St. G. Saunders.

squadron opened fire. Here were H.M.S. *Warspite* and the two 15-inch-gun monitors *Erebus* and *Roberts*, with a squadron of armed landing-craft. These latter came close inshore, and, despite harsh casualties, kept up their fire until the two leading Commandos were safely ashore. No. 41, landing at the northern end of the gap in the sea-wall, captured the village of Westkapelle and drove on towards Domburg. No. 48, landing south of the gap, soon met fierce resistance. Invaluable though the naval covering fire had been, a principal adjunct was lacking. A heavy bombardment had been planned for the previous day, but mist prevented our aircraft from taking off. Very effective fighter bomber attacks helped the landing at a critical moment, but the Marines met much stronger opposition, from much less damaged defences, than we had hoped.

That evening No. 48 Commando had advanced two miles along the fringe towards Flushing, but was held up by a powerful battery embedded in concrete. The whole of the artillery of the IInd Canadian Corps, firing across the water from the Breskens shore, was brought to bear, and rocket-firing aircraft attacked the embrasures. In the gathering darkness the Commando killed or captured the defenders. Next morning it pressed on and took Zouteland by midday. There No. 47 took up the attack, and, with a weakening defence, reached the outskirts of Flushing. On November 3 they joined hands with No. 4 Commando after its stiff house-to-house fighting in the town. In a few days the whole island was in our hands, with 8,000 prisoners.

Many other notable feats were performed by Commandos during the war, and though other troops and other Services played their full part in this remarkable operation the extreme gallantry of the Royal Marines stands forth. The Commando idea was once again triumphant.

*   *   *

Minesweeping began as soon as Flushing was secure, and in the next three weeks a hundred craft were used to clear the seventy-mile channel. On November 28 the first convoy arrived, and Antwerp was opened for the British and American Armies. Flying bombs and rockets plagued the city for some time, and caused many casualties, but interfered with the furtherance of the war no more than in London.

Antwerp's ordeal was not the only reason for trying to thrust the Germans farther away. When the 2nd Canadian Division swung west into South Beveland there were still four German divisions in a pocket south of the river Meuse and west of the Nijmegen corridor. It was an awkward salient, which by November 8 was eliminated by the Ist and the XIIth Corps.* On the other flank of the Nijmegen corridor there was still an obstinate enemy, west of the Meuse, in a pocket centred on Venlo. Farther south the First U.S. Army breached the Siegfried Line north of Aachen in the first week of October. The town was attacked from three sides and surrendered on October 21. On their flank the Third Army were twenty miles east of the Moselle. The Seventh Army and the First French Army had drawn level and were probing towards the High Vosges and the Belfort Gap. The Americans had all but outrun their supplies in their lightning advances of September, and a pause was essential to build up stocks and prepare for large-scale operations in November.

*　　*　　*

The Strategic Air Forces played a big part in the Allied advance to the frontiers of France and Belgium. In the autumn they reverted to their primary *rôle* of bombing Germany, with oil installations and the transportation systems as specific targets. The enemy's Radar screen and early warning system had been thrust back behind his frontier, and our own navigation and bombing aids were correspondingly advanced. Our casualty rate decreased ; the weight and accuracy of our attacks grew. The long-continued onslaught had forced the Germans to disperse their factories very widely. For this they now paid a heavy penalty, since they depended all the more on good communications. Urgently needed coal piled up at pitheads for lack of wagons to move it. Every day a thousand or more freight trains were halted for lack of fuel. Industry, electricity, and gas plant were beginning to close down. Oil production and reserves dropped drastically, affecting not only the mobility of the troops, but also the activities and even the training of their air forces.

In August Speer had warned Hitler that the entire chemical industry was being crippled through lack of by-products from the synthetic oil plants, and the position grew worse as time went on. In November he reported that if the decline in railway

* The 1st Corps at this time was a remarkable example of Allied integration. It consisted of four divisions, English, Canadian, American, and Polish.

traffic continued it would result in 'a production catastrophe of decisive significance', and in December he paid a tribute to our 'far-reaching and clever planning'.* At long last our great bombing offensive was reaping its reward.

* Tedder, *Air-Power in War*, pp. 118, 119.

CHAPTER 14

Prelude to a Moscow Visit

Progress of the Russian Offensive – The Red Army Reaches the Baltic – The Liberation of Belgrade, October 20 – My Desire for Another Meeting with Stalin – Our Concern with the Future of Poland and Greece – The World Organisation and the Deadlock at Dumbarton Oaks – Telegrams from General Smuts – I Plan a Visit to Moscow – The President Approves – Stalin Sends a Cordial Invitation – Russia and the Far East – I Start for Moscow, October 5 – The Campaign in Italy.

The story of the immense Russian offensive of the summer of 1944 has been told in these pages only to the end of September, when, aided by the Roumanian revolution, the Soviet armies drove up the valley of the Danube to the frontier of Hungary and paused to consolidate their supply. We must now carry it forward to the end of the autumn.

We followed with deep interest and growing hopes the fortunes of this tremendous campaign. The German garrisons in the northern Baltic States had been practically cut off by the Russian advances far to the south, and were extracted with difficulty. The first attacks fell upon them in mid-September from either end of Lake Peipus. These spread swiftly outwards, and in three weeks reached all the Baltic shore from Riga to the north.

On September 24 the southern front again flared into activity. The offensive began with an advance south of the Danube into Yugoslav territory. The Russians were supported on their left flank by the Bulgarian Army, which had readily changed sides. Jointly they made contact with Tito's irregular forces and helped to harry the Germans in their hard but skilful withdrawal from Greece. Hitler, despite the obvious dangers impending in Poland, set great store on the campaign in Hungary, and reinforced it obstinately. The main Russian attack, supported by the Roumanian Army, began on October 6, and was directed on Budapest from the south-east, with a subsidiary thrust from the Carpathians in the north. Belgrade, by-passed on both banks of

e Danube, was liberated on October 20 and its German gar-
on annihilated.

* * *

The arrangements which I had made with the President in
e summer to divide our responsibilities for looking after
rticular countries affected by the movements of the armies
d tided us over the three months for which our agreement ran.
t as the autumn drew on everything in Eastern Europe be-
me more intense. I felt the need of another personal meeting
ith Stalin, whom I had not seen since Teheran, and with whom,
spite of the Warsaw tragedy, I felt new links since the success-
l opening of 'Overlord'. The Russian armies were now press-
g heavily upon the Balkan scene, and Roumania and Bulgaria
ere in their power. As the victory of the Grand Alliance
ecame only a matter of time it was natural that Russian am-
itions should grow. Communism raised its head behind the
undering Russian battle-front. Russia was the Deliverer, and
ommunism the gospel she brought.

I had never felt that our relations with Roumania and Bul-
aria in the past called for any special sacrifices from us. But
e fate of Poland and Greece struck us keenly. For Poland we
ad entered the war; for Greece we had made painful efforts.
oth their Governments had taken refuge in London, and we
nsidered ourselves responsible for their restoration to their
wn country, if that was what their peoples really wished. In the
ain these feelings were shared by the United States, but they
ere very slow in realising the upsurge of Communist influence,
hich slid on before, as well as followed, the onward march of
e mighty armies directed from the Kremlin. I hoped to take
dvantage of the better relations with the Soviets to reach satis-
actory solutions of these new problems opening between East
nd West.

Besides these grave issues which affected the whole of Central
urope, the questions of World Organisation were now thrust-
ng themselves upon all our minds. A lengthy conference had
een held at Dumbarton Oaks, near Washington, between
ugust and October, at which the United States, Great Britain,
he U.S.S.R., and China had produced the now familiar scheme
or keeping the peace of the world. They proposed that all
eace-loving States should join a new organisation called the
Jnited Nations. This would consist of a General Assembly

and a Security Council. The Assembly would discuss and consider how to promote and preserve world peace and advise the Security Council what to do about it. Each State would belong to the Assembly and have a vote, but the Assembly could only recommend and pass declarations; it could take no executive action. The Security Council would investigate any disputes between the United Nations, and in effect settle them by force if they could not be settled in peace. This was very different from the League of Nations. Under the new scheme the Assembly could discuss and recommend; the Council alone could act. The discretion of the Council was unfettered by definitions of 'aggression' and rules about when force could be used and when sanctions could be applied.

There had been much discussion about who should belong to the Council and how they should use its great authority. Eventually it had been settled that the 'Big Three' and China should be permanent members, joined by France in due course, and that the Assembly should elect six more States to sit on it for two years at a time. There remained the question of votes. Every member of the Assembly should have a vote, but they could only deliberate and make recommendations, and in this there was little substance. It had been much more difficult to settle the method of voting in the Security Council. The discussions had revealed many differences between the three great Allies, which will appear as this account proceeds. The Kremlin had no intention of joining an international body on which they would be out-voted by a host of small Powers, who, though they could not influence the course of the war, would certainly claim equal status in the victory. I felt sure we could only reach good decisions with Russia while we had the comradeship of a common foe as a bond. Hitler and Hitlerism were doomed; but after Hitler what?

*　　　*　　　*

General Smuts' meditations at his farm in the veldt led him along the same paths of thought, and during the conference he had telegraphed to me:

Field-Marshal Smuts to Prime Minister   20 Sept 44
    The crisis arising from the deadlock with Russia in World Organisation talks fills me with deep concern, and in any case comes at a most unfortunate moment before the final end of

the war. In this, as in other cases, we are, I fear, being hurried at breakneck pace into momentous decisions. Telecommunications, international aviation, etc., all tell the same tale. As the consequences of this *impasse* may however be particularly calamitous here, I may be excused for sending a warning note.

The Soviet attitude struck me at first as absurd and their contention as one not to be conceded by other Great Powers, and likely to be turned down by smaller Powers also. But second thoughts have inclined the other way. I assume that Molotov sincerely states the Soviet attitude, and that it is correctly interpreted by Cadogan and Clark Kerr as one which involves the honour and standing of Russia among her Allies. She questions whether she is trusted and treated as an equal or whether she is still the pariah and outcast. A misunderstanding here amounts to more than a mere difference. It may, by touching Russian *amour propre* and inducing an inferiority complex, poison European relations, with far-reaching results. Knowing her power, Russia may become more grasping than ever. Her reaction and sense of power are shown by the lack of any attempt on her part to discover a solution. What will be her future relations with countries such as Germany and Japan, even France, not to mention lesser countries? Should a World Organisation be formed which does not include Russia she will become the power centre of another group. We shall then be heading towards a third World War. If the United Nations do not set up such an organisation they will stand stultified before history. This creates a very grave dilemma, and we must at all costs avoid the position into which we may be drifting.

Mindful of these dangers, the small Powers should be prepared to make a concession to Russia's *amour propre*, and on this issue should not demand theoretical equality of status. Such a demand, if pressed, may carry with it for smaller Powers the most devastating results. It would be most unwise in dealing with questions which involve power and security to raise theoretical issues of sovereign equality, and it is for the United States of America and the United Kingdom to use their influence in favour of common sense and safety first rather than the small countries' status.

On the merits the principle of unanimity among the Great Powers has much to recommend it, at least for the years immediately following on this war. If this principle proves unworkable in practice the situation could subsequently be reviewed when mutual confidence has been established and a more workable basis laid down. A clash at the present juncture should be avoided at all costs. In the event of unanimity for

the Powers being adopted, even including their voting
questions directly concerning their interests, the result w
require that the U.S.A. and the United Kingdom should exe
all their influence to get Russia to act moderately and sensib
and not to flout world opinion. And in this it is likely that the
will be largely successful. Should Russia prove intransigent
may be necessary for the Organisation to act, but the blan
will attach to her. The principle of unanimity will at the wor
only have the effect of a veto, of stopping action where it ma
be wise, or even necessary. Its effect will be negative; it w
retard action. But it will also render it impossible for Russ
to embark on courses not approved of by the U.S.A. and th
United Kingdom.

A brake like unanimity may not be so bad a thing to hav
where people are drunk with new-won power. I do not defen
it; I dislike it; but I do not consider it at present so bad a
instrument that on this issue the future of world peace an
security should be sacrificed.

The talks have so far been conducted on an official advisor
level, although there may no doubt have been interventio
on a higher level. Before definite decisions are reached on th
highest level the whole situation should, I think, be most care
fully reviewed in all its far-reaching implications, and th
Great Powers should endeavour to find some *modus vivend*
even if only of a temporary character, which would preven
a catastrophe of the first magnitude. Where so much is a
stake for the future we simply must agree, and cannot affor
to differ.

And further:

Field-Marshal Smuts to Prime Minister   26 Sept 4
May the results of your arduous labours in Canada justif
your efforts. ... My warm congratulations on your and Mr
Churchill's safe return.

While the campaign in Italy again has gone much slowe
than was anticipated, and the approaching rainy season ma
even further upset your hopes in that area, Alexander coul
still press on and maintain our prestige in the Balkan area. I
spite of all the help Tito has obtained only from us, he has no
behaved loyally to us. I fear that our interests will suffer by
his supremacy in Yugoslavia.

What is happening in Greece seems still worse. There th
E.A.M. is obtaining control, unfortunately largely with ou
help. I hope this may still be prevented from the point of view
of our great Mediterranean interests, as well as those of the
suffering people of Greece, and that our loyal Greek friend

may be heartened by positive action on our part. Papandreou is rapidly coming under the power of the E.A.M. elements, who no doubt rely on Soviet backing. You will, I hope, find time to discuss with the King of Greece the best means of safeguarding our and Greek vital interests. The shape of the future Mediterranean set-up is rapidly developing, and in a way not favourable to us.

I do not say this in any spirit of hostility to Russia. It is upon close co-operation between the Big Three that our best hope rests for the near future, and my advice given in the *impasse* at Dumbarton Oaks is a proof of that. But the more firmly Russia can establish herself in the saddle now the farther she will ride in the future and the more precarious our holdfast will become. Our position in the Mediterranean and in Western Europe must be strengthened rather than weakened. In neither of these areas we may have the support of Russia, or even of de Gaullist France. From this standpoint the future dispositions as regards Germany assume an importance for us which may be far greater than and very different from that which they appear to have at present. A new situation will be created for us in Europe and the world by the elimination of Germany through this war. This calls for a searching reconsideration of our entire foreign policy for the future. While a World Organisation is necessary, it is equally essential that our Commonwealth and Empire should emerge from this ordeal as strong and influential as possible, making us an equal partner in every sense for the other Big Two.

From this viewpoint also I much regret the increasing tendency towards the breaking up of your Inter-Party Pact, which has had such magnificent war-time success. Your great influence will, I hope, prevent a break-up prematurely and before the new settlement of Europe and the world has been achieved. The end is not yet. So please take care of your health.

Field-Marshal Smuts to Prime Minister   27 Sept 44
Thank you very much for all your four messages, which I received after sending you my message on your return. The *impasse* at Dumbarton Oaks is dealt with in the first two, and I note your view and the course proposed for later meeting, which from many points of view appears admirable. As regards war plans in Europe and Asia, dealt with in the third message, I am pleased with your arrangements for the campaigns in Italy and the Balkans. Since the enemy appears to be retiring from Greece, it would seem advisable for us to appear there soon and prevent Greece coming under the heel of E.A.M.

and charging us with having deserted them. This matter ᵥ
mentioned in my previous message as one of particular c
cern for the British Empire.

As regards the Pacific war, it has to be feared that after
war against Germany is won war fever in the United Sta
will cool off and American ardour be transferred to trade ₐ
industry. So they should be grateful for your full participati
I am also glad to know that Mountbatten, who has had a ₘ
deal, will get his chance in Burma and Malaya. As events
now developing in China, it is possible that Japan, while be
driven from the occupied islands, will become entrenched
the Chinese mainland, from which it will be no easy task
eject her. Stalin will come in very useful there. Unless he d
so the Japanese war may last longer than is at present expect

Division of zones in Germany between United Kingd
and United States appears fair. The destiny of Prussia un
occupation by the Russians seems likely to be a Bolshevi
Soviet province or protectorate. So much for Hitler's drea
But it shows that Europe's two-thousand-year-old problem
Germany will remain as great as ever.

*   *   *

The Dumbarton Oaks conference ended without agreeme
but I felt acutely the need to see Stalin, with whom I alw
considered one could talk as one human being to another.

Prime Minister to Chief of the Air Staff   27 Sept
(*For your eyes alone*)

It may be necessary for me to go to Moscow with ₘ
Eden. It would be a comfort to have the new machine, wh
was promised by October 15, but we might want to go ev
earlier than that. I imagine we could fly from here to Cairo
one bound in the new machine, and in two in the York, fu
ling, I suppose, at Naples or Malta. From Cairo one wou
have to watch the weather most carefully. In clear weath
the President was able to go over the mountains at five or ₐ
thousand feet. I can certainly do eight or ten thousand for
short time. When we went in August 1942 at what height ᵤ
'Commando' cross the Caucasus Mountains? My idea is
flew at 11,000 feet, and then only for a short time. The wh
passage of the mountains took, I think, under three hou
After that it is good low-flying over the Caspian and the pla
of Russia. There would be no need to make the *détour* th
we did on the last occasion. What is essential is to wait
Cairo or Teheran till there is absolutely clear weather.

Please let me have a report and clear plan.

I telegraphed to Stalin on the same day:

Prime Minister to Marshal Stalin   27 Sept 44

I was gratified to hear from Ambassador Clark Kerr the praise which you gave to British and American operations in France. We value very much such expressions from the leader of the heroic Russian armies. I shall take occasion to repeat to-morrow in the House of Commons what I have said before, that it is the Russian Army that tore the guts out of the German military machine, and is at the present moment holding by far the larger portion of the enemy on its front.

2. I have just returned from long talks with the President, and I can assure you of our intense conviction that on the agreement of our three nations, Britain, United States of America, and U.S.S.R., stand the hopes of the world. I was very sorry to learn that you had not been feeling well lately, and that your doctors did not like your taking long journeys by air. The President had the idea that The Hague would be a good place for us to meet. We have not got it yet, but it may be the course of the war, even before Christmas, may alter the picture along the Baltic shore to such an extent that your journey would not be tiring or difficult. However, we shall have much hard fighting to do before any such plan can be made.

3. *Most Private*. The President intends to visit England, and thereafter France and the Low Countries, immediately after the election, win or lose. My information leads me to believe that he will win.

4. I most earnestly desire, and so, I know, does the President, the intervention of Soviet Russia in the Japanese war, as promised by you at Teheran as soon as the German Army was beaten and destroyed. The opening of a Russian military front against Japan would force them to burn and bleed, especially in the air, in a manner which would vastly accelerate their defeat. From all I have learnt about the internal state of Japan and the sense of hopelessness weighing on their people, I believe it might well be that once the Nazis are shattered a triple summons to Japan to surrender, coming from our three Great Powers, might be decisive. Of course, we must go into all these plans together. I will gladly come to Moscow in October if I can get away from here. If I cannot, Eden will be very ready to take my place. Meanwhile I send you and Molotov my most sincere good wishes.

*   *   *

Roosevelt was impressed with Smuts' views.

President Roosevelt to Prime Minister   28 Sept
I have read with great interest your telegram [of Septemb
20] from Field-Marshal Smuts, and I think we are all in agre
ment with him as to the necessity of having the U.S.S.R. as
fully accepted and equal member of any association of th
Great Powers formed for the purpose of preventing inte
national war.

It should be possible to accomplish this by adjusting o
differences through compromise by all the parties concerne
and this ought to tide things over for a few years until th
child learns how to toddle.

The 'child' in this case was the World Instrument.

I replied:

Prime Minister to President Roosevelt   29 Sept
... In a conversation with Clark Kerr and Harriman th
other night U.J. [Stalin] was most expansive and friendly. H
however 'grumbled about his own health'. He said he nev
kept well except in Moscow, and even his visits to the front d
him harm. His doctors were averse to his flying, and it too
him a fortnight to recover from Teheran, etc.

In these circumstances Anthony and I are seriously thinkin
of flying there very soon. The route is shorter now. Stalin h
not yet replied to our suggestion. The two great objects v
have in mind would be, firstly, to clinch his coming in again
Japan, and, secondly, to try to effect an amicable settleme
with Poland. There are other points too concerning Yug
slavia and Greece which we would also discuss. We shou
keep you informed of every point. Averell's assistance wou
of course be welcomed by us, or perhaps you could se
Stettinius or Marshall. I feel certain that personal contact
essential.

That Germany is not going to be conquered this year seen
to me pretty clear. In a telegram I have seen Omar Bradley
already thinking in terms of an operation across the Rhine
the middle of November, and I have noted other signs
stiffening German resistance.

Off the record: It was with much gusto that I read you
speech, and I was delighted to see you in such vigorous form
Every good wish.

On the same day came the following:

Marshal Stalin to Prime Minister   29 Sept
I have received the message from you and Mr. Roosev
about the Conference at Quebec, with information about yo

further military plans. It is clear from your communication what important tasks have to be settled by American and British armed strength. Permit me to wish you and your armies every kind of success.

At the present time the Soviet armies are busy with the liquidation of the group of German armies along the Baltic which threaten our right flank. Without the liquidation of this group it is not possible for us to penetrate deeply into Eastern Germany. Besides that, our armies have two nearer tasks: to remove Hungary from the war, and to probe the defence of the Germans on the Eastern Front by means of an attack by our troops, and, given favourable conditions, to overcome it.

The President liked our plan of going to Moscow. On September 30 he cabled:

Please let me know after you hear from Uncle J. the date when you and Anthony will arrive in Moscow. It is my opinion that Stalin is at the present time sensitive about any doubt as to his intention to help us in the Orient.

At your request I will direct Harriman to give you any assistance that you may desire. It does not appear practicable or advantageous for me to be represented by Stettinius or Marshall.

Stalin now sent me a cordial invitation.

Marshal Stalin to Prime Minister   30 Sept 44

I have received your message of September 27.

I share your conviction that firm agreement between the three leading Powers constitutes a true guarantee of future peace and answers to the best hopes of all peace-loving peoples. The continuation of our Government in such a policy in the post-war period as we have achieved it during this great war will, it seems to me, have a decisive influence. Of course I have a great desire to meet with you and the President. I attach great importance to it from the point of view of the interests in our common business. But, as far as I am concerned, I must make one reservation. The doctors advise me not to undertake long journeys. For a certain period I must take account of this.

I warmly welcome your wish to come to Moscow in October. We shall have to consider military and other questions, which are of great importance. If anything prevents you from coming to Moscow we should of course be very ready to meet Mr. Eden. Your information about the President's plans for a journey to Europe is of great interest to me. I also am sure of his success in the election. As regards Japan, our position the same as it was at Teheran.

I and Molotov send you our best wishes.

On this I put matters in train.

Prime Minister to Sir A. Clark Kerr (Moscow)   1 Oct ·
    You will have seen Marshal Stalin's telegram of Septemb 30, which is most friendly. Anthony and I propose to sta weather permitting, on Saturday night. The journey is mu shorter now, as we can avoid the *détour* by the Atlantic ar Spain, and also that by the mountains and Teheran. It shou not take more than three days, or perhaps two. The A Ministry will make the arrangements with Moscow.

    2. I think it would be better to go as the guests of t Russian Government, because their high sense of hospitali helps business. But of course we must have festivities at t Embassy. Will you sound them on this?

    3. I am thinking that Mrs. Churchill might come with n She has her Red Cross there now, and people in Engla would be glad to know she was on the spot to look after m I wonder how this would fit in. Of course she would not expe to go to the Kremlin banquet, which would be men only. B I presume there are things she could see apart from her ov Red Cross. Would it be an embarrassment to the Russiar as there is no Mrs. Stalin? Pray advise me quite freely on th
    Reply most urgent.

The Ambassador replied next day that he and the Russia were delighted that I had decided to come, and that Antho would be with me. 'The iron stands hot for the striking. T Russians expect you to be their guest. The idea that Mrs. Chu chill should come with you has been warmly welcomed.'

My wife however decided not to go at this moment. I ask Roosevelt to tell Stalin that he approved of our mission, ar that Mr. Harriman would take part in the discussions. I i quired what I could say about the United States' Far Easte war plans.

Prime Minister to President Roosevelt   4 Oct ·
    ... We want to elicit the time it will take after the Germa downfall for a superior Russian Army to be gathered opposi the Japanese on the frontiers of Manchukuo, and to hear fro them the problems of this campaign, which are peculiar owir to the lines of communication being vulnerable in the lat stages.
    Of course the bulk of our business will be about the Pole

ut you and I think so much alike about this that I do not need
ny special guidance as to your views.

The point of Dumbarton Oaks will certainly come up, and
must tell you that we are pretty clear that the only hope is
hat the Great Powers are agreed [*i.e.,* unanimous]. It is with
egret that I have come to this conclusion, contrary to my first
hought. Please let me know if you have any wishes about this
natter, and also instruct Averell accordingly.

The President then sent his fullest assurances of approval and
odwill.

President Roosevelt to Prime Minister   4 Oct 44

I can well understand the reasons why you feel that an
mmediate meeting between yourself and Uncle Joe is neces-
ary before the three of us can get together. The questions
which you will discuss there are ones which are of course of
eal interest to the United States, as I know you will agree. I
ave therefore instructed Harriman to stand by and to partici-
ate as my observer, if agreeable to you and Uncle Joe, and I
ave so informed Stalin. While naturally Averell will not be in
a position to commit the United States—I could not permit
anyone to commit me in advance—he will be able to keep me
fully informed, and I have told him to return and report to
ne as soon as the conference is over.

I am only sorry that I cannot be with you myself, but I am
prepared for a meeting of the three of us any time after the
lections here, for which your meeting with Uncle Joe should
be a useful prelude, and I have so informed Uncle Joe.

Like you, I attach the greatest importance to the continued
unity of our three countries. I am sorry that I cannot agree
with you however that the voting question should be raised at
this time. That is a matter which the three of us can, I am sure,
work out together, and I hope you will postpone discussion of
it until our meeting. There is, after all, no immediate urgency
about this question, which is so directly related to public
opinion in the United States and Great Britain and in all the
United Nations.

I am asking our military people in Moscow to make available to you our Chiefs' statement to Stalin.

You carry my best wishes with you, and I will eagerly await
word of how it goes.

Prime Minister to President Roosevelt   5 Oct 44

Thank you very much for what you say, and for your good
wishes. I am very glad that Averell should sit in at all principal
conferences, but you would not, I am sure, wish this to preclude private *tête-à-tête* between me and U.J. or Anthony and

Molotov, as it is often under such conditions that the l
progress is made. You can rely on me to keep you constar
informed of everything that affects our joint interests, a
from the reports which Averell will send.

2. I gather from your last sentence but one that you h
sent some general account of your Pacific plans to your pe
in Moscow, which will be imparted to U.J., and which I si
see on arrival. This will be most convenient.

3. Should U.J. raise the question of voting, as he v
likely will do, I will tell him that there is no hurry about
and that I am sure we can get it settled when we are all th
together.

*　　　*　　　*

All the major issues had thus been settled. It only remai
to plan the journey.

Prime Minister to Marshal Stalin　　　　　　　　　　4 Oct

Your people are anxious about the route I have b
advised to take. It is not good for me to go much above 8,
feet, though I can, if necessary, do so for an hour or so.
think it less of a risk to fly across the Ægean and Black Se
have satisfied myself that on the whole this is the best
involves no inappropriate risk.

2. So long as we can get down safely to refuel if necess
at Simferopol or at any other operational landing-ground
the coast which you may prefer, I shall be quite content w
the facilities available. I have everything I want in my pla
The only vital thing is that we may send an aeroplane on ah
to establish with you a joint signal station regulating
homing and landing. Please have the necessary orders given

3. I am looking forward to returning to Moscow under
much happier conditions created since August 1942.

Marshal Stalin to Prime Minister　　　　　　　　　　5 Oct

The landing on the aerodrome Sarabuz, near Simfero;
has been arranged. Send your signal aircraft to that ae
drome.

*　　　*　　　*

Eden and I with Brooke and Ismay started in two planes
the night of the 5th. At Naples we had four hours' discuss
with Generals Wilson and Alexander. I was much distressed
their tale. Five weeks had passed since I left Italy at the outset
Alexander's offensive in the last days of August. It will be c
venient to carry the story forward to its end in the autumn.

The Eighth Army attack had prospered and augured well. It surprised the Germans, and by September 1 had penetrated the Gothic Line on a twenty-mile front. Kesselring, as ever, was quick to recover, and began to send reinforcements from the central sector. Just in time they manned the Coriano Ridge, barring the way to Rimini, and for a week they resisted all attacks. Then we took it.

Prime Minister to General Alexander   15 Sept 44
Many congratulations upon the storming of the Coriano Ridge and the passage of the Marano. I can see that this has been a grand feat of arms upon the part of the troops involved. Pray give them my compliments. I hope this success may cast a brighter light on your immediate prospects.

From his centre and right Kesselring sent across seven divisions, and there were three days of heavy fighting at San Fortunato. When it was taken, by skilful combination of ground and air attack, the enemy withdrew, and Rimini fell on September 20.

By weakening his centre Kesselring gave Alexander the occasion he had awaited for the Fifth Army. The enemy had withdrawn from their forward positions to economise troops, and we were able to close up to the main position without having to make preliminary attacks. On September 13 the Fifth Army struck, and two days later the 8th Indian Division, leading our XIIIth Corps, advanced across trackless mountains and broke into the Gothic Line on the road to Faenza. By the 18th both the British and the IInd U.S. Corps on their left were on top of the watershed. The Gothic Line, turned at its eastern end by the Eighth Army, had now been pierced in the centre.

Though at the cost of grievous casualties, great success had been achieved and the future looked hopeful. But Kesselring received further reinforcements, until his German divisions amounted to twenty-eight in all. Scraping up two divisions from quiet sectors, he started fierce counter-attacks, which, added to our supply difficulties over the mountain passes, checked the XIIIth Corps' advance on Imola. General Clark thereupon shifted the weight of his onslaught to the Bologna road, and the IInd U.S. Corps advanced on October 1 with four divisions. In a few days they reached Loiano. The defence was stubborn, the ground very difficult, and it was raining hard. The climax came between October 20 and 24, when they reached a point south-east of Bologna only four miles from the Imola road. We

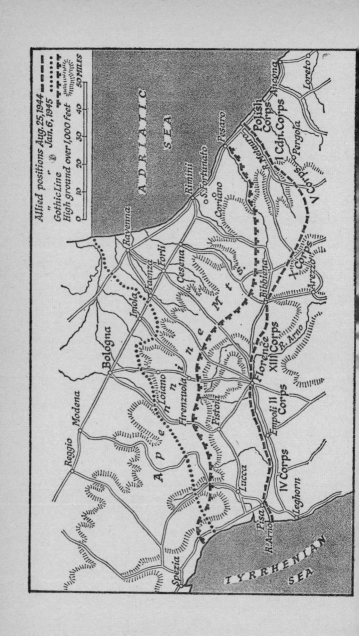

Allied positions Aug. 25, 1944 ━━━
"   "   " Jan. 6, 1945 ●●●●●●●
Gothic Line ┬┬┬┬┬┬┬
High ground over 1,000 feet

0   10   20   30   40   50 MILES

ADRIATIC
SEA

Loreto
Ancona
Pergola
Pesaro
1 Cdn. Corps
Polish Corps
2 Corps
S. Fortunato
Rimini
Corriano
Arezzo
V Corps
Ravenna
Bibbiena
Forlì
Faenza
Cesena
M t s.
Imola
X Corps
Bologna
Loiano
Florence
XIII Corps
R. Arno
Reggio
Modena
Frenzuola
Pistoja
Empoli II Corps
A p e n n i n e s
Lucca
IV Corps
Leghorn
Spezia
Pisa
R. Arno
TYRRHENIAN
SEA

ery nearly succeeded in cutting in behind the enemy facing he Eighth Army. Then, in Alexander's words, 'assisted by orrential rains and winds of gale force, and the Fifth Army's exhaustion, the German line held firm'.

For the Eighth Army too October was a month of frustration. General McCreery had taken over the command from General Leese, who had been transferred to a higher appointment in South-East Asia. On October 7 his advance began along the axis of the Rimini–Bologna road, with the British Vth Corps, joined later by the Canadians, while the Xth Corps operated in he mountains to the south. The weather was appalling. Heavy rains had swollen the numberless rivers and irrigation channels and turned the reclaimed agricultural land into the swamp it had originally been. Off the roads movement was often impossible. It was with the greatest difficulty that the troops toiled forward towards Bologna.

Despite all, Cesena was reached on October 19, and the Polish Corps, who had replaced the Xth Corps on the southern flank, struggled forward towards the Forli–Florence road, important because it would give a shorter lateral communication with Mark Clark's army. That army, as we have seen, was drawing very close to Bologna, and in the critical situation the German commander took the courageous decision to transfer three good divisions from the eastern to his central front. These doubtless just saved the day in the centre of his line. The Eighth Army also had its subtractions. The 4th Indian Division and the Greek Brigade had to be detached to deal with the crisis in Greece, the story of which falls to a later chapter.

*   *   *

I reported to the President about all this from Moscow, so far as it had developed, on October 10, adding:

> The pressure in Dutch salient seems to me to be growing very severe, and our advances are slow and costly. In these circumstances we have with much sorrow had to recommend that we should put off 'Dracula' [the amphibious attack on Rangoon] from March to November and leave the British 3rd Division in France, as well as sending there the 52nd Division, one of our best, about 22,000 strong in fighting troops, and the 6th Airborne Division to the Netherlands. Eisenhower is counting on these for the impending operation on the Rhine, and of course this was much the quickest way to bring additional troops into France.

3. Could you not deflect two, or better still three, American divisions to the Italian front, which would enable them to join Mark Clark's Fifth Army and add the necessary strength to Alexander? They would have to be there in three or four weeks. I consider the fact that we shall be sending Eisenhower these extra two divisions gives me a case for your generous consideration.

4. With regard to Istria, Trieste, etc., General Wilson is forwarding his plan to Combined Chiefs of Staff. This plan will be in accord with overall strategic objective, namely, the expulsion from or destruction in Italy of Kesselring's army.

He replied some days later:

President Roosevelt to Prime Minister (*Moscow*)   16 Oct 44

I appreciate your report on the Italian campaign, where, up to the present, our combined effort has cost us nearly 200,000 battle casualties, 90,000 of them American. My Chiefs of Staff accept Wilson's estimate that we cannot now expect to destroy Kesselring's army this winter and that the terrain and weather conditions in the Po valley will prevent any decisive advance this year. They further consider that the Germans are free to transfer five or six divisions from Italy to the Western Front whenever they consider such action more profitable than using these divisions in containing our forces south of the Po. Provision of additional U.S. divisions will not affect the campaign in Italy this year. All of us are now faced with an unanticipated shortage of man-power, and overshadowing all other military problems is the need for quick provision of fresh troops to reinforce Eisenhower in his battle to break into Germany and end the European war. While the divisions in Italy are undoubtedly tiring as the result of fighting in the present battle since August 25, Eisenhower is now fighting the decisive battle of Germany with divisions which have been in continuous combat since they landed on the Normandy beaches in the first part of June. The need for building up additional divisions on the long front from Switzerland to the North Sea is urgent. Even more urgent is the need for fresh troops to enable Eisenhower to give some rest to our front-line soldiers, who have been the spear-point of the battle since the first days in Normandy. On the basis of General Marshall's reports on the present situation we are now taking the very drastic step of sending the infantry regiments of the divisions ahead of the other units in order that General Eisenhower may be able to rotate some of our exhausted front-line soldiers.

Diversion of any forces to Italy would withhold from France vitally needed fresh troops, while committing such forces to the high attrition of an indecisive winter campaign in Northern Italy. I appreciate the hard and difficult task which our armies in Italy have faced and will face, but we cannot withhold from the main effort forces which are needed in the Battle of Germany.

From General Marshall's reports on the problem now facing General Eisenhower, I am sure that both of them agree with my conviction that no divisions should be diverted from their destination in France.

The rest of the story is soon told. Although hopes of decisive victory had faded, it remained the first duty of the armies in Italy to keep up the pressure and deter the enemy from sending help to the hard-pressed German armies on the Rhine. And so the Eighth Army fought forward whenever there was a spell of reasonably fine weather, taking Forli on November 9, and soon afterwards clearing all the road to Florence. Thereafter no major offensive was possible. Small advances were made as opportunity offered, but not until the spring were the armies rewarded with the victory they had so well earned, and so nearly won, in the autumn.

CHAPTER 15

October in Moscow

We alighted at Moscow on the afternoon of October 9, and were received very heartily and with full ceremonial by Molotov and many high Russian personages. This time we were lodged in Moscow itself, with every care and comfort. I had one small, perfectly appointed house, and Anthony another near by. We were glad to dine alone together and rest. At ten o'clock that night we held our first important meeting in the Kremlin. There were only Stalin, Molotov, Eden, and I, with Major Birse and Pavlov as interpreters. It was agreed to invite the Polish Prime Minister, M. Romer, the Foreign Minister, and M. Grabski, a grey-bearded and aged academician of much charm and quality, to Moscow at once. I telegraphed accordingly to M. Mikolajczyk that we were expecting him and his friends for discussions with the Soviet Government and ourselves, as well as with the Lublin Polish Committee. I made it clear that refusal to come to take part in the conversations would amount to a definite rejection of our advice and would relieve us from further responsibility towards the London Polish Government.

The moment was apt for business, so I said, 'Let us settle about our affairs in the Balkans. Your armies are in Roumania and Bulgaria. We have interests, missions, and agents there. Don't let us get at cross-purposes in small ways. So far as Britain and Russia are concerned, how would it do for you to have ninety per cent. predominance in Roumania, for us to have ninety per cent. of the say in Greece, and go fifty-fifty about Yugoslavia?' While this was being translated I wrote out on a half-sheet of paper:

Roumania
Russia	.	.	.	.	90%
The others	.	.	.	.	10%

Greece
Great Britain	.	.	.		90%
(in accord with U.S.A.)					
Russia	.	.	.	.	10%
Yugoslavia	.	.	.	.	50–50%
Hungary	.	.	.	.	50–50%

Bulgaria
Russia	.	.	.	.	75%
The others	.	.	.	.	25%

I pushed this across to Stalin, who had by then heard the translation. There was a slight pause. Then he took his blue pencil and made a large tick upon it, and passed it back to us. It was all settled in no more time than it takes to set down.

Of course we had long and anxiously considered our point, and were only dealing with immediate war-time arrangements. All larger questions were reserved on both sides for what we then hoped would be a peace table when the war was won.

After this there was a long silence. The pencilled paper lay in the centre of the table. At length I said, 'Might it not be thought rather cynical if it seemed we had disposed of these issues, so fateful to millions of people, in such an offhand manner? Let us burn the paper.' 'No, you keep it,' said Stalin.

I also raised the question of Germany, and it was agreed that our two Foreign Ministers, together with Mr. Harriman, should go into it. I told Stalin that the Americans would be outlining to him during the course of our future discussions their plan of operations in the Pacific for 1945.

* * *

We then sent a joint message to Roosevelt on our first talk.

10 Oct 44

We have agreed not to refer in our discussions to Dumbarton Oaks issues, and that these shall be taken up when we three can meet together. We have to consider the best way of reaching an agreed policy about the Balkan countries, including Hungary and Turkey. We have arranged for Mr. Harriman to sit in as an observer at all meetings where business of importance is to be transacted, and for General Deane to be present whenever military topics are raised. We have arranged for technical contacts between our high officers and General Deane on military aspects, and for any meetings which may be necessary later in our presence and that of the two Foreign Secretaries, together with Mr. Harriman. We shall keep you fully informed ourselves about the progress we make.

We take this occasion to send you our heartiest good wishes, and to offer our congratulations on the prowess of United States forces and upon the conduct of the war in the West by General Eisenhower.

I now reported privately to the President.

11 Oct 44

We have found an extraordinary atmosphere of goodwill here, and we have sent you a joint message. You may be sure we shall handle everything so as not to commit you. The arrangements we have made for Averell are, I think, satisfactory to him, and do not preclude necessary intimate contacts, which we must have to do any good. Of all these I shall give you a faithful report.

2. It is absolutely necessary we should try to get a common mind about the Balkans, so that we may prevent civil war breaking out in several countries, when probably you and I would be in sympathy with one side and U.J. with the other. I shall keep you informed of all this, and nothing will be settled except preliminary agreements between Britain and Russia, subject to further discussion and melting down with you. On this basis I am sure you will not mind our trying to have a full meeting of minds with the Russians.

3. I have not yet received your account of what part of the Pacific operations we may mention to Stalin and his officers. I should like to have this, because otherwise in conversation with him I might go beyond what you wish to be said. Meanwhile I will be very careful. We have not touched upon Dumbarton Oaks, except to say it is barred, at your desire. However, Stalin at lunch to-day spoke in praise of the meeting and of the very great measure of agreement that has been arrived at there. Stalin also in his speech at this same luncheon animadverted harshly upon Japan as being an aggressor nation. I have little doubt from our talks that he will declare war upon them as soon as Germany is beaten. But surely Averell

and Deane should be in a position not merely to ask him to do certain things, but also to tell him, in outline at any rate, the kind of things you are going to do yourself, and we are going to help you to do.

* * *

In the evening of October 11 Stalin came to dine at the British Embassy. This was the first time that the British Ambassador had succeeded in making such an arrangement. Every precaution was taken by the police. One of my guests, M. Vyshinsky, on passing some of the N.K.V.D. armed guards on our staircase, remarked, 'Apparently the Red Army has had another victory. It has occupied the British Embassy.' Till the small hours of the morning we ranged over the whole field of discussion in an informal atmosphere. Among other topics we discussed the next General Election in England. Stalin said that he had no doubt about the result: the Conservatives would win. It is even harder to understand the politics of other countries than those of your own.

* * *

I also cabled to Hopkins on various matters.

Prime Minister to Mr. Harry Hopkins   12 Oct 44
Everything is most friendly here, but the Balkans are in a sad tangle. Tito, having lived under our protection for three or four months at Vis, suddenly levanted, leaving no address, but keeping sentries over his cave to make out that he was still there. He then proceeded to Moscow, where he conferred, and yesterday M. Molotov confessed this fact to Mr. Eden. The Russians attribute this graceless behaviour to Tito's suspicious peasant upbringing, and say that they did not tell us out of respect for his wish for secrecy. The Bulgarians are treating our people ill, having arrested some of our officers still remaining both in Greece and Yugoslavia. I saw a tale of their having treated very cruelly American officers when prisoners of theirs. Russian attitude is that they are of course willing to indict Bulgaria for her many offences, but only in spirit of a loving parent—'This hurts me more than it does you.' They are taking great interest in Hungary, which, they mentioned erroneously, was their neighbour. They claim fullest responsibility in Roumania, but are prepared largely to disinterest themselves in Greece. All these matters are being flogged out by Mr. Eden and Molotov.

2. Under dire threats from us we persuaded Mikolajczyk

and the Poles to accept the invitation we had extracted from the Russians. We hope they will be here to-morrow.

3. We are seeing a great deal of Averell, and he is giving a dinner to-morrow night on Teheran lines—*i.e.*, only the secret ones there. He is sitting in on the military discussions and on the future of Germany talks, as well of course as the Polish conversations when they begin. We have so many bones to pick about the Balkans at the present time that we would rather carry the matter a little further *à deux* in order to be able to talk more bluntly than at a larger gathering. I will cable fully to the President about this in a day or two. Will you very kindly show this to him? I shall be very glad to hear from him.

The President now sent us an encouraging message.

President Roosevelt to Prime Minister and   12 Oct 44
Marshal Stalin

Thanks for your joint message of October 10.

I am most pleased to know that you are reaching a meeting of your two minds as to international policies in which, because of our present and future common efforts to prevent international wars, we are all interested.

*   *   *

After our first meeting I reflected on our relations with Russia throughout Eastern Europe, and in order to clarify my ideas drafted a letter to Stalin on the subject, enclosing a memorandum stating our interpretation of the percentages which we had accepted across the table. In the end I did not send this letter, deeming it wiser to let well alone. I print it only as an authentic account of my thought.

Moscow
October 11, 1944

I deem it profoundly important that Britain and Russia should have a common policy in the Balkans which is also acceptable to the United States. The fact that Britain and Russia have a twenty-year alliance makes it especially important for us to be in broad accord and to work together easily and trustfully and for a long time. I realise that nothing we can do here can be more than preliminary to the final decisions we shall have to take when all three of us are gathered together at the table of victory. Nevertheless I hope that we may reach understandings, and in some cases agreements, which will help us through immediate emergencies, and will afford a solid foundation for long-enduring world peace.

These percentages which I have put down are no more than a method by which in our thoughts we can see how near we are together, and then decide upon the necessary steps to bring us into full agreement. As I said, they would be considered crude, and even callous, if they were exposed to the scrutiny of the Foreign Offices and diplomats all over the world. Therefore they could not be the basis of any public document, certainly not at the present time. They might however be a good guide for the conduct of our affairs. If we manage these affairs well we shall perhaps prevent several civil wars and much bloodshed and strife in the small countries concerned. Our broad principle should be to let every country have the form of government which its people desire. We certainly do not wish to force on any Balkan State monarchic or republican institutions. We have however established certain relations of faithfulness with the Kings of Greece and Yugoslavia. They have sought our shelter from the Nazi foe, and we think that when normal tranquillity is re-established and the enemy has been driven out the peoples of these countries should have a free and fair chance of choosing. It might even be that Commissioners of the three Great Powers should be stationed there at the time of the elections so as to see that the people have a genuine free choice. There are good precedents for this.

However, besides the institutional question there exists in all these countries the ideological issue between totalitarian forms of government and those we call free enterprise controlled by universal suffrage. We are very glad that you have declared yourselves against trying to change by force or by Communist propaganda the established systems in the various Balkan countries. Let them work out their own fortunes during the years that lie ahead. One thing however we cannot allow —Facism or Nazism in any of their forms, which give to the toiling masses neither the securities offered by your system nor those offered by ours, but, on the contrary, lead to the build-up of tyrannies at home and aggression abroad. In principle I feel that Great Britain and Russia should feel easy about the internal government of these countries, and not worry about them or interfere with them once conditions of tranquillity have been restored after this terrible blood-bath which they, and indeed we, have all been through.

It is from this point of view that I have sought to adumbrate the degrees of interest which each of us takes in these countries with the full assent of the other, and subject to the approval of the United States, which may go far away for a long time and then come back again unexpectedly with gigantic strength.

In writing to you, with you experience and wisdom, I do not need to go through a lot of arguments. Hitler had tried to

exploit the fear of an aggressive, proselytising Communism
which exists throughout Western Europe, and he is being
decisively beaten to the ground. But, as you know well, this
fear exists in every country, because, whatever the merits of
our different systems, no country wishes to go through the
bloody revolution which will certainly be necessary in nearly
every case before so drastic a change could be made in the life
habits, and outlook of their society. We feel we were right in
interpreting your dissolution of the Comintern as a decision
by the Soviet Government not to interfere in the internal
political affairs of other countries. The more this can be
established in people's minds the smoother everything will go.
We, on the other hand, and I am sure the United States as
well, have Governments which stand on very broad bases
where privilege and class are under continual scrutiny and
correction. We have the feeling that, viewed from afar and
on a grand scale, the differences between our systems will
tend to get smaller, and the great common ground which
we share of making life richer and happier for the mass of
the people is growing every year. Probably if there were peace
for fifty years the differences which now might cause such
grave troubles to the world would become matters for
academic discussion.

At this point, Mr. Stalin, I want to impress upon you the
great desire there is in the heart of Britain for a long, stable
friendship and co-operation between our two countries, and
that with the United States we shall be able to keep the world
engine on the rails.

To my colleagues at home I sent the following:

12 Oct 44
The system of percentage is not intended to prescribe the
numbers sitting on commissions for the different Balkan
countries, but rather to express the interest and sentiment with
which the British and Soviet Governments approach the
problems of these countries, and so that they might reveal
their minds to each other in some way that could be comprehended. It is not intended to be more than a guide, and of
course in no way commits the United States, nor does it
attempt to set up a rigid system of spheres of interest. It may
however help the United States to see how their two principal
Allies feel about these regions when the picture is presented
as a whole.

2. Thus it is seen that quite naturally Soviet Russia has
vital interests in the countries bordering on the Black sea, by
one of whom, Roumania, she has been most wantonly attacked

with twenty-six divisions, and with the other of whom, Bulgaria, she has ancient ties. Great Britain feels it right to show particular respect to Russian views about these two countries, and to the Soviet desire to take the lead in a practical way in guiding them in the name of the common cause.

3. Similarly, Great Britain has a long tradition of friendship with Greece, and a direct interest as a Mediterranean Power in her future. In this war Great Britain lost 30,000 men in trying to resist the German-Italian invasion of Greece, and wishes to play a leading part in guiding Greece out of her present troubles, maintaining that close agreement with the United States which has hitherto characterised Anglo-American policy in this quarter. Here it is understood that Great Britain will take the lead in a military sense and try to help the existing Royal Greek Government to establish itself in Athens upon as broad and united a basis as possible. Soviet Russia would be ready to concede this position and function to Great Britain in the same sort of way as Britain would recognise the intimate relationship between Russia and Roumania. This would prevent in Greece the growth of hostile factions waging civil war upon each other and involving the British and Russian Governments in vexatious arguments and conflict of policy.

4. Coming to the case of Yugoslavia, the numerical symbol 50–50 is intended to be the foundation of joint action and an agreed policy between the two Powers now closely involved, so as to favour the creation of a united Yugoslavia after all elements there have been joined together to the utmost in driving out the Nazi invaders. It is intended to prevent, for instance, armed strife between the Croats and Slovenes on the one side and powerful and numerous elements in Serbia on the other, and also to produce a joint and friendly policy towards Marshal Tito, while ensuring that weapons furnished to him are used against the common Nazi foe rather than for internal purposes. Such a policy, pursued in common by Britain and Soviet Russia, without any thought of special advantages to themselves, would be of real benefit.

5. As it is the Soviet armies which are obtaining control of Hungary, it would be natural that a major share of influence should rest with them, subject of course to agreement with Great Britain and probably the United States, who, though not actually operating in Hungary, must view it as a Central European and not a Balkan State.

6. It must be emphasised that this broad disclosure of Soviet and British feelings in the countries mentioned above is only an interim guide for the immediate war-time future, and will be

surveyed by the Great Powers when they meet at the armistice or peace table to make a general settlement of Europe.

* * *

At five o'clock on the evening of October 13 we had our meeting at the Soviet Government Hospitality House, known as Spiridonovka, to hear Mikolajczyk and his colleagues put their case. These talks were held as a preparation for a further meeting at which the British and American delegations would meet the Lublin Poles. I pressed Mikolajczyk hard to consider two things, namely, *de facto* acceptance of the Curzon Line, with inter-change of population, and a friendly discussion with the Lublin Polish Committee so that a united Poland might be established. Changes, I said, would take place, but it would be best if unity were established now, at this closing period of the war, and I asked the Poles to consider the matter carefully that night. Mr. Eden and I would be at their disposal. It was essential for them to make contact with the Polish Committee and to accept the Curzon Line as a working arrangement, subject to discussion at the Peace Conference.

At ten o'clock the same evening we met the so-called Polish National Committee. It was soon plain that the Lublin Poles were mere pawns of Russia. They had learned and rehearsed their part so carefully that even their masters evidently felt they were overdoing it. For instance, M. Bierut, the leader, spoke in these terms: 'We are here to demand on behalf of Poland that Lvov shall belong to Russia. This is the will of the Polish people.' When this had been translated from Polish into English and Russian I looked at Stalin and saw an understanding twinkle in his expressive eyes, as much as to say, 'What about that for our Soviet teaching!' The lengthy contribution of another Lublin leader, Osóbka-Morawski, was equally depressing. Mr. Eden formed the worst opinion of the three Lublin Poles.

The whole conference lasted over six hours, but the achievement was small.

* * *

On the 14th there was a Command Performance at the Bolshoi Theatre—first a ballet, then opera, and finally some splendid dancing and singing by the Red Army choir. Stalin and I occupied the Royal Box, and we had a rapturous ovation from the entire audience. After the theatre we had a most interesting and successful military discussion at the Kremlin. Stalin had with him Molotov and General Antonov. Harriman brought General Deane. I had Brooke, Ismay, and General Burrows, head of our Military Mission in Moscow.

We began by telling them our future intentions in North-West Europe, Italy, and Burma. Deane followed with a statement about the campaign in the Pacific, and gave an outline of the sort of help which would be particularly valuable from the Soviets, once they were at war with Japan. General Antonov then made a very frank statement about the situation on the Eastern Front, the difficulties which confronted Russian armies, and their plans for the future. Stalin intervened from time to time to emphasise points of special significance, and concluded by assuring us that the Russian armies would press vigorously and continuously into Germany and that we need not have the slightest anxiety that the Germans would be able to withdraw any troops from their Eastern Front.

There was no doubt whatever that the Soviets intended to enter the war against Japan as soon after the defeat of Germany as they could collect the necessary forces and supplies in the Far East. Stalin would not commit himself definitely to a date. He spoke of a period of 'several months' after the German defeat. We got the impression that this might be interpreted as about three or four. The Russians agreed to an immediate start in building up stocks of food and fuel in their Far Eastern oil-fields, and to let the Americans use the airfields and other facilities in the maritime provinces which they needed for their Strategical Air Force. Stalin did not seem anxious about the effect of these preparations on the Japanese. In fact, he hoped they would make a 'premature attack', as this would encourage the Russians to fight their best. 'The Russians,' he remarked, 'would have to know what they were fighting for.'

On the 15th I had a high temperature and could not attend the second military meeting, which was held in the Kremlin that evening. Eden took my place, and had with him Brooke, Ismay, and Burrows; while Stalin, in addition to Molotov and Antonov, had Lieut.-General Shevchenko, Chief of Staff of the Soviet Army in the Far East. Harriman was again there, with General Deane. The only subject discussed was Soviet participation against Japan. Substantial conclusions were reached.

Stalin first of all agreed that we should concert our war plans. He asked for United States help in building up a two to three months' reserve of fuel, food, and transport in the Far East, and said that if this could be done and the political issues could be clarified the U.S.S.R. would be ready to attack Japan about three months after Germany had been defeated. He also promised to prepare airfields in the maritime provinces for the United States and Soviet Strategic Air Forces, and to receive American four-engined planes and instructors without delay. Meetings between the Soviet and American military staffs in Moscow would begin at once, and he promised to take part in the first one himself.

* * *

As the days passed only slight improvement was made with the festering sore of Soviet-Polish affairs. The Poles were willing to accept the Curzon Line 'as a line of demarcation between Russia and Poland'. The Russians insisted on the words 'as a basis of frontier between Russia and Poland'. Neither side would give way. Mikolajczyk declared that he would be repudiated by his own people, and Stalin at the end of a talk of two hours and a quarter which I had with him alone remarked that he and Molotov were the only two of those he worked with who were favourable to dealing 'softly' with Mikolajczyk. I was sure there were strong pressures in the background, both party and military.

Stalin did not think it desirable to proceed with an attempt to form a united Polish Government without the frontier question being agreed. Had this been settled he would have been quite willing that Mikolajczyk should head the new Government. I myself thought that difficulties not less obstinate would arise in a discussion for a merger of the Polish Government with the Lublin Poles, whose representatives continued to make the worst possible impression on us, and who, I told Stalin, were 'only an expression of the Soviet will'. They had no doubt also the ambition to rule Poland, and were thus a kind of Quislings. In all the circumstances the best course was for the two Polish delegations to return whence they had come. I felt very deeply the responsibility which lay on me and the Foreign Secretary in trying to frame proposals for a Russo-Polish settlement. Even forcing the Curzon Line upon Poland would excite criticism.

In other directions considerable advantages had been gained. The resolve of the Soviet Government to attack Japan on the overthrow of Hitler was obvious. This would have suprem value in shortening the whole struggle. The arrangements made about the Balkans were, I was sure, the best possible. Coupled with successful military action, they should now be effective in saving Greece, and I had no doubt that our agreement to pursue a fifty-fifty joint policy in Yugoslavia was the best solution for our difficulties in view of Tito's behaviour and of the arrival of Russian and Bulgarian forces under Russian command to help his eastern flank.

There is no doubt that in our narrow circle we talked with an ease, freedom, and cordiality never before attained between our two countries. Stalin made several expressions of personal regard which I feel sure were sincere. But I became even more convinced that he was by no means alone. As I said to my colleagues at home, 'Behind the horseman sits black care.'

*   *   *

Prime Minister to the King   16 Oct 44

With humble duty, the Prime Minister hopes His Majesty has had a successful and interesting visit to the armies in the Netherlands and is now safely back home. He trusts His Majesty is well after these exertions.

2. Here in Moscow the weather is brilliant but crisp, and the political atmosphere is extremely cordial. Nothing like it has been seen before. The Prime Minister and Mr. Eden in their various talks with Marshal Stalin and M. Molotov have been able to deal with the most delicate problems in a frank, outspoken manner without the slightest sign of giving offence. The Prime Minister attended a special performance of the ballet, which was very fine, and received a prolonged ovation from an enormous audience. Presently when Marshal Stalin came into the box for the first time in this war and stood beside him there was an almost passionate demonstration. At or after the very lengthy feasts, with very numerous cordial toasts, it has been possible to touch on many grave matters in an easy fashion. The nights are very late, lasting till three or even four o'clock ; but the Prime Minister also keeps late hours, and much work is done from about noon onwards, with conferences of various kinds.

3. We had three hours on the entire military scene. After Field-Marshal Brooke and the Prime Minister had explained the situation and plans in the West, in Italy, and in Burma, Mr. Harriman and General Deane, U.S.A., gave a full account of the Pacific, past, present, and future, which appeared to interest Marshal Stalin greatly. Later the Russian Deputy Chief of Staff told us much about Russian plans against

Germany which we had never heard before, the gist of which was extremely satisfactory. On account of secrecy I will defer all further reference to what he said until I get home. To-night at six o'clock we are to have a Russian statement on the Far Eastern theatre, which is likely to be satisfactory and of the greatest interest.

4. The day before yesterday was 'All Poles' Day'. Our lot from London are, as your Majesty knows, decent but feeble, but the delegates from Lublin could hardly have been under any illusions as to our opinion of them. They appeared to me to be purely tools, and recited their parts with well-drilled accuracy. I cross-examined them fairly sharply, and on several points Marshal Stalin backed me up. We shall be wrestling with our [London] Poles all to-day, and there are some hopes that we may get a settlement. If not we shall have to hush the matter up and spin it out until after the [American] Presidential election.*

5. There are still many subjects to be discussed, like the future treatment of Germany.

Mr. Churchill, with his humble duty, remains Your Majesty's faithful servant.

*   *   *

On the evening of October 17 we held our last meeting. The news had just arrived that Admiral Horthy had been arrested by the Germans as a precaution now that the whole German front in Hungary was disintegrating. I remarked that I hoped the Ljubljana Gap could be reached as fast as possible, and added that I did not think the war would be over before the spring. We then had our first talk on the question of Germany. We discussed the merits and drawbacks of the Morgenthau Plan. It was decided that the European Advisory Commission should study the problem in detail.

*   *   *

While flying home I gave the President further details of our talks.

Prime Minister to President Roosevelt   22 Oct 44
On our last day at Moscow Mikolajczyk saw Bierut, who admitted his difficulties. Fifty of his men had been shot in the last month. Many Poles took to the woods rather than join his forces. Approaching winter conditions behind the front would be very hard as the Russian Army moved forward, using all

* This took place on November 7. Mr. Roosevelt was re-elected President of the United States for the fourth time by a majority of over three and a half million votes.

transport. He insisted however that if Mikolajczyk were Premier he (Bierut) must have 75 per cent. of the Cabinet. Mikolajczyk proposed that each of the five Polish parties should be represented, he having four out of the five of their best men, whom he would pick from personalities not obnoxious to Stalin.

2. Later, at my request, Stalin saw Mikolajczyk and had an hour and a half's very friendly talk. Stalin promised to help him, and Mikolajczyk promised to form and conduct a Government thoroughly friendly to the Russians. He explained his plan, but Stalin made it clear that the Lublin Poles must have the majority.

3. After the Kremlin dinner we put it bluntly to Stalin that unless Mikolajczyk had fifty-fifty plus himself the Western World would not be convinced that the transaction was *bona fide* and would not believe that an independent Polish Government had been set up. Stalin at first replied he would be content with fifty-fifty, but rapidly corrected himself to a worse figure. Meanwhile Eden took the same line with Molotov, who seemed more comprehending. I do not think the composition of the Government will prove an insuperable obstacle if all else is settled. Mikolajczyk had previously explained to me that there might be one announcement to save the prestige of the Lublin Government and a different arrangement among the Poles behind the scenes.

4. Apart from the above, Mikolajczyk is going to urge upon his London colleagues the Curzon Line, including Lvov, for the Russians. I am hopeful that even in the next fortnight we may get a settlement. If so I will cable you the exact form so that you can say whether you want it published or delayed.

5. On major war criminals U.J. took an unexpectedly ultra-respectable line. There must be no executions without trial; otherwise the world would say we were afraid to try them. I pointed out the difficulties in international law, but he replied if there were no trials there must be no death sentences, but only lifelong confinements.

6. We also discussed informally the future partition of Germany. U.J. wants Poland, Czecho, and Hungary to form a realm of independent, anti-Nazi, pro-Russian States, the first two of which might join together. Contrary to his previously expressed view, he would be glad to see Vienna the capital of a federation of South German States, including Austria, Bavaria, Württemburg, and Baden. As you know, the idea of Vienna becoming the capital of a large Danubian federation has always been attractive to me, though I should prefer to add Hungary, to which U.J. is strongly opposed.

7. As to Prussia, U.J. wished the Ruhr and the Saar detached

and put out of action and probably under international con
trol, and a separate State formed in the Rhineland. He woul
also like the internationalisation of the Kiel Canal. I am no
opposed to this line of thought. However, you may be sur
that we came to no fixed conclusions pending the tripl
meeting.

8. I was delighted to hear from U.J. that you had suggeste
a triple meeting towards the end of November at a Black Se
port. I think this a very fine idea, and hope you will let m
know about it in due course. I will come anywhere you tw
desire.

9. U.J. also raised formally the Montreux Convention
wishing for modification for the free passage of Russian war
ships. We did not contest this in principle. Revision is clearl
necessary, as Japan is a signatory and Inönü missed his marke
last December. We left it that detailed proposals should b
made from the Russian side. He said they would be moderate

10. About recognising the present French Administration
as the Provisional Government of France, I will consult th
Cabinet on my return. Opinion of United Kingdom is ver
strongly for immediate recognition. De Gaulle is no longe
sole master, but is better harnessed than ever before. I sti
think that when Eisenhower proclaims a large zone of th
interior for France it would not be possible to delay thi
limited form of recognition. Undoubtedly de Gaulle has th
majority of the French nation behind him, and the Frenc
Government need support against potential anarchy in larg
areas. I will however cable you again from London.

I am now in the air above Alamein of Blessed Memory
Kindest regards.

He replied:

President Roosevelt to Prime Minister   22 Oct 4

I am delighted to learn of your success at Moscow i
making progress toward a compromise solution of the Polis
problem.

When and if a solution is arrived at I should like to be con
sulted as to the advisability from this point of view of delayin
its publication for about two weeks. You will understand.

Everything is going well here at the present time.

Your statement of the present attitude of Uncle J. towar
war criminals, the future of Germany, and the Montreu
Convention is most interesting. We should discuss thes
matters, together with our Pacific war effort, at the forth
coming three-party meeting.

*   *   *

On leaving after this profoundly interesting fortnight, in which
ve got closer to our Soviet Allies than ever before—or since—I
ad written to Stalin:

20 Oct 44

Eden and I have come away from the Soviet Union refreshed
and fortified by the discussions which we had with you,
Marshal Stalin, and with your colleagues. This memorable
meeting in Moscow has shown that there are no matters that
cannot be adjusted between us when we meet together in frank
and intimate discussion. Russian hospitality, which is re-
nowned, excelled itself on the occasion of our visit. Both in
Moscow and in the Crimea, where we spent some enjoyable
hours, there was the highest consideration for the comfort of
myself and our mission. I am most grateful to you and to all
those who were responsible for these arrangements. May we
soon meet again.

CHAPTER 16

Paris

As our armies moved eastwards and southwards it became increasingly urgent to set up a unified and broadly representative Administration in France. We were anxious not to impose a ready-made Committee from abroad, and we tried first to gauge the feelings of the people themselves as the liberation progressed. I had long pondered this problem, and as early as July 10 had minuted to Mr. Eden:

Prime Minister to Foreign Secretary   10 July 44
    Surely it would be most unwise of us to make up our minds on this [proposal to ask the U.S.A. and the U.S.S.R. to join with us in recognising the French Committee of National Liberation as the Provisional Government of France] until the result of the President's honeymoon with de Gaulle is made known. Clearly we shall have to go as far as the United States go, and after their decision is declared we may press them to go farther. Should the President make a *volte-face* and come to terms with de Gaulle we shall have a very good case to present to Parliament, showing how foolish it would have been to have had a premature debate which might have spoiled all this happy kissing.

Five weeks later the break-out from Normandy had been ccomplished and Patton was at the gates of Paris, but I was till averse to taking any decisive steps and minuted again:

Prime Minister to Foreign Secretary   18 Aug 44

I should deprecate taking any decisions about France till we can see more clearly what emerges from the smoke of battle. Should the great success of our operations secure the liberation of the West and South of France, including Paris, as may easily be the case, there will be a large area from which a real Provisional Government might be drawn instead of one being composed entirely of the French National Liberation Committee, whose interest in seizing the title-deeds of France is obvious.

I therefore strongly deprecate commitments of any kind at this stage to the French National Committee beyond those which have already been agreed to. One does not know at all what may happen, and it is as well to keep our hands free. I think a broader basis should be established before we commit ourselves.

Throughout the following weeks we watched the rallying of he Maquis and of public opinion to General de Gaulle's National Committee. Hitherto, by force of circumstances, it could not be a body representative of France as a whole, but by the end of September progress had been made, and on the 28th I said in my review of the war to the House of Commons:

Naturally that body has new elements, especially among those who formed the Maquis and Resistance movements, and among those who raised the glorious revolt in Paris, which reminded us of the famous days of the Revolution, when France and Paris struck a blow that opened the path broadly for all the nations of the world. Naturally, we, and, I believe, the United States and the Soviet Union, are most anxious to see emerge an entity which can truly be said to speak in the name of the people of France—the whole people of France. It would now seem possible to put into force the decree of the Algiers Committee whereby, as an interim stage, the Consultative Assembly would be transformed into an elected body, reinforced by the addition of new elements drawn from inside France. To this body the French Committee of National Liberation would be responsible. Such a step, once taken, when seen to have the approval of the French people, would greatly strengthen the position of France, and would render possible that recognition of the Provisional

Government of France, and all those consequences thereof, which we all desire to bring about at the earliest moment. I close no doors upon a situation which is in constant flux and development.

The welcome which the Maquis gave to the Committee seemed to me to be a decisive point in favour of its more formal recognition. I therefore telegraphed to the President:

Prime Minister (Moscow) to President Roosevelt   14 Oct 44

I have been reflecting about the question of the recognition of the French Provisional Government. I think events have now moved to a point where we could take a decision on the matter consistently with your own policy and my latest statement in the House of Commons.

2. In your telegram you said that you thought that we should wait until France was cleared of the enemy, and you implied that in any case de Gaulle must first show himself ready to take over from Eisenhower full responsibility for the administration of part of France as an interior zone. I for my part took the line in Parliament that the reorganisation of the Consultative Assembly on a more representative basis ought to precede recognition.

3. I understand that Eisenhower is anxious to comply with the request he has already had from the French to constitute a large part of France into an interior zone. Negotiations between Supreme Headquarters and the French are making good progress, and it appears that we may expect about three-quarters of France to become an interior zone very shortly.

4. The enlargement of the Consultative Assembly is also making good progress. Duff Cooper reports that owing to very real difficulties of communications in France the French have found it impracticable to proceed with the original Algiers plan of getting members of an enlarged Assembly confirmed in their mandates by elections in liberated departments. They propose instead to add selected delegates from the Resistance Movement and Parliamentary groups. I understand it is hoped to settle the matter shortly and publish a new decree defining attributions of the reformed Assembly and giving it increased powers over the Executive. It is thought that the enlarged Assembly should be able to meet at the end of this month.

5. There is no doubt that the French have been co-operating with Supreme Headquarters and that their Provisional Government has the support of the majority of French people. I suggest therefore that we can now safely recognise General de Gaulle's Administration as the Provisional Government of France.

6. One procedure might be to tell the French now that we will recognise [it] as soon as the enlarged Assembly has met and has given de Gaulle's Administration a vote of confidence.

7. An alternative procedure would be to recognise as soon as the interior zone has been formally established. I am inclined to think that this alternative is preferable, as it would connect recognition with what will be a mark of satisfactory co-operation between the French authorities and the Allied Armies in the common cause against Germany.

8. Please tell me what you think. If you agree that we should settle the matter by one or other of the procedures suggested above, the Foreign Office and State Department might at once compare their ideas upon the actual terms in which we should give recognition. It is important that we should take the same line, although we need not necessarily adopt exactly the same wording. We should of course have also to inform the Soviet Government of what we intend.

9. Recognition would not of course commit us on the separate question of French membership of the European Advisory Commission or similar bodies.

The President replied:

President Roosevelt to Prime Minister   20 Oct 44
I think until the French set up a real zone of interior that we should make no move towards recognising them as a Provisional Government. The enlargement of the Consultative Assembly, which has already been extended and made more representative, is almost as important, and I should be inclined to hang recognition on the effective completion of both these acts. I would not be satisfied with de Gaulle merely saying that he was going to do it.

I agree with you that there must be no implication, if and when we do recognise a Provisional Government, that this means a seat on the European Advisory Council, etc. These matters can be taken up later on their merits.

I am anxious to handle this matter, for the present, directly between you and me, and would prefer, for the moment, that the *modus operandi* should not become a matter of discussion between the State Department and your Foreign Office.

I do hope you are free of the temperature and really feeling all right again.

*   *   *

Our discussions proceeded on these lines. The French Assembly was strengthened and enlarged by members of the resistance organisations and the old Parliamentary group.

Already in August we had concluded a Civil Affairs Agreemer
with the French Provisional Administration, dividing Franc
into a forward zone, under the Supreme Allied Commande
and an interior zone, where the administration would be in th
hands of the French authorities. On October 20 it was ar
nounced that, with the agreement of the Allied High Comman
an interior zone comprising the larger part of France, includir
Paris, had been set up. The Committee of National Liberatio
was thus finally transformed into a Provisional Government
France.

I was now prepared to recommend, in concert with our Allie
the official acceptance of this body as the Government c
Liberated France. After last-minute hesitations by the Sta
Department the public announcement was made during m
visit to Moscow, where I discussed the final stages of form
recognition with the Russians. This came sooner than I expecte
and I telegraphed to the President:

Prime Minister (*Moscow*) *to President Roosevelt*   23 Oct ⋅

I was naturally surprised at the very sharp turn taken l
the State Department, and on arrival here I find the announc
ment is to be made to-morrow. We shall of course take simil;
and simultaneous action. I think it likely that the Russians w
be offended. Molotov in conversation said that he expecte
they would be made to appear the ones who were obstructin
whereas they [the Russians] would have recognised long ag
but had deferred to American and British wishes. I hor
therefore it has been possible to bring them in too.

*   *   *

I said in my speech in the House of Commons on October 27

I have been myself for some weeks past satisfied not onl
that the present French Government, under General de Gaull
commands the full assent of the vast majority of the Frenc
people, but that it is the only Government which can possibl
discharge the very heavy burdens which are being cast upon i
and the only Government which can enable France to gathe
its strength in the interval which must elapse before the cor
stitutional and Parliamentary processes, which it has declare
its purpose to reinstate, can again resume their norm;
functions.

Thus we completed the processes begun in the dark and fa
off days of 1940.

*   *   *

It was thought fitting that my first visit to Paris should be on Armistice Day, and this was publicly announced. There were many reports that collaborators would make attempts on my life and extreme precautions were taken. On the afternoon of November 10 I landed at Orly airfield, where de Gaulle received me with a guard of honour, and we drove together through the outskirts of Paris and into the city itself until we reached the Quai d'Orsay, where my wife and Mary and I were entertained in state. The building had long been occupied by the Germans, and I was assured I should sleep in the same bed and use the same bathroom as had Goering. Everything was mounted and serviced magnificently, and inside the palace it was difficult to believe that my last meeting there, described in a previous book, with Reynaud's Government and General Gamelin in May 1940 was anything but a bad dream. At eleven o'clock on the morning of November 11 de Gaulle conducted me in an open car across the Seine and through the Place de la Concorde, with a splendid escort of Gardes Républicains in full uniform with all their breastplates. They were several hundred strong, and provided a brilliant spectacle, on which the sun shone brightly. The whole of the famous avenue of the Champs Elysées was crowded with Parisians and lined with troops. Every window was filled with spectators and decorated with flags. We proceeded through wildly cheering multitudes to the Arc de Triomphe, where we both laid wreaths upon the tomb of the Unknown Warrior. After this ceremony was over the General and I walked together, followed by a concourse of the leading figures of French public life, for half a mile down the highway I knew so well. We then took our places on a dais, and there was a splendid march past of French and British troops. Our Guards detachment was magnificent. When this was over I laid a wreath beneath the statue of Clemenceau, who was much in my thoughts on this moving occasion.

De Gaulle entertained me at a large luncheon at the Ministry of War, and made a most flattering speech about my war services. But many problems had still to be settled.

On the night of the 12th after dinner at the Embassy I left with General de Gaulle for Besançon. The General was anxious for me to see the attack on a considerable scale which was planned for the French Army under General de Lattre de Tassigny. All the arrangements for the journey in a luxurious special train were most carefully made, and we arrived in plenty of

time for the battle. We were to go to an observation point in th
mountains, but owing to bitter cold and deep snow the road
were impassable and the whole operation had to be delayed.
passed the day driving with de Gaulle, and we found plenty t
talk about in a long and severe excursion, inspecting troops a
intervals. The programme continued long after dark. Th
French soldiers seemed in the highest spirits. They marched pas
in great style and sang famous songs with moving enthusiasn
My personal party—my daughter Mary and my naval aid
Tommy—feared that I should have another go of pneumonia
since we were out at least ten hours in terrible weather. But a
went well, and in the train the dinner was pleasant and interes
ing. I was struck by the awe, and even apprehension, with whic
half a dozen high generals treated de Gaulle in spite of the fac
that he had only one star on his uniform and they had lots.

During the night our train divided. De Gaulle returned t
Paris, and our half went on to Rheims, arriving next morning
when I went to Ike's headquarters. In the afternoon I flew bac
to Northolt.

*   *   *

On my return to London I sent the President a report. A cop
was also passed to Stalin.

Prime Minister to President Roosevelt   15 Nov 4
  ... Thank you for your kind wishes about the Paris-c
Gaulle trip. I certainly had a wonderful reception from abov
half a million French in the Champs Élysées and also from th
partly Opposition Centre at the Hôtel de Ville. I re-establishe
friendly private relations with de Gaulle.

I see statements being put out in the French Press and othe
quarters that all sorts of things were decided by us in Pari
You may be sure that our discussions about important thing
took place solely on an *ad referendum* basis to the three Grea
Powers, and of course especially to you, who have by far th
largest forces in France. Eden and I had a two hours' talk wit
de Gaulle and two or three of his people after luncheon on th
11th. De Gaulle asked a number of questions which made m
feel how very little they were informed about anything tha
had been decided or was taking place. He is of course anxiou
to obtain full modern equipment for eight more division
which can only be supplied by you. S.H.A.E.F. reasonabl
contends that these will not be ready for the defeat of Ger
many in the field and that shipping must be devoted to the u

keep of the actual forces that will win the battles of the winter and spring. I reinforced this argument.

At the same time I sympathise with the French wish to take over more of the line, to have the best share they can in the fighting or what is left of it—and there may be plenty—and not to have to go into Germany as a so-called conqueror who has not fought. I remarked that this was a sentimental point which ought nevertheless to receive consideration. The important thing for France was to have an Army prepared for the task which it would actually have to discharge, namely, their obligation first to maintain a peaceful and orderly country behind the front of our armies, and secondly to assist in the holding down of parts of Germany later on.

On this second point the French pressed very strongly to have a share in the occupation of Germany, not merely as sub-participation under British or American command, but as a French command. I expressed my sympathy with this, knowing well that there will be a time not many years distant when the American armies will go home and when the British will have great difficulty in maintaining large forces overseas, so contrary to our mode of life and disproportionate to our resources, and I urged them to study the type of army fitted for that purpose, which is totally different in form from the organisation by divisions required to break the resistance of a modern war-hardened enemy army. They were impressed by this argument, but nevertheless pressed their view.

I see a Reuter message, emanating no doubt unofficially from Paris, that it was agreed France should be assigned certain areas—the Ruhr, the Rhineland, etc.—for their troops to garrison. There is no truth in this, and it is obvious that nothing of this kind can be settled on such a subject except in agreement with you. All I said to de Gaulle on this was that we had made a division of Germany into Russian, British, and United States spheres; roughly, the Russians had the east, the British the north, and the Americans the south. I further said that speaking for His Majesty's Government, the less we had of it the better we should be pleased, and that we should certainly favour the French taking over as large a part as their capacity allowed, but that all this must be settled at an inter-Allied table. I could of course issue something which would be a disclaimer of any loose statements made by Reuter, but you may not think this necessary in view of the obvious facts. I am telegraphing to U.J. in the same sense. We did not attempt to settle anything finally or make definite agreements.

It is evident however that there are a number of questions which press for decision at a level higher than that of the High Commands, without which decision no clear guidance can be

given. Here is another reason why we should have a triple mee
ing if U.J. will not come, or a quadruple meeting if he will. I
the latter case the French would be in on some subjects a
out on others. One must always realise that before five yea
are out a French army must be made to take on the main ta
of holding down Germany. The main question of discussic
between Eden and Bidault was Syria, which was troublesom
lengthy, and inconclusive, but primarily our worry.

I thought I would give you this account at once in case
further tendentious statements being put out in the Press.

I thought very well of Bidault. He looks like a young
Reynaud, especially in speech and smiling. He made a ve
favourable impression on all of us, and there is no doubt th
he has a strong share in the power. Giraud was at the banqu
and apparently quite content. What a change in fortune sin
Casablanca! Generally I felt in the presence of an organise
Government, broadly based and of rapidly growing strengt
and I am certain that we should be most unwise to do anythi
to weaken it in the eyes of France at this difficult, critical tim
I had a considerable feeling of stability in spite of Communi
threats, and that we could safely take them [the French] mo
into our confidence. I hope you will not consider that I a
putting on French clothes when I say this. Let me know yo
thoughts. I will cable you later about the meeting. . . .

I also exchanged warm messages with General de Gaulle.

Prime Minister to General de Gaulle   16 Nov

Now that I am back home, let me express to Your Excellen
and to your colleagues of the French Government my pr
found appreciation of the splendid hospitality and innume
able kindnesses and courtesies shown me and my frien
during the memorable days which I have just spent in Franc
I shall always recall as one of the proudest and most movi
occasions of my life the wonderful reception which the peop
of Paris gave to their British guests on this our first visit
your capital after its liberation. I was also most grateful f
the opportunity of seeing for myself something of the ardo
and high quality of French troops, which are completing th
liberation of their native soil under the skilful leadership
General de Lattre de Tassigny. The welcome extended to
was indeed a happy augury for that continued friendsh
between our two countries essential to the safety and to th
future peace of Europe.

General de Gaulle to Prime Minister   20 Nov

Je vous remercie au nom du Gouvernement de votre mes

age. La France, sa capitale, et son Armée, ont été heureuses d'acclamer dans votre personne non seulement le Premier Ministre d'un grand pays qui leur est cher, mais encore le glorieux combattant qui a maintenu la coalition dans la guerre aux jours les plus sombres et lui vaut ainsi la victoire. Laissez-moi vous dire combien j'ai été personnellement heureux de vous revoir.

Prime Minister to General de Gaulle (Paris)   25 Nov 44
   If you think well, please give the following message from me to de Lattre:
   I send all my congratulations on the brilliant exploits of your young Army. It must be wonderful to be a Frenchman twenty years old with good weapons in his hands and France to avenge and save.

*   *   *

On November 20 Stalin sent a friendly reply to my telegram f November 15.

Marshal Stalin to Prime Minister   20 Nov 44
   Thank you for your information about your conversations with de Gaulle. I have acquainted myself with your communication with interest. I have nothing against your proposal about a possible meeting between us three and the French, provided the President also agrees with this, but it is necessary first to settle definitely about the time and place of the meeting between us three.
   General de Gaulle expressed recently his wish to come to Moscow to establish contact with the leaders of the Soviet Government. We replied agreeing to this. The French are expected to arrive in Moscow towards the end of this month. The French have not yet specified the questions which they would wish to discuss. In any case, after our conversations with General de Gaulle I will let you know about it.

This raised the whole issue of the future organisation of urope. There had been many rumours in the Press and else-/here about forming a Western *bloc* when the war was over. uch a plan seemed to be particularly popular in Foreign Office rcles, although it would burden us with heavy military com-itments. I felt that the Cabinet should be consulted very soon, articularly as Franco-Soviet talks were approaching.
   In consultation with Mr. Eden I now sent the following reply Stalin:

Prime Minister to Marshal Stalin 25 Nov 4

Your message of November 20. I am glad de Gaulle
coming to see you, and I hope you will talk over the whole fiel
together. There has been some talk in the Press about
Western *bloc*. I have not yet considered this. I trust first of a
to our Treaty of Alliance and close collaboration with th
United States to form the mainstays of a World Organisatio
to ensure and compel peace upon the tortured world. It
only after and subordinate to any such world structure tha
European arrangements for better comradeship should be se
on foot, and in these matters we shall have no secrets fro
you, being well assured that you will keep us equally informe
of what you feel and need.

2. The battle in the West is severe and the mud frightfu
The main collision is on the axis Aix-la-Chapelle–Cologn
This is by no means decided in our favour yet, though Eisen
hower still has substantial reserves to throw in. To the north
west Montgomery's armies are facing north, holding back th
Germans on the line of the Dutch Maas. This river permits u
an economy of force on this front. To the east we are makin
slow but steady progress and keeping the enemy in continuc
battle. One must acclaim the capture of Metz and the drivin
of the enemy back towards the Rhine as a fine victory for th
Americans. In the south the French have had brilliant succes
particularly in reaching the Rhine on a broad front and i
taking Strasbourg, and these young French soldiers, fror
eighteen to twenty-one years old, are showing themselve
worthy of their glorious chance to cleanse the soil of Franc
I think highly of General de Lattre de Tassigny. De Gaull
and I travelled there in order to see the opening of this battl
from a good viewpoint. However, a foot of snow fell in th
night and everything was put off for three days.

3. In a week or ten days it should be possible to estimat
whether the German armies will be beaten decisively west c
the Rhine. If they are we can go on in spite of the weathe
Otherwise there may be some lull during the severity of th
winter, after which one more major onslaught should brea
the organised German resistance in the West.

4. Do you think it is going to be a hard winter, and will th
suit your strategy? We all greatly liked your last speech. Pleas
do not fail to let me know privately if anything troublesom
occurs, so that we can smooth it away and keep the closin
grip on Nazidom at its most tense degree.

General de Gaulle had meanwhile arrived in Moscow an
conversations with the Russians had begun. Stalin lost no tim
in informing me of the general points.

Marshal Stalin to Prime Minister   2 Dec 44

There is every evidence that de Gaulle and his French friends, having arrived in the Soviet Union, will raise two questions:

1. The conclusion of a French-Soviet Pact of Mutual Assistance similar to the Anglo-Soviet Pact.

We can hardly object. But I should like to know your view on this subject. Please give your advice.

2. De Gaulle will probably raise the question of changing France's eastern frontier and extending the French frontier to the left bank of the Rhine. It is also common knowledge that there is a scheme for forming a Rhenish-Westphalian province under international control. Possibly French participation in this control is also contemplated. Thus the proposal of the French to transfer the boundary line to the Rhine will compete with the scheme for creating a Rhine province under international control.

Please give your advice on this question also.

I have sent a similar message to the President.

And again the following day:

Marshal Stalin to Prime Minister   3 Dec 44

The meeting with General de Gaulle has provided an opportunity for a friendly exchange of views on questions of Franco-Soviet relations. During the conversations General de Gaulle persisted, as I had expected, with two main questions: the frontier of France on the Rhine and the conclusion of a Franco-Soviet Pact of Mutual Assistance of the type of the Anglo-Soviet Treaty.

As regards the frontier of France on the Rhine, I expressed myself to the effect that it was impossible to decide this question without the knowledge and agreement of our chief Allies, whose armies are waging a battle of liberation against the enemy on the territory of France. I emphasised the complexity of a solution of this question.

With regard to the proposal of a Franco-Soviet Pact of Mutual Assistance, I pointed out the necessity of a study of this question from all sides, and the necessity for clarification of the juridical aspect of such a pact, in particular of the question who would ratify such a pact in France in present conditions.

Consequently the French still have to furnish a number of explanations, which we have up till now not received from them.

In sending you this information I shall be grateful for a reply from you and for your comments on these questions.

I have conveyed the same message to the President.

I send you my best wishes.

T—s.w.w.—11—к

On December 4 the Cabinet met to survey the possibilities of a Western *bloc* and de Gaulle's talks in Moscow. I read out to my colleagues the latest exchange of correspondence with Stalin, and the results of our deliberations were embodied in a message which I sent him in the early hours of December 5.

Prime Minister to Marshal Stalin   5 Dec 44

Your telegram about de Gaulle's visit and the two questions he will raise. We have no objection whatever to a Franco-Soviet Pact of Mutual Assistance similar to the Anglo-Soviet Pact. On the contrary, His Majesty's Government consider it desirable and an additional link between us all. Indeed, it also occurs to us that it might be best of all if we were to conclude a tripartite treaty between the three of us which would embody our existing Anglo-Soviet Treaty, with any improvements. In this way the obligations of each one of us would be identical and linked together. Please let me know if this idea appeals to you, as I hope it may. We should both of course tell the United States.

2. The question of changing the eastern frontier of France to the left bank of the Rhine, or alternatively of forming a Rhenish-Westphalian province under international control, together with other alternatives, ought to await settlement at the peace table. There is however no reason why when three heads of Governments meet we should not come much closer to conclusions about all this than we have done so far. As you have seen, the President does not expect de Gaulle to come to the meeting of the Three. I would hope that this could be modified to his coming in later on, when decisions especially affecting France were under discussion.

3. Meanwhile would it not be a good thing to let the European Advisory Commission sitting in London, of which France is a member, explore the topic for us all without committing in any way the heads of Governments?

4. I am keeping the President informed.

Mr. Roosevelt also kept in close touch with me.

President Roosevelt to Prime Minister   6 Dec 44

I have this date sent the following message to Uncle Joe:

'Thank you for your two informative messages of December 2 and December 3.

'In regard to a proposed Franco-Soviet Pact along the lines of the Anglo-Soviet Pact of Mutual Assistance, this Government would have no objection in principle if you and General de Gaulle considered such a pact in the interests of both your countries and European security in general.

'I am in complete agreement with your replies to General de Gaulle with regard to the post-war frontier of France. It appears to me at the present time that no advantage to our common war effort would result from an attempt to settle this question now and that its settlement subsequent to the collapse of Germany is preferable.'

And later:

President Roosevelt to Prime Minister   6 Dec 44

You will have seen from my reply to Stalin on his talks with de Gaulle that our views are identical on the two questions which he raised.

I still adhere to my position that any attempt to include de Gaulle in the meeting of the three of us would merely introduce a complicating and undesirable factor.

In regard to your suggestion to Uncle Joe that the question of France's post-war frontiers be referred to the European Advisory Commission, I feel that since the Commission is fully occupied with questions relating to the surrender of Germany it would be a mistake to attempt to bring up at this stage before it any questions of post-war frontiers. It seems to me preferable to leave this specific topic for further exploration between us.

I fully appreciate the advantages which you see in a possible tripartite Anglo-Franco-Soviet Pact. I am somewhat dubious however as to the effect of such an arrangement on the question of international Security Organisation, to which, as you know, I attach the very highest importance. I fear that a tripartite pact might be interpreted by public opinion here as a competitor to a future World Organisation, whereas a bilateral arrangement between France and the Soviet Union similar to the Soviet-British Pact would be more understandable. I realise however that this is a subject which is of primary concern to the three countries involved.

Stalin telegraphed next day:

Marshal Stalin to Prime Minister   7 Dec 44

I have received your reply to my message about a Franco-Soviet Pact and about the frontier of France on the Rhine. I thank you for your advice.

At the time of receiving your reply we had already begun discussions with the French about the pact. Your proposal in preference for a tripartite Anglo-Franco-Soviet Pact as an improvement in comparison with the Anglo-Soviet Pact has been approved by myself and my colleagues. We have made a proposal to de Gaulle for the conclusion of such a tripartite pact, but we have not yet had his reply.

I have delayed my reply to your other messages. I hope to reply soon.

But events took a slightly different course. The French were determined for domestic reasons to come away from Moscow with a strictly Franco-Soviet pact. This was signed on December 10, and Stalin telegraphed the same day:

Marshal Stalin to Prime Minister　　　　　　　　　10 Dec 44
I communicated to General de Gaulle your opinion about your preference for an Anglo-French-Soviet Pact of Mutual Assistance, and spoke in favour of accepting your proposal. However, General de Gaulle insisted on concluding a Franco-Soviet Pact, saying that a three-party pact should be concluded at the next stage, as that question demanded preparation. At the same time a message came from the President, who informed me that he had no objection to a Franco-Soviet Pact. In the result we reached agreement about concluding a pact, and it was signed to-day. The pact will be published after General de Gaulle's arrival in Paris.

I think that General de Gaulle's visit has had positive results, and will assist not only in strengthening Franco-Soviet relations, but will also be a contribution to the common work of the Allies.

It was for the French now to make a similar agreement with us, if they felt so inclined. I informed Stalin of this possibility in a jocular way.

Prime Minister to Marshal Stalin　　　　　　　　　19 Dec 44
I saw last night for the second time the film which you have given me called *Kutuzov*. The first time I greatly admired it, but as it was all in Russian I could not understand the exact meaning of each situation. Last night I saw it with the English captions, which made exactly intelligible the whole thing, and I must tell you that in my view this is one of the most masterly film productions I have ever witnessed. Never has the conflict of two will-powers been more clearly displayed. Never has the importance of fidelity in commanders and men been more effectively inculcated by the film pictures. Never have the Russian soldiers and the Russian nation been presented by this medium so gloriously to the British nation. Never have I seen the art of the camera better used.

2. If you thought it fit privately to communicate my admiration and thanks to those who have laboured in producing this work of art and high morale I should thank you. Meanwhile I congratulate you.

3. I like to think we were together in that deadly struggle, as in this Thirty Years War. I do not suppose that you showed the film to de Gaulle, any more than I shall show him *Lady Hamilton* when he comes over here to make a similar treaty to that which you have made with him, and we have made together.

Salutations.

On December 25 he replied that he would 'of course welcome the conclusion of an Anglo-French treaty'. I felt that there was no hurry about this and that we should await a move from the French. On December 31 I minuted to Mr. Eden:

You may feel inclined to see how the proposals which have come on the *tapis* meanwhile for a bilateral treaty between Britain and France shape themselves. You said to me that if de Gaulle attempted to say that there could be no Anglo-French Treaty until we had settled everything about Syria you would let him wait. It is for him to make the proposal, not us.

Meantime we are losing nothing from the point of view of security, because the French have practically no Army and all the other nations concerned are prostrate or still enslaved. We must be careful not to involve ourselves in liabilities which we cannot discharge and in engagements to others for which there is no corresponding return. I do not know what our financial position will be after the war, but I am sure we shall not be able to maintain armed forces sufficient to protect all these helpless nations even if they make some show of recreating their armies. Anyhow, the first thing to do is to set up the World Organisation, on which all depends.

CHAPTER 17

Counter-stroke in the Ardennes

November brought the Allied cause the loss of Field-Marshal Sir John Dill, the head of our Inter-Service Mission in Washington. After forty years of a full Army life, which began in the South African War, he was appointed Chief of the Imperial General Staff in May 1940. In that great position his balanced judgment and steadfast temperament were a great stand-by in our days of peril. After Pearl Harbour he was transferred to Washington, where he interpreted our views to the United States Chiefs of Staff. He soon endeared himself there, and formed a firm personal friendship with General Marshall, which proved invaluable in overcoming the frets and frictions that inevitably arise between Allies. This was the climax of his career. He would surely have lived far beyond his sixty-three years but for his selfless devotion to duty ; but even when a very sick man he would not give in. As a last tribute to him and to all he stood for, he was accorded the signal distinction of burial in the National Cemetery at Arlington, where America's great men lie. An equestrian statue was erected to his memory by the American Army.

The President sent me a message saying, 'America joins with Great Britain in sorrow at the loss of your distinguished soldier, whose personal admirers here are legion.' I thanked him, and to General Marshall I said: 'I read with emotion the message which the United States Joint Chiefs of Staff have addressed to their British colleagues about the death of our friend Sir John Dill. Let me express my own thanks for all your kind thoughts. He did all he could to make things go well, and they went well.'

To fill the gap required important changes in our commands.

Prime Minister to General Wilson (Italy)   21 Nov 44

It is of great importance that Field-Marshal Dill's position should be filled by someone who would have access to the President from time to time and a status which would enable him to be in very close touch with General Marshall. It goes without saying that the officer selected must be one who works well with Americans and be in full possession of the general outlook upon the war as a whole. I can find only one officer with the necessary credentials and qualities, namely, yourself. I have therefore proposed to the President that you should succeed Dill as Head of the British Military Mission and my official representative in military matters at Washington. The President has cordially agreed, and you are assured of a warm welcome in Washington. I hope therefore that you will feel able to let me know at once that you accept this extremely important appointment.

2. I also proposed to the President that General Alexander should become Allied Supreme Commander in the Mediterranean in succession to you, with General McNarney as his Deputy, and that General Mark Clark should take over the group of armies on the Italian front.

3. The President has replied that these proposals are entirely agreeable to the United States Chiefs of Staff and to himself.

4. I should like you to come home this next week for a day or two for a preliminary discussion. I hope that you can manage this. My 'York' will come out at once. I hope you will bring Macmillan with you.

'I appreciate the compliment,' the President had cabled, 'you pay General Clark in suggesting that he take over the Army Group in Italy as General Alexander's successor.'

*   *   *

There had meanwhile been much preparation on the Western

Front for the advance to the Rhine. The November rains were the worst for many years, flooding the rivers and streams, and making quagmires through which the infantry had to struggle. In the British sector Dempsey's Second Army drove the enemy from their large salient west of Venlo back across the Meuse. Farther south our XXXth Corps had come into the line between Maeseyck and Geilenkirchen, where they joined hands with the Ninth U.S. Army. Together they took Geilenkirchen on November 19, after intensive artillery preparation, and then toiled over saturated country towards the river Roer. The right of the Ninth Army reached the river near Jülich on December 3, while the First Army on their flank had a bitter struggle in the Hürtgen Forest. Seventeen Allied divisions were engaged. The enemy had almost as many and the fighting was severe.

It would have been rash as yet to cross the river, because its level was controlled by massive dams a score of miles to the south. These were still in enemy hands, and by opening the sluices he could have cut off our troops on the far bank. Heavy bombers tried to burst the dams and release the water, but in spite of several direct hits no gap was made, and on December 13 the First U.S. Army had to renew their advance to capture them.

South of the Ardennes Patton's Third Army had meanwhile crossed the Moselle on each side of Thionville and thrust eastwards to the German frontier. Metz was entered on November 20, though the Germans still clung to the surrounding forts, of which the last held out till December 13. From Metz and Nancy the Army swung up towards the river Saar, which they reached on a broad front, and threw bridgeheads across it near Saarlautern on December 4. Here they confronted the strongest part of the Siegfried defences, consisting of a forward line along the north bank of the river, and behind it a zone over two miles deep of mutually supporting concrete works. Against such formidable and obstinately held fortifications the Third Army came to a halt.

On the right of the line General Devers's Sixth Army Group, from Luneville and Épinal, forced their way through the Vosges and the Belfort Gap. The American Seventh Army had a stiff fight for the mountain crests, but the French First Army, after a week's battle, the opening of which I had hoped to see, captured Belfort on November 22 and reached the Rhine north of Bâle. Thence they swung down the river towards Colmar. This turned

The Frontier Regions

the German flank in the Vosges and the enemy withdrew. Stras
bourg was entered on November 23, and during the next fe
weeks the Seventh Army cleared all Northern Alsace, wheele
up on the right of the Third Army, and, crossing the Germa
frontier on a wide front, penetrated the Siegfried Line nea
Wissembourg. There was still a large pocket of Germans o
French soil at Colmar, thirty miles deep and broad, which th
French had been unable to clear. This was to prove an emba
rassment a few weeks later.

* * *

I sent my comments on the whole situation to Smuts.

Prime Minister to Field-Marshal Smuts 3 Dec 4

... 2. In spite of Metz and Strasbourg and other successe
we have of course sustained a strategic reverse on the Wester
Front. Before this offensive was launched we placed on recor
our view that it was a mistake to attack against the who
front and that a far greater mass should have been gathere
at the point of desired penetration. Montgomery's commen
and predictions beforehand have in every way been borne ou
I imagine some readjustments will be made giving back 1
Montgomery some of the scope taken from him after th
victory he gained in Normandy. You must remember howeve
that our armies are only about one-half the size of th
American and will soon be little more than one-third. All
friendly and loyal in the military sphere in spite of the di
appointment sustained. We must now re-group and reinforc
the armies for a spring offensive. There is at least one full-sca
battle to fight before we get to the Rhine in the north, whic
is the decisive axis of advance. I am trying meanwhile to hav
Holland cleaned up behind us. But it is not so easy as it use
to be for me to get things done.

3. Our armies in Italy were delayed by 'Anvil' and great
weakened for its sake. Consequently we cleared the Apennin
only to find the valley of the Po a bog. Thus both in the mou
tains and on the plains our immense armour superiority ha
been unable to make itself felt, and now the bad weather
Italy, as on the Western Front, greatly diminishes the tactic
air-power in which we have so great a predominance. Hithert
in Italy we have held twenty-eight German divisions, an
therefore no reproach can be made against our activities. O
the contrary, General Marshall is astonished we have done s
well. This is only however because the Germans have delaye
a withdrawal through the Brenner and Ljubljana, presumab
in order to bring their forces home from the Balkans. W

cannot look for any very satisfactory events in Northern Italy at present, though we are still attacking. . . .

5. In Burma too we have been compelled to work downwards from the north through the jungles I had hoped to avoid, and Mountbatten was doing pretty well. Now however the disasters in China have overtaken Kunming, and may soon affect Chungking. The Generalissimo is withdrawing his best Chinese troops from the southward advance in Burma to defend his capital, his air terminus, and, I expect, his life and *régime*. I cannot blame him, but this gravely affects the success of Mountbatten's well-conducted but already unappetising operations. We seem condemned to wallow at half-speed through these jungles, and I cannot so far procure agreement for a far-flung amphibious strategical movement across the Bay of Bengal. Everything has to be chewed up by the Combined Staffs and 'Safety first' overloads every plan. The Americans are having hard fighting at Leyte, but their advance in the Pacific has been admirable during the year, and I hope our Fleet will join them in growing strength in 1945. As old Fisher said, 'The Royal Navy always travels first class,' and you can imagine the enormous demands in man-power, ancillary vessels, and preparations of all kinds which the Admiralty blithely put forward.

6. Meanwhile there approaches the shadow of the General Election, which before many months have passed will certainly break up the most capable Government England has had or is likely to have. Generally we have a jolly year before us. Our financial future fills in any spaces in the horizon not already overcast with clouds. However, I am sure we shall master all these troubles as they come upon us, singly or in company, even though the tonic element of mortal danger is lacking.

7. Of all the messages which reached me on my birthday, none was more movingly phrased or gave me more encouragement than yours, my old and trusted friend.

Three days later I addressed myself to the President.

Prime Minister to President Roosevelt   6 Dec 44
As we are unable to meet, I feel that the time has come for me to place before you the serious and disappointing war situation which faces us at the close of this year. Although many fine tactical victories have been gained on the Western Front and Metz and Strasbourg are trophies, the fact remains that we have definitely failed to achieve the strategic object which we gave to our armies five weeks ago. We have not yet reached the Rhine in the northern part and most important sector of the front, and we shall have to continue the great battle for many weeks before we can hope to reach the Rhine

and establish our bridgeheads. After that, again, we have t
advance through Germany.

2. In Italy the Germans are still keeping twenty-six division
—equivalent to perhaps sixteen full strength or more—on ou
front. They could however at any time retreat through th
Brenner and Ljubljana and greatly shorten their line by holdir
from Lake Garda to, say, the mouth of the Adige. By this the
might save half their Italian forces for home defence. Eve
after that there are the Alps to which they could fall bac
thus saving more men. It seems to me that their reason fo
standing so long in Italy may have been to extricate the twel
divisions in the Balkans, etc., which are now fighting their wa
back to Hungary and Austria. Apart from the Air and Partisar
and small Commando forces, there are no means of preventir
this, and my opinion is that the greater part will escape. Abor
half of these might be available for adding to what may
saved from Italy. This would be a powerful reinforcement
the German homeland, available, according to events, either
the East or in the West.

3. We have secured weighty advantages from 'Dragoo
[the landing in Southern France] for the battle on the ma
front, but the reason why the Fifteenth Group of Armies h
not been able to inflict a decisive defeat on Kesselring is tha
owing to the delay caused by the weakening of our forces fr
the sake of 'Dragoon', we did not get through the Apennin
till the valley of the Po had become water-logged. Th
neither in the mountains nor on the plains have we been ab
to use our superiority in armour.

4. On account of the obstinacy of the German resistance c
all fronts, we did not withdraw the five British and Britis
Indian divisions from Europe in order to enable Mountbatte
to attack Rangoon in March, and for other reasons also th
operation became impracticable. Mountbatten therefo
began, as we agreed at Quebec, the general advance throug
Burma downstream from the north and the west, and this h
made satisfactory progress. Now, owing to the advance of th
Japanese in China, with its deadly threat to Kunming ar
perhaps Chungking, to the Generalissimo and his *régime,* tw
and possibly more Chinese divisions have to be withdrawn fr
the defence of China. I have little doubt that this was inevi
able and right. The consequences however are serious so fa
as Mountbatten's affairs are concerned, and no decision h
yet been taken on how to meet this new misfortune, which
one stroke endangers China and your air terminal as well
the campaign in Northern Burma. All my ideas about a real
weighty blow across the Adriatic or across the Bay of Beng
have equally been set back.

5. The vast-scale operations which you have conducted in the Pacific are at present the only part of the war where we are not in a temporary state of frustration.

6. We have however, happily, to consider what the Russians will do. We have Stalin's promise for a winter campaign, starting, I presume, in January. On most of his immense front he seems to have been resting and preparing, though only about three or four German divisions have come over to face Eisenhower. I am not in a position to measure the latest attacks he has launched to the south-west of Budapest. We may however, I think, look forward to more assistance from this and other Russian action than we have had lately, and the German position is so strained that any heavy penetration might bring about a partial if not a total collapse.

7. I have tried to survey the whole scene in its scope and proportion, and it is clear that we have to face, in varying degrees of probability:

(a) A considerable delay in reaching, still more in forcing, the Rhine on the shortest road to Berlin.

(b) A marked degree of frustration in Italy.

(c) The escape home of a large part of the German forces from the Balkan peninsula.

(d) Frustration in Burma.

(e) Elimination of China as a combatant.

When we contrast these realities with the rosy expectations of our peoples, in spite of our joint efforts to damp them down, the question very definitely arises, 'What are we going to do about it?' My anxiety is increased by the destruction of all hopes of an early meeting between the three of us and the indefinite postponement of another meeting of you and me with our Staffs. Our British plans are dependent on yours, our Anglo-American problems at least must be surveyed as a whole, and the telegraph and the telephone more often than not only darken counsel. Therefore I feel that if you are unable to come yourself before February I am bound to ask you whether you could not send your Chiefs of Staff over here as soon as practicable, where they would be close to your main armies and to General Eisenhower and where the whole stormy scene can be calmly and patiently studied with a view to action as closely concerted as that which signalised our campaigns of 1944.

Though sympathetic, Mr. Roosevelt did not appear to share my anxieties.

President Roosevelt to Prime Minister   10 Dec 44
    ... Perhaps I am not close enough to the picture to feel as

240

disappointed about the war situation as you are, and perhaps
also because six months ago I was not as optimistic as you
were on the time element.

On the European front I always felt that the occupation of
Germany up to the left bank of the Rhine would be a very
stiff job. Because in the old days I bicycled over most of the
Rhine terrain, I have never been as optimistic as to the ease
of getting across the Rhine with our joint armies as many of
the commanding officers have been.

However, our agreed broad strategy is developing according
to plan. You and I are now in the position of Commanders-in-
Chief who have prepared their plans, issued their orders, and
committed their resources to battle according to those plans
and orders. For the time being, even if a little behind schedule,
it seems to me the prosecution and outcome of the battles lie
with our Field Commanders, in whom I have every confidence.
We must remember that the winter season is bringing great
difficulties, but our ground and air forces are day by day
chewing up the enemy's dwindling man-power and resources,
and our supply flow is much improved with the opening of
Antwerp. General Eisenhower estimates that on the Western
front line he is inflicting losses in excess of the enemy's
capability to form new units. I still cannot see clearly just
when, but soon a decisive break in our favour is bound to
come.

As to the Italian front, Alexander's forces are doing their
bit in keeping those German divisions in Italy, and we must
remember that the Germans are really free to withdraw to the
line of the Alps if they decide.

The same thing applies to their troops in the Balkans. I have
never believed that we had the power to capture any large
German forces in the Balkans without assistance by the
Russians.

On the Russian front we must also give full allowance to the
vile weather, and the Russians seem to be doing their bit at
the present time. This of course you know more about than I
do.

The Far Eastern situation is of course on a somewhat
different footing, and I am not at all happy about it.

From the long-range point of view, other than the measures
Wedemeyer is now taking, we can do very little to prepare
China to conduct a worth-while defence, but Japan is suffering
losses in men and ships and materials in the Pacific area that
are many times greater than ours, and they too cannot keep
this up. Even the Almighty is helping. This magnificent earth-
quake and tidal wave is a proof.

The time between now and spring, when the freeze is over,

will develop many things. We shall know a lot more than we know now.

My Chiefs of Staff are now devoting all of their abilities and energies in directing their organisations towards carrying out the plans we have made and in supporting our forces throughout the world. Practically all of these forces are, for the time being, committed. That is why I do not feel that my Chiefs should leave their posts at this time, since no requirement exists for broad strategic decisions to guide our Field Commanders. ...

*   *   *

A heavy blow now impended. Within six days a crisis burst upon us. The Allied decision to strike hard from Aachen in the north as well as through Alsace in the south had left our centre very weak. In the Ardennes sector a single corps, the VIIIth American, of four divisions, held a front of seventy-five miles. The risk was foreseen and deliberately accepted, but the consequences were grave and might have been graver. By a remarkable feat the enemy gathered about seventy divisions on their Western Front, of which fifteen were armoured. Many were under strength and needed rest and re-equipment, but one formation, the Sixth Panzer Army, was known to be strong and in good fettle. This potential spear-head had been carefully watched while it lay in reserve east of Aachen. When the fighting on that front died down in early December it vanished for a while from the ken of our Intelligence, and bad flying weather hindered our efforts to trace it. Eisenhower suspected that something was afoot, though its scope and violence came as a surprise.

The Germans had indeed a major plan. Rundstedt assembled two Panzer armies, the Fifth and Sixth, and the Seventh Army, a total of ten Panzer and fourteen infantry divisions. This great force, led by its armour, was intended to break through our weak centre in the Ardennes to the river Meuse, swing north and north-west, cut the Allied line in two, seize the port of Antwerp, and sever the life-line of our northern armies. This bold bid was planned by Hitler, who would brook no changes in it on the part of his doubting generals. In its support the remnants of the German Air Force were assembled for a final effort, while paratroops, saboteurs, and agents in Allied uniforms were all given parts to play.

The attack began on December 16 under a heavy artillery

barrage. At its northern flank the Sixth Panzer Army ran into the right of the First U.S. Army in the act of advancing towards the Roer dams. After a swaying battle the enemy were held. Farther south the Germans broke through on a narrow front, but the determined defence of St. Vith, where the 7th U.S. Armoured Division specially distinguished itself, hindered them for several critical days. The Sixth Panzer Army launched a new spear-head to strike west and then northwards at the Meuse above Liége. The Fifth Panzer Army meanwhile drove through the centre of the VIIIth U.S. Corps, by-passed St. Vith and Bastogne, and penetrated deeply to Marche and towards the Meuse at Dinant.

Although the time and weight of the attack surprised the Allied High Command its importance and purpose were quickly recognised. They resolved to strengthen the 'shoulders' of the breakthrough, hold the Meuse crossings both east and south of Namur, and mass mobile troops to crush the salient from north and south. Eisenhower acted speedily. He stopped all Allied attacks in progress and brought up four American divisions from reserve, and six more from the south. Two airborne divisions, one of them the 6th British, came from England. North of the salient the British XXXth Corps, of four divisions, which had just come out of the line on the river Roer, was concentrated between Liége and Louvain behind the American First and Ninth Armies. These latter threw in all their reserves to extend a defensive flank westwards from Malmedy.

By severing the front of General Bradley's Twelfth Army Group the Germans had made it impossible for him to exercise effective command from his headquarters in Luxembourg over his two armies north of the bulge. General Eisenhower therefore very wisely placed Montgomery in temporary command of all Allied troops in the north, while Bradley retained the Third U.S. Army and was charged with holding and counter-attacking the enemy from the south. Corresponding arrangements were made for the tactical air forces.

I telegraphed to Smuts.

Prime Minister to Field-Marshal Smuts   22 Dec 44
   Montgomery and also we here in England have, as you are aware, pressed for several months for the emphasis of the advance to the north of the Ruhr, and have on repeated occasions urged that our strength did not enable us to undertake two major offensives such as the one against Cologne

and that across the Saar. In spite of appalling weather conditions our friends however pushed on confidently, and were very much spread from north to south when the enemy began his counter-stroke. I spoke to Eisenhower on the telephone during the afternoon of the 20th and suggested that he give to Montgomery the whole command north of the breakthrough, and to Omar Bradley everything south of the breakthrough, keeping control himself of the concerted operation. He replied that he had issued orders exactly on these lines in the morning. Montgomery now in fact has under his command eighteen American divisions plus his Twenty-first Army Group comprising about sixteen divisions. He is forming substantial reserves and is assuming entire charge of the battle in the area of his command. He should be able to intervene heavily. There is nothing so far to suggest that the Germans have the power to mount a full-scale offensive against the Twenty-first Army Group's main front.

2. Matters are not by any means so clear south of the gap. The Americans are putting up stubborn resistance, but there is a good deal of disorganisation. Naturally an army has been gathered from the Metz region to march north under Patton. The position of the enemy does not strike me as good. As usual I am optimistic ; the tortoise has thrust his head out very far.

*   *   *

Three of our reinforcing divisions lined the Meuse south of Namur. Bradley concentrated a corps at Arlon and sent the American 101st Airborne Division to secure the important road junctions at Bastogne. The German armour swung north of Bastogne and sought to break their way north-westwards, leaving their infantry to capture the town. The 101st, with some armoured units, were isolated, and for a week beat off all attacks.

The wheel of the Fifth and Sixth Panzer Armies produced bitter fighting around Marche, which lasted till December 26. By then the Germans were exhausted, although at one time they were only four miles from the Meuse and had penetrated over sixty miles. Bad weather and low ground fogs had kept our air forces out of the first week of the battle, but on December 23 flying conditions got better and they intervened with tremendous effect. Heavy bombers attacked railways and centres of movement behind the enemy lines, and tactical air forces played havoc in his forward areas, starving him of reinforcements, fuel, food, and ammunition. Strategic raids on German refineries helped to deny him petrol and slacken the advance.

Baulked of their foremost objective, the Meuse, the Panzers turned savagely on Bastogne. The American 101st Division had been reinforced on December 26 by part of the 4th U.S. Armoured Division, and though vastly outnumbered held the town grimly for another week. Before the end of December the German High Command must have realised, however unwillingly, that the battle was lost, for Patton's counter-offensive from Arlon, which started on the 22nd, was steadily if slowly progressing over the snow-choked countryside towards Houffalize. The enemy made one last bid, this time in the air. On January 1 they made a violent low-level surprise attack on all our forward airfields. Our losses were heavy, though promptly replaced, but the Luftwaffe lost more than they could afford in their final massed attack of the war.

* * *

On January 3 Montgomery also launched his northern counter-offensive against Houffalize to join Patton's attack from the south. I visited the front at this time, and telegraphed to the President:

Prime Minister to President Roosevelt   6 Jan 45
C.I.G.S. and I have passed the last two days with Eisenhower and Montgomery, and they both feel the battle very heavy, but are confident of success. I hope you understand that, in case any troubles should arise in the Press, His Majesty's Government have complete confidence in General Eisenhower and feel acutely any attacks made on him.

2. He and Montgomery are very closely knit, and also Bradley and Patton, and it would be disaster which broke up this combination, which has in 1944 yielded us results beyond the dreams of military avarice. Montgomery said to me to-day that the break-through would have been most serious to the whole front but for the solidarity of the Anglo-American Army.

3. Although I regret our divisions only amount to seventeen and two-thirds, all units are absolutely up to strength, and we have seven or eight thousand reinforcements all ready in addition in France awaiting transfer to their units. The measures we have taken to bring another 250,000 into or nearer the front line enable me to say with confidence that at least our present strength will be maintained throughout the impending severe campaign.

4. I am deeply impressed with the need of sustaining the Foot, who bear two-thirds of the losses but are very often the last to receive reinforcements. More important even than the sending over of large new units is the keeping up of the infantry strength of divisions already engaged. We are therefore preparing a number of infantry brigades, including several from the Marines, of whom the Navy has 80,000. These brigades will liberate mobile divisions from quasi-static sectors, and at the same time do the particular work which is needed in them. Montgomery welcomed this idea most cordially as regards the Twenty-first Army Group. I gathered from General Eisenhower that he takes the same view, and that he is longing for more infantry drafts—*i.e.*, rifle and bayonet—to maintain the United States divisions at their proper establishment.

5. I most cordially congratulate you on the extraordinary gallantry which your troops have shown in all this battle, particularly at Bastogne and two other places which Montgomery mentioned to me on his own front, one at the peak of the salient, where the 1st and 9th American Divisions fought on and won after extremely heavy losses, and the other in connection with the 7th United States Armoured Division, which seems to have performed the highest acts of soldierly devotion. Also many troops of the First Army have fought to the end, holding cross-roads in the area of incursion, which averted serious perils to the whole armies of the north at heavy personal sacrifice.

6. As I see there have been criticisms in the American papers of our troops having been kept out of the battle, I take this occasion to assure you that they stand absolutely ready at all times to obey General Eisenhower's commands. I believe that the dispositions which he and Field-Marshal Montgomery under him have made are entirely in accordance with strict military requirements, both as regards the employment of troops in counter-attack and their lateral movement, having regard to criss-cross communications. I have not found a trace of discord at the British and American headquarters ; but, Mr. President, there is this brute fact: we need more fighting troops to make things move.

7. I have a feeling this is a time for an intense new impulse, both of friendship and exertion, to be drawn from our bosoms and to the last scrap of our resources. Do not hesitate to tell me of anything you think we can do.

*   *   *

At this time Eisenhower and his staff were of course acutely anxious to know whether the Russians could do anything from their side to take off some of the pressure against us in the West. All efforts through the liaison officers in Moscow had failed to obtain any reply from their opposite numbers. In order to put the case to the Soviet Chiefs of Staff in the most effective manner Eisenhower had sent his Deputy, Air Marshal Tedder, with a special mission. They were considerably delayed by the weather. As soon as I heard of this I said to Eisenhower, 'You may find many delays on the staff level, but I expect Stalin would tell me if I asked him. Shall I try?' He asked me to do so, and I therefore sent the following message:

Prime Minister to Marshal Stalin   6 Jan 45
The battle in the West is very heavy, and at any time large decisions may be called for from the Supreme Command. You know yourself from your own experience how very anxious the position is when a very broad front has to be defended after the temporary loss of the initiative. It is Eisenhower's great desire and need to know in outline what you plan to do, as this obviously affects all his and our major decisions. Our envoy, Air Chief Marshal Tedder, was last night reported weather-bound in Cairo. His journey has been much delayed through no fault of yours. In case he has not reached you yet I shall be grateful if you can tell me whether we can count on a major Russian offensive on the Vistula front, or elsewhere, during January, with any other points you may care to mention. I shall not pass this most secret information to anyone except Field-Marshal Brooke and General Eisenhower, and only under conditions of the utmost secrecy. I regard the matter as urgent.

When one considers how serious was the decision asked for, and how many people were involved, it is remarkable that the answer should have been sent me the very next day.

Marshal Stalin to Prime Minister   7 Jan 45
I received your message of January 6, 1945, on the evening of January 7.
Unfortunately Air Marshal Tedder has not yet arrived in Moscow.
It is most important that we should be able to take advantage of our supremacy over the Germans in artillery and in the air. This demands clear flying weather and an absence of low mists, which hinder aimed artillery fire. We are preparing an offensive, but the weather is at present unfavourable. Never-

theless, taking into account the position of our Allies on the Western Front, G.H.Q. of the Supreme Command has decided to accelerate the completion of our preparation, and, regardless of the weather, to commence large-scale offensive operations against the Germans along the whole Central Front not later than the second half of January. You may rest assured that we shall do everything possible to render assistance to the glorious forces of our Allies.

Prime Minister to Marshal Stalin   9 Jan 45
I am most grateful to you for your thrilling message. I have sent it over to General Eisenhower for his eyes only. May all good fortune rest upon your noble venture.
2. The battle in the West goes not too badly. There is a good chance of the Huns being crushed out of their salient with very heavy losses. It is preponderantly an American battle, and their troops have fought splendidly, with heavy losses. We are both shoving everything in we can. The news you give me will be a great encouragement to General Eisenhower, because it gives him the assurance that the German reinforcements will have to be split between both our flaming fronts. The battle in the West will be continuous, according to the generals responsible for fighting it.

I quote this interchange as a good example of the speed at which business could be done at the summit of the Alliance, and also because it was a fine deed of the Russians and their chief to hasten their vast offensive, no doubt at a heavy cost in life. Eisenhower was very pleased indeed at the news I was able to send him. He asked however for any reinforcements that could be sent. Nearly three weeks beforehand the country had been told that another 250,000 men would be found to nourish and sustain troops in contact with the enemy, and that for the first time in our long struggle the British Government proposed to use its powers to compel the women of our fighting services to serve abroad. Not much compulsion was needed. The keenest zeal prevailed. But these drastic measures took time to mature, and although we could make good our autumn losses in the field and keep up a full supply of material, we had little left in hand. The Americans for their part, in addition to 60,000 infantry reinforcements, prepared to send nine fresh divisions from the United States.

*   *   *

From the north two American corps, with the XXXth British on their western flank, pressed down upon the enemy. On January 7 they crossed the Laroche–Vielsalm road, an important escape route for the Germans. Struggling through snowstorms the two wings of the Allied attack slowly drew closer, until they met at Houffalize on January 16. The Germans were forced steadily eastwards and harassed continually from the air, until by the end of the month they were back behind their frontier with nothing to show for their supreme effort except ruinous losses of material and casualties amounting to a hundred and twenty thousand men.

One awkward situation during the battle must be recorded, although happily it did not affect the issue. In order to release divisions from the Third Army Eisenhower had ordered Devers's Sixth Army Group to take over part of Patton's front and authorised, if necessary, a withdrawal from the Rhine to the Vosges. This meant leaving Strasbourg open to the enemy. There was understandable consternation in French political and military circles. What vengeance would fall upon the citizens of Strasbourg, who had rallied so passionately to their deliverers! I chanced to be at Eisenhower's headquarters at St. Germains at this juncture, and he and Bedell Smith listened attentively to my appeal. The enemy did indeed spring into action on the Army Group's front, especially in the Colmar pocket, but were repulsed. Eisenhower cancelled his instructions, and the military necessity which might have made the evacuation of Strasbourg imperative never arose. De Gaulle expressed his gratitude.

This was the enemy's final offensive of the war. At the time it caused us no little anxiety. Our own advance had to be postponed, but we benefited in the end. The Germans could not replace their losses, and our subsequent battles on the Rhine, though severe, were undoubtedly eased. The German High Command, and even Hitler, must have been disillusioned. Taken by surprise, Eisenhower and his commanders acted swiftly, but they will agree that the major credit lies elsewhere. In Montgomery's words, 'The Battle of the Ardennes was won primarily by the staunch fighting qualities of the American soldier.'*

For my own part, I will quote from a speech I made to the House of Commons on January 18:

'I have seen it suggested that the terrific battle which has been proceeding since December 16 on the American front is an

* *Normandy to the Baltic*, Field-Marshal Montgomery, p. 181.

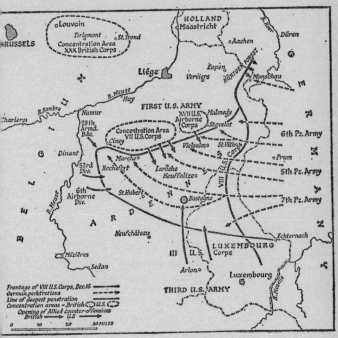

Rundstedt's Counter-Offensive

Anglo-American battle. In fact however the United States troops have done almost all the fighting, and have suffered almost all the losses. ... I never hesitate ... to stand up for our own soldiers when their achievements have been cold-should-ered or neglected or overshadowed, as they sometimes are ; but we must not forget that it is to American homes that the tele-grams of personal losses and anxiety have been going during the past month. ... According to the professional advice which I have at my disposal, what was done to meet von Rundstedt's counter-stroke was resolute, wise, and militarily correct. A gap was torn open, as a gap can always be in a line hundreds of miles long. General Eisenhower at once gave the command to the north of the gap to Field-Marshal Montgomery, and to the south of it to General Omar Bradley. . . . In the result both these highly skilled commanders handled the very large forces at their disposal in a manner which I think I may say without exaggeration may become the model for military students in the future. . . .'

British Intervention in Greece

*efore leaving Italy at the end of August I had asked the Chief
*f the Imperial General Staff to work out the details of a
*ritish expedition to Greece in case the Germans there col-
psed. We gave it the code-name 'Manna'. Its planning was
omplicated by our strained resources and the uncertainty of
*iermany's strategic position in the Balkans, but I directed that
*ur forces should be ready to act by September 11, and that the
*ireek Prime Minister and representatives of the Greek Govern-
*nent in Italy should be prepared to enter Athens without delay.
*y the end of the first week of September they were installed in
*villa near Caserta. Here Papandreou set to work with his new
*.A.M. colleagues.† It was essential that there should be no
*olitical vacuum in Greece. As I minuted on August 29, 'It is
*nost desirable to strike out of the blue without any preliminary
*risis. It is the best way to forestall the E.A.M.' The essence of
*he plan was to occupy Athens and its airfield with a parachute

---

* See Chapter 7.
† E.A.M., the Greek 'National Liberation Front'.

brigade, bring in four squadrons of fighter aircraft, clear Piræ harbour for further reinforcements from Egypt, and ensure th early arrival of the Greek Ministers. We would then hasten relief supplies and bring over the Greek Brigade from Italy.

German delay in quitting Athens forced us to modify o project. The garrison of ten thousand men showed no sign moving, and on September 13 I telegraphed to General Wilsc instructing him to prepare a preliminary descent in the Pelopo nese, where the Germans were withdrawing northwards to th Corinth area. As from midnight September 13–14 the troo for 'Manna' were placed at forty-eight hours' notice. They we commanded by General Scobie, and consisted initially of th 2nd Parachute Brigade from Italy, the 23rd Armoured Brigad acting as infantry, administrative troops from Egypt, and wha ever Greek forces were at the disposal of their recognise Government. The 15th Cruiser Squadron, with minesweepir flotillas, and four British and three Greek air squadrons, t gether with United States transport aircraft, were to sustain th expedition.

The tardy German withdrawal from Athens enabled us ho ever to consolidate the direction of Greek affairs on the eve the decisive stroke. I was glad that the Greek Government wa now at hand in Italy. At the end of September General Wilsc summoned Saraphis, the E.L.A.S. general,* and his Nationali rival Zervas to meet Papandreou at Caserta. Mr. Macmillan, Minister Resident in the Mediterranean, together with M Leeper, our Ambassador to the Greek Government, were preser to advise and direct the political side of this important con ference, which had to create a unified command of all Gree forces available in Italy and inside Greece, together with th British forces now poised for the landing.

A comprehensive agreement was signed on September 26. laid down that all guerrilla forces in the country should plac themselves under the orders of the Greek Government, who their turn put them under the command of General Scobie The Greek guerrilla leaders declared that none of their me would take the law into their own hands. Any action in Ather would be taken only on the direct orders of the British con mander. This document, known as the Caserta Agreemen governed our future action.

* E.L.A.S., the Greek 'People's National Army of Liberation'. (Both E.A.M. an E.L.A.S. were Communist-controlled.)

The liberation did not begin until October. Commando units were then sent into Southern Greece, and in the early hours of October 4 our troops occupied Patras. This was our first foothold since the tragic exit of 1941. The troops then worked their way along the southern shores of the Gulf of Corinth. On October 12 General Wilson learnt that the Germans were evacuating Athens, and next day British parachutists landed on the Megara airfield, about eight miles west of the capital. On the 14th the rest of the paratroopers arrived, and occupied the city on the heels of the German withdrawal. Our naval forces entered the Piræus, bringing with them General Scobie and the main part of his force, and two days later the Greek Government arrived, together with our Ambassador.

*   *   *

The testing time for our arrangements had now come. At the Moscow conference I had obtained Russian abstention at a heavy price. We were pledged to support Papandreou's Provisional Administration, in which E.A.M. was fully represented. All parties were bound by the Caserta Agreement, and we wished to hand over authority to a stable Greek Government without loss of time. But Greece was in ruins. The Germans destroyed roads and railways as they withdrew northwards. Our Air Force harassed them as they went, but on land we could do little to interfere. E.L.A.S. armed bands filled the gap left by the departing invaders, and their central command made little effort to enforce the solemn promises which had been given. Everywhere was want and dissension. Finances were disordered and food exhausted. Our own military resources were stretched to the limit.

At the end of the month Mr. Eden visited Athens on his way home from Moscow, and received a tumultuous welcome in memory of his efforts for Greece in 1941. With him were Lord Moyne the Minister Resident in Cairo, and Mr. Macmillan. The whole question of relief was discussed and everything humanly possible was done. Our troops willingly went on half-rations to increase the food supplies, and British sappers started to build emergency communications. By November 1 the Germans had evacuated Salonika and Florina, and ten days later the last of their forces had crossed the northern frontier. Apart from a few isolated island garrisons, Greece was free.

But the Government in Athens had not enough troops to

control the country and compel E.L.A.S. to observe the Casert
Agreement. Disorder grew and spread. On November 7
minuted to the Foreign Secretary:

Prime Minister to Foreign Secretary   7 Nov 4
   In my opinion, having paid the price we have to Russia fo
freedom of action in Greece, we should not hesitate to us
British troops to support the Royal Hellenic Governmer
under M. Papandreou.
   2. This implies that British troops should certainly inter
vene to check acts of lawlessness. Surely M. Papandreou ca
close down E.A.M. newspapers if they call a newspaper strik
   3. I hope the Greek Brigade will soon arrive, and will no
hesitate to shoot when necessary. Why is only one India
brigade of the Indian Division to be sent in? We need anothe
eight or ten thousand foot-soldiers to hold the capital an
Salonika for the present Government. Later on we mus
consider extending the Greek authority. I fully expect a clas
with E.A.M., and we must not shrink from it, provided th
ground is well chosen.

And the following day:

Prime Minister to General Wilson (Italy) and   8 Nov 4
Mr. Leeper (Athens)
   In view of increasing threat of Communist elements i
Greece and indications that they plan to seize power by force
I hope that you will consider reinforcing our troops in Athen
area by immediate dispatch of the 3rd Brigade of 4th India
Division or some other formation. . . .

                    *   *   *

A revolt by E.A.M. was imminent, and on November 1
General Scobie was directed to make counter-preparations
Athens was to be declared a military area, and authority wa
given to order all E.L.A.S. troops to leave it. The 4th India
Division was sent from Italy to Salonika, Athens, and Patra
The Greek Brigade also came from Italy, and became the centr
of controversy between Papandreou and his E.A.M. colleague
The only chance of averting civil war was to disarm the guerri
las and other forces by mutual agreement and establish a ne
National Army and police force under the direct control of th
Government in Athens. Arrangements were made to raise an
equip National Guard battalions, each 500 strong. Ultimate
there were thirty of these; they proved very useful in roundin

armed hostile civilians and guarding areas cleared by our
troops.

A draft decree for the demobilisation of the guerrillas, drawn
up at M. Papandreou's request by the E.A.M. Ministers themselves, was presented to the distracted Cabinet. The regular
Greek Mountain Brigade and the Sacred Squadron were to
remain. E.L.A.S were to keep a brigade of their own, and
E.D.E.S.* were to be given a small force. But at the last moment
the E.A.M. Ministers went back on their own proposals, on
which they had wasted a precious week, and demanded that the
Mountain Brigade should be disbanded. The Communist tactic
was now in full swing. On December 1 the six Ministers associated with E.A.M. resigned, and a general strike in Athens was
proclaimed for the following day. The rest of the Cabinet passed
a decree dissolving the guerrillas, and the Communist Party
moved its headquarters from the capital. General Scobie issued
a message to the people of Greece stating that he stood firm
behind the present constitutional Government 'until the Greek
State can be established with a legally armed force and free
elections can be held'. I issued a similar personal statement from
London.

On Sunday, December 3, Communist supporters, engaging in
a banned demonstration, collided with the police and civil war
began. The next day General Scobie ordered E.L.A.S. to
evacuate Athens and the Piræus forthwith. Instead their troops
and armed civilians tried to seize the capital by force.

At this moment I took a more direct control of the affair. On
learning that the Communists had already captured almost all
the police stations in Athens, murdering the bulk of their occu-
pants not already pledged to their attack, and were within half a
mile of the Government offices, I ordered General Scobie and
his 5,000 British troops, who ten days before had been received
with rapture as deliverers by the population, to intervene and
fire upon the treacherous aggressors. It is no use doing things like
this by halves. The mob violence by which the Communists
sought to conquer the city and present themselves to the world
as the Government demanded by the Greek people could only
be met by firearms. There was no time for the Cabinet to be
called.

Anthony and I were together till about two o'clock, and were
entirely agreed that we must open fire. Seeing how tired he was,

* E.D.E.S., the 'Greek National Democratic Army'.

I said to him, 'If you like to go to bed, leave it to me.' He did, a
at about 3 a.m. I drafted the following telegram:

> *Prime Minister to General Scobie (Athens).*   5 Dec
> *Repeated to General Wilson (Italy)**
>
> I have given instructions to General Wilson to make su
> that all forces are left with you and all possible reinforceme
> are sent to you.
>
> 2. You are responsible for maintaining order in Athens a
> for neutralising or destroying all E.A.M.-E.L.A.S. ban
> approaching the city. You may make any regulations you li
> for the strict control of the streets or for the rounding up
> any number of truculent persons. Naturally E.L.A.S. will try
> put women and children in the van where shooting may occ
> You must be clever about this and avoid mistakes. But do r
> hesitate to fire at any armed male in Athens who assails t
> British authority or Greek authority with which we are wor
> ing. It would be well of course if your command were re
> forced by the authority of some Greek Government, a
> Papandreou is being told by Leeper to stop and help. *Do n*
> *however hesitate to act as if you were in a conquered c*
> *where a local rebellion is in progress.*†
>
> 3. With regard to E.L.A.S. bands approaching from the o
> side, you should surely be able with your armour to give son
> of these a lesson which will make others unlikely to try. Y
> may count upon my support in all reasonable and sensil
> action taken on this basis. *We have to hold and domino*
> *Athens. It would be a great thing for you to succeed in th*
> *without bloodshed if possible, but also with bloodshed*
> *necessary.*

This telegram was dispatched at 4.50 a.m. on the 5th. I m
admit that it was somewhat strident in tone. I felt it so necessa
to give a strong lead to the military commander that I inte
tionally worded it in the sharpest terms. The fact that he ha
such an order in his possession would not only encourage hi
to decisive action, but gave him the certain assurance that
should be with him in any well-conceived action he might tak
whatever the consequences might be. I felt grave concern abo
the whole business, but I was sure that there should be no roo
for doubts or hedging. I had in my mind Arthur Balfou
celebrated telegram in the eighties to the British authorities
Ireland: 'Don't hesitate to shoot.' This was sent through t

---

* The Command had not yet changed hands.
† Author's subsequent italics throughout.

en telegraph offices. There was a furious storm about it in the
⸽use of Commons of those days, but it certainly prevented loss
⸽ life. It was one of the key stepping-stones by which Balfour
⸽vanced to power and control. The setting of the scene was
⸽w entirely different. Nevertheless 'Don't hesitate to shoot'
⸽ng in my mind as a prompter from those far-off days.

Later that day I telegraphed to our Ambassador:

Prime Minister to Mr. Leeper (*Athens*)   5 Dec 44

This is no time to dabble in Greek politics or to imagine that
Greek politicians of varying shades can affect the situation.
You should not worry about Greek Government compositions.
The matter is one of life and death.

2. You must urge Papandreou to stand to his duty, and
assure him he will be supported by all our forces if he does so.
The day has long gone past when any particular group of
Greek politicians can influence this mob rising. His only
chance is to come through with us.

3. I have put the whole question of the defence of Athens
and the maintenance of law and order in the hands of General
Scobie, and have assured him that he will be supported in the
use of whatever force is necessary. Henceforward you and
Papandreou will conform to his directions in all matters
affecting public order and security. You should both support
Scobie in every possible way, and you should suggest to him
any means which occur to you of making his action more
vigorous and decisive.

Every good wish.

*   *   *

E.L.A.S. had quickly gained control of most of Athens, except
⸽ly its very centre, where our troops first held them and then
⸽gan to counter-attack. Scobie reported:

8 Dec 44

Increased activities on the part of the rebels and widespread sniping limited progress during the fighting, which
continued throughout yesterday. By midday the total of rebel
prisoners under military guard was 35 officers, 524 other ranks.
These figures do not include those held by the police, as it is
difficult to obtain accurate figures for them.

Some progress was made by the 23rd Brigade in house-to-
house clearing throughout the afternoon. A further sector in
the centre of the city was cleared by the Parachute Brigade.

Marine reinforcements had to be landed from H.M.S. *Orion*
to deal with serious sniping of Navy House, Piræus, by rebels
who infiltrated into the area south of Port Leontos. In face of

strong opposition our troops were forced to withdraw in o
area.

In the area being cleared by the Greek Mountain Briga
an attack was made by the rebels from the flank. The atta
was held, but delayed progress of the brigade.

This showed the scale of the fighting on which we had nc
embarked.

Prime Minister to General Wilson (Italy)   9 Dec
You should send further reinforcements to Athens witho
the slightest delay. The prolongation of the fight has ma
dangers. I warned you of the paramount political importan
of this conflict. At least two more brigades should hurry to tl
scene.

2. In addition to the above, why does not the Navy help a
the time instead of only landing a small number in a crisi
You guaranteed most strongly that you had already se
enough soldiers.

Prime Minister to General Scobie   8 Dec
There is much talk in the Press to-night of a peace offer
E.L.A.S. Naturally we should be glad to have this matt
settled, but you should make quite sure, so far as your influen
goes, that we do not give away for the sake of kindness wh
has been won or can still be won by our troops. It would see
that anything less satisfactory than the terms agreed up
before the revolt took place should not be accepted. Also it
difficult to see how E.A.M. leaders, with their hands wet wi
Greek and British blood, should resume their places in tl
Cabinet. This might however be got over. The great thing
to proceed with caution and to consult us upon the term
when they are made. The clear objective is the defeat
E.A.M. The ending of the fighting is subsidiary to this. I a
ordering large reinforcements to come to Athens, and Fiel
Marshal Alexander will probably be with you in a few day
Firmness and sobriety are what are needed now, and n
eager embraces, while the real quarrel is unsettled.

Keep us informed before any compromise is settled in whi
you or Leeper are concerned.

Rumours were spread by Communists and their like in Lo
don that British troops were in sympathy with E.A.M. The
was no truth in them.

On the peace offer the answer was:

General Scobie to Prime Minister   10 Dec
We would at once inform you should any peace offer

made by E.L.A.S., but neither the Ambassador nor I know of any such approach.

I have clearly before me the main objective you mention. While any one party is able to back its views with a private army Greece can never achieve peace and stability. Fighting may, I hope, be restricted to Athens-Piræus, but I am ready to see it through in the rest of the country if necessary. It is a pity that tear gas may not be used. It would be of great help in this city fighting.

Your assurance that large reinforcements are being sent is most welcome. I have been informed by Allied Force Head-quarters that the 4th Division is being dispatched early.

* * *

Now that the free world has learnt so much more than was ~~be~~en understood about the Communist movement in Greece ~~a~~nd elsewhere, many readers will be astonished at the vehement ~~a~~ttacks to which His Majesty's Government, and I in particular ~~a~~t its head, were subjected. The vast majority of the American ~~p~~ress violently condemned our action, which they declared ~~fa~~lsified the cause for which they had gone to war. If the editors ~~o~~f all these well-meaning organs will look back at what they ~~w~~rote then and compare it with what they think now they will, ~~I~~ am sure, be surprised. The State Department, in the charge of ~~M~~r. Stettinius, issued a markedly critical pronouncement, which ~~th~~ey in their turn were to regret, or at least reverse, in after-years. ~~In~~ England there was much perturbation. *The Times* and the *~~M~~anchester Guardian* pronounced their censures upon what they ~~co~~nsidered our reactionary policy. Stalin however adhered strict-~~ly~~ and faithfully to our agreement of October, and during all the ~~lo~~ng weeks of fighting the Communists in the streets of Athens ~~n~~ot one word of reproach came from *Pravda* or *Isvestia*.

In the House of Commons there was a great stir. I accepted ~~w~~illingly the challenge flung at us in an amendment moved by ~~S~~ir Richard Acland, the leader and sole member in Parliament ~~o~~f the Commonwealth Party, supported by Mr. Shinwell and ~~M~~r. Aneurin Bevan. There was a strong current of vague ~~o~~pinion, and even passion, of which these and other similar ~~fi~~gures felt themselves the exponents. Here again any Govern-~~m~~ent which had rested on a less solid foundation than the ~~N~~ational Coalition might well have been shaken to pieces. But ~~th~~e War Cabinet stood like a rock against which all the waves ~~a~~nd winds might beat in vain.

When we recall what has happened to Poland, to Hungar
and Czechoslovakia in these later years we may be grateful
Fortune for giving us at this critical moment the calm, unit
strength of determined leaders of all parties. Space does n
allow me to quote more than a few extracts from the speech
made on December 8 against the amendment to the Vote
Confidence which we had demanded.

Let me present to the House the charge which is ma
against us. It is that we are using His Majesty's forces to d
arm the friends of democracy in Greece and in other parts
Europe and to suppress those popular movements which ha
valorously assisted in the defeat of the enemy. Here is a pre
direct issue, and one on which the House will have to pr
nounce before we separate this evening. Certainly F
Majesty's Government would be unworthy of confidence
His Majesty's forces were being used by them to disarm t
friends of democracy.

The question however arises, and one may be permitted
dwell on it for a moment, who are the friends of democrac
and also how is the word 'democracy' to be interpreted? M
idea of it is that the plain, humble, common man, just t
ordinary man who keeps a wife and family, who goes off
fight for his country when it is in trouble, goes to the poll
the appropriate time, and puts his cross on the ballot-pap
showing the candidate he wishes to be elected to Parliament
that he is the foundation of democracy. And it is also essenti
to this foundation that this man or woman should do th
without fear, and without any form of intimidation
victimisation. He marks his ballot-paper in strict secrecy, a
then elected representatives meet and together decide wh
Government, or even, in times of stress, what form of gover
ment, they wish to have in their country. If that is democra
I salute it. I espouse it. I would work for it. ... I stand up
the foundation of free elections based on universal suffra
and that is what we consider the foundation for democrac
But I feel quite differently about a swindle democracy,
democracy which calls itself democracy because it is L
Wing. It takes all sorts to make democracy, not only L
Wing, or even Communist. I do not allow a party or a bo
to call themselves democrats because they are stretchi
farther and farther into the most extreme forms of revolutio
I do not accept a party as necessarily representing democra
because it becomes more violent as it becomes less numero

One must have some respect for democracy and not use t
word too lightly. The last thing which resembles democra

is mob law, with bands of gangsters, armed with deadly weapons, forcing their way into great cities, seizing the police stations and key points of government, endeavouring to introduce a totalitarian *régime* with an iron hand, and clamouring, as they can nowadays if they get the power— [*Interruption*.]

I am sorry to be causing so much distress. I have plenty of time, and if any outcries are wrung from hon. Members opposite I can always take a little longer over what I have to say, though I should regret to do so. I say that the last thing that represents democracy is mob law and the attempt to introduce a totalitarian *régime* which clamours to shoot everyone who is politically inconvenient as part of a purge of those who are said to have collaborated with the Germans during the occupation. Do not let us rate democracy so low, do not let us rate democracy as if it were merely grabbing power and shooting those who do not agree with you. That is the antithesis of democracy.

Democracy is not based on violence or terrorism, but on reason, on fair play, on freedom, on respecting the rights of other people. Democracy is no harlot to be picked up in the street by a man with a tommy gun. I trust the people, the mass of the people, in almost any country, but I like to make sure that it is the people and not a gang of bandits who think that by violence they can overturn constituted authority, in some cases ancient Parliaments, Governments, and States. . . .

We march along an onerous and painful path. Poor old England! (Perhaps I ought to say 'Poor old Britain!') We have to assume the burden of the most thankless tasks, and in undertaking them to be scoffed at, criticised, and opposed from every quarter ; but at least we know where we are making for, know the end of the road, know what is our objective. It is that these countries shall be freed from the German armed power, and under conditions of normal tranquillity shall have a free universal vote to decide the Government of their country—except a Fascist *régime*—and whether that Government shall be of the Left or of the Right.

There is our aim—and we are told that we seek to disarm the friends of democracy. We are told that because we do not allow gangs of heavily armed guerrillas to descend from the mountains and install themselves, with all the bloody terror and vigour of which they are capable, in power in great capitals, we are traitors to democracy. I repulse that claim too. I shall call upon the House as a matter of confidence in His Majesty's Government, and of confidence in the spirit with which we have marched from one peril to another till victory is in sight, to reject such pretensions with the scorn that they deserve. . . .

If I am blamed for this action I will gladly accept my dismissal at the hands of the House; but if I am not so dismissed—make no mistake about it—we shall persist in the policy of clearing Athens and the Athens region of all who are rebels against the authority of the constitutional Government of Greece—of mutineers against the orders of the Supreme Commander in the Mediterranean under whom all the guerrillas have undertaken to serve. I hope I have made the position clear, both generally as it affects the world and the war and as it affects the Government.

Only thirty members faced us in the division lobby. Nearly three hundred voted confidence. Here again was a moment in which the House of Commons showed its enduring strength and authority.

I telegraphed the following:

Prime Minister to Mr. Leeper (*Athens*)　　　　　　9 Dec 4
　Do not be at all disquieted by criticisms made from various quarters in the House of Commons. No one knows better than I the difficulties you have had to contend with. I do not yield to passing clamour, and will always stand with those who execute their instructions with courage and precision. In Athens as everywhere else our maxim is 'No peace without victory'.

*　　　*　　　*

There is no doubt that the emotional expression of American opinion and the train of thought at that time being followed by the State Department affected President Roosevelt and his immediate circle. The sentiments I had expressed in the House of Commons have now become commonplaces of American doctrine and policy and command the assent of the United Nations. But in those days they had an air of novelty which was startling to those who were governed by impressions of the past and did not feel the onset of the new adverse tide in human affairs. In the main the President was with me, and Hopkins sent me a friendly message about the speech.

Earl of Halifax to Prime Minister　　　　　　　　8 Dec 4
　Harry and Jim Forrestal have just telephoned enthusiastic approval of your speech on Greece, which they both think will have done immense good. I am sure they are right.

Prime Minister to Mr. Harry Hopkins　　　　　　　9 Dec 4
　I am very glad you were pleased by my speech. I was much

upset by the last sentence of the Stettinius Press release,* which seemed to reflect on the whole of our foreign policy in Belgium, where we acted under your orders, and in Greece, where our action was fully approved at Quebec. Naturally the prolongation and severity of the fighting in Athens with E.L.A.S. causes me anxiety.

Every good wish.

And again the same day:

I hope you will tell our great friend that the establishment of law and order in and around Athens is essential to all future measures of magnanimity and consolation towards Greece. After this has been established will be the time for talking. My guiding principle is 'No peace without victory'. It is a great disappointment to me to have been set upon in this way by E.L.A.S. when we came loaded with good gifts and anxious only to form a united Greece which could establish its own destiny. But we have been set upon, and we intend to defend ourselves. I consider we have a right to the President's support in the policy we are following. If it can be said in the streets of Athens that the United States are against us, then more British blood will be shed and much more Greek. It grieves me very much to see signs of our drifting apart at a time when unity becomes ever more important, as danger recedes and faction arises.

2. For you personally. Do not be misled by our majority yesterday. I could have had another eighty by sending out a three-line whip instead of only two. On Fridays, with the bad communications prevailing here, Members long to get away for the week-end. Who would not?

Every good wish.

British troops were still fighting hard in the centre of Athens, hemmed in and outnumbered. We were engaged in house-to-house combat with an enemy at least four-fifths of whom were in plain clothes. Unlike many of the Allied newspaper correspondents in Athens, our troops had no difficulty in understanding the issues involved.

---

*This was dated December 5, and ran as follows:
'The Department of State has received a number of inquiries from correspondents in regard to the position of this Government concerning the recent Cabinet crisis in Italy.
'The position of this Government has been consistently that the composition of the Italian Government is purely an Italian affair, except in the case of appointments where important military factors are concerned. This Government has not in any way intimated to the Italian Government that there would be any opposition on its part to Count Sforza. Since Italy is an area of combined responsibility, we have reaffirmed to both the British and Italian Governments that we expect the Italians to work out their problems of Government along democratic lines without influence from outside. *This policy would apply to an ever more pronounced degree with regard to Governments of the United Nations in their liberated territories.*

Papandreou and his remaining Ministers had lost all authority. Previous proposals to set up a Regency under the Archbishop Damaskinos had been rejected by the King, but on December 10 Mr. Leeper revived the idea. King George however was against it, and we were reluctant at the time to press him.

Amid these tumults Field-Marshal Alexander and Mr. Macmillan arrived in Athens. We received the first reports of their mission on December 11. Our plight was worse than we had expected. Alexander telegraphed, 'The British forces are in fact beleaguered in the heart of the city.' The road to the airfield was not secure. We were not in control of Piræus harbour, so no ships could be unloaded there. Only six days' rations and three days' reserve of ammunition were left for the troops fighting in the city. Alexander proposed to clear the port and the road to Athens at once, bring in immediate reinforcement from Italy, and build up supply dumps, and, 'having linked up securely both ends of the dumb-bell, to undertake the necessary operations to clear the whole of Athens and Piræus'. He also pressed Leeper's proposal to appoint the Archbishop as Regent and asked for stern measures against the rebels and permission to bomb areas inside Athens.

On December 12 the War Cabinet gave Alexander a free hand in all military measures. The 4th British Division, on passage from Italy to Egypt, was diverted, and their arrival during the latter half of the month turned the scale. I told Alexander that the Greek King would not agree to the plan for a Regency. The suggestion that the Archbishop should be called upon to form a Government satisfied no one. The political reaction at home to these events showed a clearer and calmer view.

*   *   *

At this moment an astonishing leakage of official secrets occurred. The reader will remember my telegram to General Scobie dispatched at 4.50 a.m. on December 5. This had been marked 'Personal and Top Secret From Prime Minister to General Scobie. Repeated to General Wilson', and of course was in cipher. A few days later an American columnist was able to publish practically an exact copy of it. All our communications were menaced thereby.

I learned on inquiry that all messages sent through General Wilson's Supreme Headquarters in Italy were communicated everal personages, including the American Ambassador in Rome, unless they bore a special restrictive marking. On reading the text of my message sent before dawn on the 5th to General Scobie the Ambassador repeated its substance to the State Department. He was fully within his rights in doing this. What happened after his paraphrase reached the State Department has never been discovered, or at any rate made known, but on the 11th the American journalist made public what might well have been, at that time, an awkward bombshell. It happened that the next day the Trades Union Congress was to meet in London. There was naturally much anxiety about our policy in Greece and Left Wing forces were astir. It seemed probable that the publication of the drastic terms of my message to General Scobie would produce a bad impression. However, the matter was not mentioned at the Trades Union Congress, nor indeed did it attract any attention in Parliament. Mr. Bevin represented the War Cabinet at the Congress, and with characteristic loyalty and courage he defended and vindicated our policy in Greece. He carried the whole conference with him, and by an overwhelming majority the trade unions gave their support to the Government and proved once again their stable and responsible qualities in great matters.

*   *   *

I had meanwhile received a most kindly worded telegram from the President.

President Roosevelt to Prime Minister   13 Dec 44

I have been as deeply concerned as you have yourself in regard to the tragic difficulties you have encountered in Greece. I appreciate to the full the anxious and difficult alternatives with which you have been faced. I regard my *rôle* in this matter as that of a loyal friend and ally whose one desire is to be of any help possible in the circumstances. You may be sure that in putting my thoughts before you I am constantly guided by the fact that nothing can in any way shake the unity and association between out two countries in the great tasks to which we have set our hands.

As anxious as I am to be of the greatest help to you in this trying situation, there are limitations, imposed in part by the traditional policies of the United States and in part by the mounting adverse reaction of public opinion in this country. No one will understand better than yourself that I, both personally and as Head of State, am necessarily responsive to

the state of public feeling. It is for these reasons that it has
not been possible for this Government to take a stand along
with you in the present course of events in Greece. Even an
attempt to do so would bring only temporary value to you
and would in the long run do injury to our basic relationships
I don't need to tell you how much I dislike this state of affairs
as between you and me. My one hope is to see it rectified so
that we can go along, in this as in everything, shoulder to
shoulder. I know that you, as the one on whom the responsibility rests, desire with all your heart a satisfactory solution of
the Greek problem, and particularly one that will bring peace
to that ravished country. I will be with you wholeheartedly
in any solution which takes into consideration the factors I
have mentioned above. With this in mind I am giving you at
random some thoughts that have come to me in my anxious
desire to be of help.

I know that you have sent Macmillan there with broad
powers to find such a solution, and it may be that he will have
been successful before you get this. I of course lack full details
and am at a great distance from the scene, but it has seemed
to me that a basic reason—or excuse perhaps—for the E.A.M.
attitude has been distrust regarding the intentions of King
George II. I wonder if Macmillan's efforts might not be greatly
facilitated if the King himself would approve the establishment of a Regency in Greece and would make a public
declaration of his intention not to return unless called for by
popular plebiscite. This might be particularly effective if
accompanied by an assurance that elections will be held at
some fixed date, no matter how far in the future, when the
people would have full opportunity to express themselves.

Meanwhile might it not be possible to secure general agreement on the disarmament and dissolution of all the armed
groups now in the country, including the Mountain Brigade
and the Sacred Squadron, leaving your troops to preserve law
and order alone until the Greek national forces can be
reconstituted on a non-partisan basis and be adequately
equipped?

I shall be turning over in my mind this whole question, and
hope you will share your thoughts and worries with me.

This however did not give me any practical help. I replied:

14 Dec 44
I will send you over the week-end a considered answer to
your telegram, for the kindly tone of which I thank you. I
hope that the British reinforcements now coming steadily into
Attica may make a more healthy situation in Athens. You will

realise how very serious it would be if we withdrew, as we easily could, and the result was a frightful massacre, and an extreme Left Wing *régime* under Communist inspiration installed itself, as it would, in Athens. My Cabinet colleagues here of all parties are not prepared to act in a manner so dishonourable to our record and name. Ernest Bevin's speech to the Labour conference won universal respect. Stern fighting lies ahead, and even danger to our troops in the centre of Athens. The fact that you are supposed to be against us, in accordance with the last sentence of Stettinius's Press release, has added, as I feared, to our difficulties and burdens. I think it probable that I shall broadcast to the world on Sunday night and make manifest the purity and disinterestedness of our motives throughout, and also of our resolves.

2. Meanwhile I send you a letter I have received from the King of Greece, to whom we have suggested the policy of making Archbishop of Athens Regent. The King refuses to allow this. Therefore an act of constitutional violence will be entailed if we finally decide upon this course. I know nothing of the Archbishop, except that our people on the spot think he might stop a gap or bridge a gully.

* * *

It was a pleasure to hear at the same time from one on whose udgment and instinct in such matters I relied.

Field-Marshal Smuts to Prime Minister   14 Dec 44

I am very distressed at the anxiety and trouble which the situation in Greece is causing you and the Cabinet. I spoke strongly yesterday at Port Elizabeth in favour of policy pursued by the United Kingdom Government. I hope my comments have been conveyed by cable in condensed form. We may, I fear, find, if private Partisan armies and underground movements are kept alive, the peace degenerating in civil convulsions and anarchy not only in Greece but elsewhere also in Europe. . . . I hope that it is possible for the Archbishop to act with greater decision and authority. At this stage firmness is in any case essential, and weakness in dealing with the Partisans may end in real civil war at a later, more inconvenient, stage.

To be frank, I dislike our Ambassador taking this important *rôle* in change of Greek Government, as it may later be used as an argument against you for undue interference in the affairs of Greece. My own view, for what it is worth, is that after the suppression of the E.A.M. revolt the Greek King should return to discharge his proper constitutional functions, and the onus of practically running Greece should no longer be borne by His Majesty's Government.

I also received from the Greek 3rd Mountain Brigade, which had been fighting loyally with us, a message of thanks for our efforts to protect their country and of grief because British blood was being shed. They asked me to become their Honorary Commander.

But from Harry Hopkins came another warning.

Public opinion here is deteriorating rapidly because of Greek situation and your statement in Parliament about the United States and Poland.

With the battle joined as it is in Europe and Asia, with every energy required on everyone's part to defeat the enemy, I confess I find myself greatly disturbed at the diplomatic turn of events, which throw into the public gaze our several difficulties.

I do not know what the President or Stettinius may have to say publicly, but it may well be that one or both of them must state in unequivocal terms our determination to do all that we can to seek a free and secure world.

We were all agreed on this aim, but the question was whether it could be achieved by allowing the Communists to seize all power in Athens. That was the issue at stake.

Prime Minister to Mr. Harry Hopkins   17 Dec 44

I am distressed and puzzled by your message. I hope you will not hesitate to telegraph me on any points on which you think we, or I personally, have been in error, and what you would advise, because I have great trust in your judgment and friendship, even if I may at times look at matters from a different angle. All the President's telegrams to me have been most kind and encouraging, and also his telegram to U.J. may do a world of good.

2. Naturally I should welcome any public statements in America which set forth the aims stated in your last sentence. These are also ours. We seek nothing for ourselves from this struggle.

I also sent my promised reply to the President.

Prime Minister to President Roosevelt   17 Dec 44

About Greece. The present position is that our representatives on the spot, Macmillan and Leeper, have strongly recommended the appointment of the Archbishop as Regent. This is obnoxious to the Papandreou Government, though they might be persuaded to advocate a Regency of three, namely, the Archbishop, General Plastiras, and Dragoumis. There is suspicion that the Archbishop is ambitious of obtaining chief political power, and that, supported by E.A.M., he will use it ruthlessly against existing Ministers. Whether this be true or not I cannot say. The facts are changing from hour to hour. I do not feel at all sure that in setting up a one-man Regency we might not be imposing a dictatorship on Greece.

2. There is also to be considered the fact that the King refuses, I think inflexibly, to appoint a Regency, certainly not a one-man Regency of the Archbishop, whom he distrusts and fears. According to the Greek constitution, the Crown Prince is Regent in the absence of the King. The King also states that all his Ministers under Papandreou advise him against such a step, and that, as a constitutional monarch, he cannot be responsible for it.

3. The War Cabinet decided to await for three or four days the course of military operations. Our reinforcements are arriving rapidly, and the British General Staff Intelligence says that there are not more than twelve thousand E.L.A.S. in Athens and the Piræus. The Greek King's estimate is fifteen to twenty-two thousand. Anyhow, we shall by the middle of next week be far superior in numbers. I am not prepared, as at present informed, to give way to unconstitutional violence in such circumstances.

4. Our immediate task is to secure control of Athens and the Piræus. According to the latest reports, E.L.A.S. may agree to depart. This will give us a firm basis from which to negotiate the best settlement possible between the warring Greek factions. It will certainly have to provide for the disarming of the guerrilla forces. The disarmament of the Greek Mountain Brigade, who took Rimini, and the Sacred Squadron, who have fought so well at the side of British and American troops, would seriously weaken our forces, and in any case we could not abandon them to massacre. They may however be removed elsewhere as part of a general settlement.

5. I am sure you would not wish us to cast down our painful and thankless task at this time. We embarked upon it with your full consent. We desire nothing from Greece but to do our duty by the common cause. In the midst of our task of bringing food and relief and maintaining the rudiments of order for a Government which has no armed forces we have become involved in a furious, though not as yet very bloody struggle. I have felt it much that you were unable to give a word of explanation for our action, but I understand your difficulties.

6. Meanwhile the Cabinet is united and the Socialist

Ministers approve Mr. Bevin's declarations at the Labour
conference, which on this matter endorsed the official plat
form by a majority of 2,455,000 votes to 137,000. I could a
any time obtain, I believe, a ten to one majority in the House
of Commons.

I am sure you will do whatever you can. I will keep you
constantly informed.

*   *   *

Mr. Mackenzie King in Canada also felt the unfavourabl
reactions to our Greek policy which had been so volubly ex
pressed in the United States. He revealed his embarrassments i
several telegrams.

Prime Minister to Prime Minister of Canada   15 Dec 4

In the House I have done my best to clarify our position. T
my mind the essential point is that, having obtained th
written assent of all parties, including the E.A.M., the Gree
Prime Minister invited British troops to enter Greece to kee
order and safeguard supplies. We accepted this invitation
and must still do our best to carry it out. The task is un
grateful, but we could not in honour shirk our responsibilities
With tempers inflamed on both sides in Athens, the situatio
is inevitably difficult. But the visit of Alexander was mos
valuable, and on the whole latest reports are more encourag
ing.

I also sent Mr. Mackenzie King the telegrams which I ha
exchanged with the President in August,* and drew his atten
tion to the Caserta Agreement, which by now had been mad
public. I told him that I had the verbal approval of Stalin to ou
entering Greece and liberating Athens. 'Although,' I concluded
'Communists are at the root of the business, Stalin has not so fa
made any public reflection on our action.'

In defence to these facts, arguments, and appeals, Mr. Mac
kenzie King refrained from any public act of dissociation.

It is odd, looking back on these events, now that some year
have passed, to see how completely the policy for which I an
my colleagues fought so stubbornly has been justified by events
Myself, I never had any doubts about it, for I saw quite plainl
that Communism would be the peril civilisation would have t
face after the defeat of Nazism and Fascism. It did not fall to u
to end the task in Greece. I little thought however at the end o
1944 that the State Department, supported by overwhelming

* Chapter 7, pp. 99–100.

merican opinion, would in little more than two years not only
lopt and carry on the course we had opened, but would make
hement and costly exertions, even of a military character, to
ing it to fruition. In his evidence before the House of Repre-
ntatives Foreign Affairs Committee, Mr. Dean Acheson, the
nited States Acting Secretary of State, is reported to have testi-
d on March 21, 1947, as follows: 'A Communist-dominated
overnment in Greece would be considered dangerous to
nited States security.'

If Greece has escaped the fate of Czechoslovakia and sur-
ves to-day as one of the free nations, it is due not only to
ritish action in 1944, but to the steadfast efforts of what was
resently to become the united strength of the English-speaking
orld.

CHAPTER 19

Christmas at Athens

In Athens the street-fighting swayed to and fro on an enlarging scale. On December 15 Field-Marshal Alexander warned me that it was most important to get a settlement quickly, and the best chance was through the Archbishop. 'Otherwise,' he telegraphed, 'I fear if rebel resistance continues at the same intensity as at present I shall handle to send further large reinforcements from the Italian front to make sure of clearing the whole of Piræus–Athens, which is fifty square miles of houses.'

> *Prime Minister to Field-Marshal Alexander (Italy)*   17 Dec 4
> The E.L.A.S. advance towards the centre of Athens seems to me a very serious feature, and I should like your appreciation of whether, with the reinforcements now arriving, we are likely to hold our own in the centre of the city and defeat the enemy. Have you any other reinforcements in view besides the 4th Division, the Tank Regiment, and the two remaining brigades of the 46th Division? Is there now any danger of a mass surrender of British troops cooped up in the city of Athens, followed by a massacre of Greeks who sided with us? The War Cabinet desire your report on the military situation in this respect.
> 2. We have no intention of subduing or occupying Greece

Our object is to afford a foundation upon which a broad-based Greek Government can function and raise a national force to preserve itself in Attica. After this we go, as we have no interests in Greece except those of sentiment and honour.

3. The King of Greece has refused categorically in a long and powerfully reasoned letter to appoint a Regent, and especially to appoint the Archbishop, of whom he has personal distrust. I have heard mixed accounts of the Archbishop, who is said to be very much in touch with E.A.M. and to have keen personal ambitions. We have not yet decided whether or in what way to overcome the King's resistance. If this cannot be overcome there will be no constitutional foundation other than an act of violence, to which we must become parties. The matter would be rendered more complicated if, as it may prove and as the King asserts, he is advised not to appoint a Regency by his Prime Minister and Government. In this case we should be punishing the King for obeying his constitutional oath and be ourselves setting up a dictator. The Cabinet have therefore decided to await further developments of the military situation before taking final and fateful decisions.

4. Personally I feel that our military predominance should be plainly established before we make terms, and in any case I should not like to make terms on grounds of weakness rather than of strength. Of course if you tell me it is impossible for us to be in control of Attica within a reasonable time the situation presents difficulties, but not such as should daunt us after all the others we have overcome.

And two days later:

Prime Minister to Field-Marshal Alexander (Italy)   19 Dec 44
    The Cabinet feel it better to let the military operations to clear Athens and Attica run for a while rather than embark all our fortunes on the character of the Archbishop. Have you looked up his full record? It is hard thing to ask me to throw over a constitutional King acting on the true advice of his Ministers, apart from British pressure, in order to install a dictator who may very likely become the champion of the extreme Left.

    We are waiting here till the scene clears a little more, after which we shall give all the necessary directions.

Alexander's reply was grave. He had now succeeded General Wilson in the Supreme Command.

Field-Marshal Alexander to Prime Minister   21 Dec 44
    In answer to your signal of December 19, I am most concerned that you should know exactly what true situation is

and what we can do and cannot do. This is my duty. You would know the strength of British forces in Greece, and what additions I can send from Italian front if forced by circumstances to do so.

Assuming that E.L.A.S. continue to fight, I estimate that it will be possible to clear the Athens–Piræus area and thereafter to hold it securely, but this will not defeat E.L.A.S. and force them to surrender. We are not strong enough to go beyond this and undertake operations on the Greek mainland. During the German occupation they maintained between six and seven divisions on the mainland, in addition to the equivalent of four in the Greek islands. Even so they were unable to keep their communications open all the time, and I doubt if we will meet less strength and determination than they encountered.

The German intentions on the Italian front require careful watching. Recent events in the West and the disappearance and silence of 16th S.S. Division opposite Fifth U.S. Army indicates some surprise move which we must guard against. I mention these factors to make the military situation clear to you, and to emphasise that it is my opinion that the Greek problem cannot be solved by military measures. The answer must be found in the political field.

Finally, I think you know that you can always rely on me to do everything in my power to carry out your wishes, but I earnestly hope that you will be able to find a political solution to the Greek problem, as I am convinced that further military action after we have cleared the Athens–Piræus area is beyond our present strength.

I replied:

Prime Minister to Field-Marshal Alexander (Italy) 22 Dec 44
There is no question of our embarking in any military operations away from the Athens–Piræus area. We must however have a military foundation there on which a Greek Government of some kind or other can function. I have personally great doubts about the Archbishop, who might quite conceivably make himself into a dictator supported by the Left Wing. However, these doubts may be removed in the next few days, and I am hopeful that in these days we shall achieve the mastery in Attica and cleanse Athens.

2. Thereafter we do not intend to stay in Greece except for such reasonable period as may be necessary to let the new Government, whatever it is, gain for itself a National Army or Militia, in the hopes that these may be able to conduct elections, plebiscites, etc. We can achieve no political solution

while negotiating from a basis of weakness and frustration. The political field in the present circumstances can only be entered by the gate of success.

I sent Field-Marshal Smuts my reactions on Greek affairs.

Prime Minister to Field-Marshal Smuts　　　　　22 Dec 44

Greece has proved a source of endless trouble to me, and we have indeed been wounded in the house of our friends. With this new chance, Communist and Left Wing forces throughout the world have stirred in sympathy, and our prestige and authority in Greece has to some extent been undermined by the American Press, reporting back. The return of the Greek King would provide no basis for a British policy. We must at all costs avoid giving the impression of forcing him on them by our bayonets.

I have serious doubts about the Regency, which may well assume the form of a dictatorship. I am unable to say whether it would be a dictatorship of the Left, as I do not know enough about the Archbishop. All Leftist forces and our people on the spot have certainly given their support to it. Alexander of course has his heart in the North and strongly dislikes the whole Greek business. But if the powers of evil prevail in Greece, as is quite likely, we must be prepared for a quasi-Bolshevised Russian-led Balkans peninsula, and this may spread to Italy and Hungary. I therefore foresee great perils to the world in these quarters, but am powerless to do anything effective without subjecting the Government to great stresses and quarrelling with America. I am hoping that the next few days may see an improvement in the progress of military operations in Attica, and thus induce a more healthy atmosphere. In the meantime our reinforcements are coming in, and of course in numbers we are already greatly superior to E.L.A.S. The situation is not however very pleasant.

*　　　*　　　*

Two days later I resolved to go and see for myself.

It was December 24, and we had a family and children's party for Christmas Eve. We had a Christmas tree—one sent from the President—and were all looking forward to a pleasant evening, the brighter perhaps because surrounded by dark shadows. But when I had finished reading my telegrams I felt sure I ought to fly to Athens, see the situation on the spot, and especially make the acquaintance of the Archbishop, around whom so much was turning. I therefore set the telephone working and arranged for an aeroplane to be ready at Northolt that night. I

also spoilt Mr. Eden's Christmas by the proposal, which he im
mediately accepted, that he should come too. After having bee
much reproached by the family for deserting the party,
motored to meet Eden at Northolt, where the Skymaster whic
General Arnold had recently sent me waited, attentive an
efficient. We slept soundly until about eight o'clock, when w
landed at Naples to refuel. Here were several generals, and w
all had breakfast together or at adjoining tables. Breakfast
not my best hour of the day, and the news we had both from th
Italian front and from Athens was bleak. In an hour we were o
again, and in perfect weather flew over the Peloponnese and th
Straits of Corinth. Athens and the Piræus unfolded like a ma
beneath us on a gigantic scale, and we gazed down upon
wondering who held what.

At about noon we landed at the Kalamaki airfield, which wa
guarded by about two thousand British airmen, all well arme
and active. Here were Field-Marshal Alexander, Mr. Leeper
and Mr. Macmillan. They came on board the plane, and w
spent nearly three hours in hard discussion of the whol
position, military and political. We were, I think, in complet
agreement at the end, and about the immediate steps to b
taken.

I and my party were to sleep on board the *Ajax*, anchore
off the Piræus, the famous light cruiser of the Plate Rive
battle,* which now seemed a long time ago. The road was re
ported clear, and with an escort of several armoured cars we
traversed the few miles without incident. We boarded the *Aja*
before darkness fell, and I realised for the first time that it wa
Christmas Day. All preparations had been made by the ship'
company for a jolly evening, and we certainly disturbed them
as little as possible.

The sailors had a plan for a dozen of them to be dressed up i
every kind of costume and disguise, as Chinese, Negroes, Red
Indians, Cockneys, clowns—all to serenade the officers and
warrant officers, and generally inaugurate revels suitable to the
occasion. The Archbishop and his attendants arrived—an enor
mous tall figure in the robes and high hat of a dignitary of the
Greek Church. The two parties met. The sailors thought he wa
part of their show of which they had not been told, and danced
around him enthusiastically. The Archbishop thought this
motley gang was a premeditated insult, and might well have

* See Book 2, Chapter 8.

eparted to the shore but for the timely arrival of the captain,
ho, after some embarrassment, explained matters satisfac-
rily. Meanwhile I waited, wondering what had happened. But
ll ended happily.

*　　*　　*

I sent an account of our various discussions to the War
abinet.

Prime Minister (Athens) to Deputy　　　　　　26 Dec 44
Prime Minister and others

On our arrival at air-port at Athens Foreign Secretary and
I held a conference with Field-Marshal Alexander, Mr. Macmillan, and Mr. Leeper.

2. Field-Marshal Alexander gave an encouraging account
of present military situation, which had been grave a fortnight
ago but was now much better. The Field-Marshal however
had formed the decided view that behind the E.L.A.S. units
there was a stubborn core of resistance, Communist in
character, which was stronger than we had thought and
would be very difficult to eradicate. If we were successful in
pushing the E.L.A.S. force outside the boundaries of Athens
we should still be faced with a tremendous task if we tried to
eliminate them altogether.

3. Mr. Macmillan and Mr. Leeper informed us they had
been considering the summoning of a conference of all the
political leaders, which E.L.A.S. would be invited to attend.
We felt that the convening of such a conference, with the
declared object of putting an end to fratricidal strife in Greece,
would, even if E.L.A.S. refused the invitation, ensure that our
intentions would have been made clear to the world. We also
agreed it would be a good move that the Archbishop should
be chairman of the conference. At our meeting [in the aero-
plane] we drew up the text of a public statement which
Messrs. Macmillan and Leeper were to show to the Greek
Prime Minister and the Archbishop, text of which has already
been telegraphed to you.

4. We expressed our wishes that the conference should
rapidly become a conference among Greeks, though we would
stay there as long as it was helpful. When the time came to put
this to the Archbishop we had been informed beforehand that
he would agree to play his part. When he came to see us [on
board the *Ajax*] he spoke with great bitterness against the
atrocities of E.L.A.S. and the dark, sinister hand behind
E.A.M. Listening to him, it was impossible to doubt that he
greatly feared the Communist, or Trotskyite as he called it,

combination in Greek affairs. He told us that he had issued an encyclical to-day condemning the E.L.A.S. crowd for taking eight thousand hostages, middle-class people, many of them Egyptians, and shooting a few every day, and that he had said that he would report these matters to the Press of the world if the women were not released. After some wrangling he understood that the women would be released. Generally he impressed me with a good deal of confidence. He is a magnificent figure, and he immediately accepted the proposal of being chairman of the conference. We are asking the U.S. and Soviet representatives in Athens to be present as observers. The conference is fixed for 4 p.m. on December 26.

5. The Archbishop, at my request, is sending me proposals for the agenda of the conference. I cannot foretell what may come out of it. It may be of course that E.L.A.S. will refuse the invitation. If they do so they will be shown before the world as making an unbridled bid for power. If they do accept I do not rate the chance of forming a united Government high. I was impressed, especially from what the Archbishop said, by the intensity of hatred for Communists in the country. We had no doubt of this before we came here. Present position is confirmed by all we have heard so far. There is no doubt how the people of Athens would vote if they had a chance, and we must keep the possibility of getting them that chance steadily in view. We will send you further reports after we have met E.L.A.S., if they come to-morrow.

I had of course kept the President informed.

Prime Minister to President Roosevelt   26 Dec 44
Anthony and I are going out to see what we can do to square this Greek entanglement. Basis of action: the King does not go back until a plebiscite in his favour has been taken. For the rest, we cannot abandon those who have taken up arms in our cause, and must if necessary fight it out with them. It must always be understood that we seek nothing from Greece, in territory or advantages. We have given much, and will give more if it is in our power. I count on you to help us in this time of unusual difficulty. In particular I should like you to tell your Ambassador in Athens to make contact with us and to help all he can in accordance with the above principles.

He replied next day.

President Roosevelt to Prime Minister   27 Dec 44
I have asked our Ambassador to call upon you as soon as

possible, and I am ready to be of all assistance I can in this difficult situation.

I hope that your presence there on the spot will result in achieving an entirely satisfactory solution.

*   *   *

On the morning of the 26th, 'Boxing Day', I set out for the mbassy. I remember that three or four shells from the fighting hich was going on a mile away on our left raised spouts of ater fairly near the *Ajax* as we were about to go ashore. Here armoured car and military escort awaited us. I said to my rivate Secretary, Jock Colville, 'Where is your pistol?' and hen he said that he had not got one I scolded him, for I rtainly had my own. In a few moments, while we were crowd-g into our steel box, he said, 'I have got a tommy gun.' 'Where d you get it from?' I asked. 'I borrowed it from the driver,' he plied. 'What is *he* going to do?' I asked. 'He will be busy driv-g.' 'But there will be no trouble unless we are stopped,' I nswered, 'and what is he going to do then?' Jock had no reply. black mark! We rumbled along the road to the Embassy ithout any trouble.

There I again met the Archbishop, on whom we were about stake so much. He agreed to all that was proposed. We lanned the procedure at the conference to be held in the after-oon. I was already convinced that he was the outstanding gure in the Greek turmoil. Among other things, I had learned at he had been a champion wrestler before he entered the rthodox Church. Mr. Leeper has noted that I said, 'It would istress me to think that any new task Your Beatitude assumes s Regent might in any way interfere with your spiritual func-ions.' He gave me all the necessary reassurance.

About six o'clock that evening, December 26, the conference pened in the Greek Foreign Office. We took our seats in a large, leak room after darkness fell. The winter is cold in Athens. here was no heating, and a few hurricane lamps cast a dim ght upon the scene. I sat on the Archbishop's right, with Mr. den, and Field-Marshal Alexander was on his left. Mr. Mac-eagh, the American Ambassador, M. Baelen, the French Minister, and the Soviet military representative had all accepted ur invitation. The three Communist leaders were late. It was ot their fault. There had been prolonged bickering at the out-osts. After half an hour we began our work, and I was already

speaking when they entered the room. They were presenta[ble]
figures in British battle dress. In my speech I said, among ot[her]
things:

When we came here yesterday we thought it would b[e a]
good thing to have a talk round a table. It is better to let ev[ery]
effort be made to remake Greece as a factor in the victo[ry]
and to do it now. Therefore we had a talk with M. Papandre[ou]
the Prime Minister. ... We proposed to him that there sho[uld]
be a conference like this. Mr. Eden and I have come all t[he]
way, although great battles are raging in Belgium and on [the]
German frontier, to make this effort to rescue Greece fro[m]
miserable fate and raise her to a point of great fame and [re-]
pute. M. Papandreou told us immediately that he wo[uld]
welcome such a conference, and we have all met here n[ow]
in this city, where the sound of firing can be heard fr[om]
minute to minute at no great distance. The next British s[tep]
was to invite the Archbishop to be the chairman of this Gr[eek]
conference. We do not intend to obstruct your deliberatio[ns.]
We British, and other representatives of the great uni[ted]
victorious Powers, will leave you Greeks to your own [dis-]
cussions under this most eminent and most venerable citiz[en,]
and we shall not trouble you unless you send for us again. [We]
may wait a little while, but we have many other tasks to p[er-]
form in this world of terrible storm. My hope is however t[hat]
the conference which begins here this afternoon in Athe[ns]
will restore Greece once again to her fame and power amo[ng]
the Allies and the peace-loving peoples of the world, w[ill]
secure the Greek frontiers from any danger from the nor[th,]
and will enable every Greek to make the best of himself a[nd]
the best of his country before the eyes of the whole wor[ld.]
For all eyes are turned upon this table at this moment, and [I]
British trust that whatever has happened in the heat of fig[ht-]
ing, whatever misunderstandings there may have been, [we]
shall preserve that old friendship between Greece and Gre[at]
Britain which played so notable a part in the establishment [of]
Greek independence.

General Alexander added a sharp touch that Greek troo[ps]
should be fighting in Italy and not against British troops [in]
Greece.

Once we had broken the ice and got the Greeks who had do[ne]
such terrible injuries to each other to parley round the tab[le]
under the presidency of the Archbishop, and the formal speech[es]
had been made, the British members of the conference wit[h-]
drew.

*   *   *

I was glad to get back to the Embassy, where there were a few oil stoves lent by G.H.Q. for the duration of my visit. While we were awaiting news from the conference and dinner I sent the following telegram to my wife, towards whom I felt penitent because of my desertion on Christmas Eve:

Prime Minister to Mrs. Churchill   **26 Dec 44**

We have had a fruitful day, and so far there is no need to give up hope of some important results. H.M.S. *Ajax* is very comfortable, and one can get a view of the fighting in North Piræus at quite short range. We have had to move a mile farther away, as we were getting too many of their trench mortar bombs in our neighbourhood. I went into the Embassy up that long road from Piræus to Athens in an armoured car with strong escort, and I addressed all the plucky women on Embassy staff, who have been in continued danger and discomfort for so many weeks, but are in gayest of moods. Mrs. Leeper is an inspiration to them.

2. You will have read about the plot to blow up H.Q. in the Hôtel Grande-Bretagne. I do not think it was for my benefit. Still, a ton of dynamite was put in sewers by extremely skilled hands and with German mechanism between the time my arrival was known and daylight: I have made friends with the Archbishop, and think it has been very clever to work him in as we have done, leaving the constitutional questions for further treatment later.

3. The conference at Greek Foreign Office was intensely dramatic. All those haggard Greek faces round the table, and the Archbishop with his enormous hat, making him, I should think, seven feet high, whom we got to preside. The American, Russian, and French Ambassadors were all very glad to be invited. You will hear speeches on radio no doubt, or see them printed in Wednesday's papers. E.L.A.S. arrived late, three in all. Thanks were proposed, with many compliments to us for coming, by the Greek Government, and supported by E.L.A.S. representative, who added reference to Great Britain, 'our great Ally'—all this with guns firing at each other not so far away.

4. After some consideration I shook E.L.A.S. delegate's hand, and it was clear from their response that they were gratified. They are the very top ones. We have now left them together, as it was a Greek show. It may break up at any moment. We shall wait for a day or two if necessary to see. At least we have done our best.

*   *   *

Bitter and animated discussions between the Greek parti[es]
occupied all the following day. At 5.30 that evening I had a fina[l]
discussion with the Archbishop. As the result of his conversa[-]
tions with the E.L.A.S. delegates it was agreed I should ask th[e]
King of Greece to make him Regent. He would set about form[-]
ing a new Government without any Communist members. W[e]
undertook to carry on the fighting in full vigour until eithe[r]
E.L.A.S. accepted a truce or the Athens area was clear of them[.]
I told him that we could not undertake any military task beyon[d]
Athens and Attica, but that we would try to keep British force[s]
in Greece until the Greek National Army was formed.

Just before this talk I had received a letter from the Com[-]
munist delegates asking for a private meeting with me. Th[e]
Archbishop begged me not to assent to this. I replied that as th[e]
conference was fully Greek in character I did not feel justifie[d]
in agreeing to their request.

On the following morning, December 28, Mr. Eden and [I]
left by air for Naples and London. I had no chance to say good[-]
bye to M. Papandreou before leaving. He was about to resign[,]
and was a serious loser by the whole business. I asked ou[r]
Ambassador to keep in friendly touch with him.

I sent the following telegram to the Chiefs of Staff:

Prime Minister (*Athens*) *to General Ismay,*   28 Dec 4[4]
for C.I.G.S. and C.O.S.

It is clear to me that great evils will follow here in Athens[,]
affecting our position all over the world, if we cannot clea[r]
up situation quickly—*i.e.*, in two or three weeks. This woul[d]
entail, according to Alexander, the moving in of the tw[o]
brigades of the 46th Division, which are already under order[s]
and standing by. On the other hand, the military situation i[n]
Western Apennines is such that any serious weakening o[f]
the reserves of Fifteenth Army Group might be attended wit[h]
danger.

2. In these circumstances I wish you to consider and b[e]
ready to discuss with me on my return allowing the leadin[g]
brigade of 5th Division to proceed from Palestine to Italy o[n]
schedule arranged before 4th Division was diverted to Greece[.]
It would be a great convenience if we could have a reply t[o]
this to-morrow, Thursday. I do not leave Caserta until afte[r]
midnight. This of course would mean that no violent action[s]
could be taken in Palestine, irritating the Jews, such as the[the]
search for arms on a large scale, until the situation is easier al[l]
round.

Just before leaving Athens I also sent the following telegram the President, from whom I had had a kindly inquiry:

Prime Minister (Athens) to President Roosevelt   28 Dec 44

Many thanks for your message, which encouraged me amidst many difficulties. Ambassador MacVeagh called yesterday and we had a resumed talk. Like everyone else here, he is convinced that a Regency under the Archbishop is the only course open at the moment. I have seen the Archbishop several times, and he made a very good impression on me by the sense of power and decision which he conveyed, as well as by his shrewd political judgments. You will not expect me to speak here of his spiritual qualities, for I really have not had sufficient opportunity to measure these.

2. The Greek conference, of which you will have had from other sources full account, was unanimous in recommending a Regency. This was strongly supported by E.A.M. However, I do not consider Archbishop is at all Left Wing in Communist sense. On the contrary, he seems to be an extremely determined man, bent on establishing a small, strong executive in Greece to prevent the continuance of civil war.

3. I am therefore returning with Anthony to England to press upon the King of Greece to appoint the Archbishop Regent. Effect of this, if King agrees, will of course mean that Archbishop will form a Government of ten or less of the 'best will'. I gathered that he would make Plastiras Prime Minister, and that Papandreou would not be included. Naturally I could not probe too far while all these matters are hypothetical.

4. On our return we shall advise our colleagues, who are already inclined to this course, that we should put the strongest pressure on the Greek King to accept advice of his Prime Minister, M. Papandreou, who changed his mind about three times a day but has now promised to send a telegram in his own words.

5. If Ambassador MacVeagh's report should on these matters correspond with mine I should greatly hope that you would feel yourself able to send a personal telegram to the King of Greece during the next few days supporting the representation we shall make to him, of which we shall keep you informed. My idea is that the Regency should be only for one year, or till a plebiscite can be held under conditions of what is called 'normal tranquillity'.

The Archbishop has left this matter entirely in my hands, so that I can put the case in most favourable manner to the King. Of course if after these difficulties have been surmounted and Archbishop is Regent you felt able to send him a telegram of support that would make our task easier. Mr.

President, we have lost over one thousand men, and thou
the greater part of Athens is now clear it is a painful sight
see this city with street-fighting raging now here, now ther
and the poor people all pinched and only kept alive in ma
cases by rations we are carrying, often at loss of life, to the
at the various depots. Anything that you can say to strength
this new lay-out as the time comes will be most valuable, ar
may bring about acceptance by E.L.A.S. of the terms
truce set forth by General Scobie. For the rest we are rei
forcing as is necessary and military conflict will go on. Th
vast majority of the people long for a settlement that will fr
them from the Communist terror.

6. We have to think of an interim arrangement which can
reviewed when our long-hoped-for meeting takes place. Th
date should not now be far distant. It will then be possible
correlate our opinions and actions. In the meanwhile we hav
no choice but to recommend creation of a new and mo
competent executive Government under the Regency of th
Archbishop, and to press on with our heavy and unsoug
task of clearing Athens from very dangerous, powerful, we
organised, and well-directed elements which are now pressin
into the area. I should value a telegram when I return o
Friday morning.

*　　　*　　　*

On December 29 we arrived back in London, and I tele
graphed again to President Roosevelt.

Ambassador Winant has sent me a copy of your message
the Greek King. We are all very much obliged to you fo
acting so promptly. Anthony and I have just returned. The Wa
Cabinet have endorsed all our actions, and have authorised u
to urge the King of Greece to-night to appoint the Arch
bishop as Regent. The Archbishop left it to me to discuss th
period of the Regency with the King, so that this gives a littl
latitude.

2. Failing agreement, His Majesty's Government will advis
the Archbishop to assume the office of Regent and assur
him that we will recognise him and the Government he form
as the Government of Greece.

Later that same night I sent him more solid news.

Prime Minister to President Roosevelt　　　30 Dec 4
Anthony and I sat up with the King of Greece till 4.30 thi
morning, at the end of which time His Majesty agreed to the
following announcement. I have sent this to Ambassado
Leeper in Athens in order that the Archbishop may go t

work at once. The Greek translation is now being made, and I will furnish you with a copy of it at the earliest moment.

This has been a very painful task to me. I had to tell the King that if he did not agree the matter would be settled without him and that we should recognise the new Government instead of him. I hope you will be able to give every support and encouragement to the Archbishop and his Government.

This was the announcement:

We, George II, King of the Hellenes, having deeply considered the terrible situation into which our well-loved people have fallen through circumstances alike unprecedented and uncontrollable, and being ourselves resolved not to return to Greece unless summoned by a free and fair expression of the national will, and having full confidence in your loyalty and devotion, do now by this declaration appoint you, Archbishop Damaskinos, to be our Regent during this period of emergency; and we accordingly authorise and require you to take all steps necessary to restore order and tranquillity throughout our kingdom. We further declare our desire that there should be ascertained, by processes of democratic government, the freely expressed wishes of the Greek people as soon as these storms have passed, and thus abridge the miseries of our beloved country, by which our heart is rent.

I sent the royal announcement at once to Mr. Leeper in Athens, saying that the Archbishop from the moment when he received it should consider himself free to proceed with all the functions of his office and could be assured of the resolute support of His Majesty's Government.

President Roosevelt replied on the same day: 'I am happy to know of your safe arrival, and wish you every success in the solution of the Greek problem, which seems very promising as a result of your journey.'

I answered:

Prime Minister to President Roosevelt   31 Dec 44
The Greek King behaved like a gentleman and with the utmost dignity, and I am sure a private message from you would give him comfort. I shall send only a civil acknowledgment to E.L.A.S. for the published message they have sent me, and hand the matter over to the Archbishop. It is clearly his job now.

The great battle in the West seems to be turning steadily in our favour, and I remain of the opinion that Rundstedt's sortie is more likely to shorten than to lengthen the war.

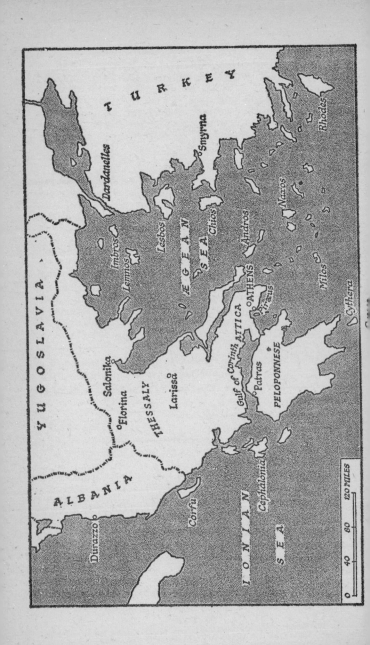

Mr. Leeper (now Sir Reginald Leeper, G.B.E., K.C.M.G.) in
account of these events in his book *When Greek Meets
eek* comments:

The King's declaration, which endorsed the unanimous
recommendation of the conference, was the direct result of
Mr. Churchill's visit. It finally scotched the legend that the
British were trying to force the King back on his people. For
that reason alone Mr. Churchill's visit to Athens had been
abundantly justified. Had his instinct not brought him to the
scene of trouble at that moment I doubt very much whether
any other influence could have induced all sides to come together in recommending the Regency to the King.

E.L.A.S. addressed a message to me on December 30 claim-
g that they had fulfilled all the conditions demanded by
eneral Scobie for a truce. This was not true, and the British
mmander insisted on a formal acceptance of his terms.
The Archbishop replied to the King accepting his mandate as
egent. There was a new and living Greek Government. On
nuary 3 General Plastiras, a vehement Republican, who was
e leader of the Army revolt against King Constantine in 1922,
came Prime Minister.

*   *   *

I also received some wise advice from Smuts.

Field-Marshal Smuts to Prime Minister and   30 Dec 44
Foreign Secretary

It is with deep interest and much anxiety that we have
followed your Athens mission. It will have a profound and
beneficial effect on world opinion. A wholly distorted picture
of the true position in Greece has unfortunately been painted
by the Press. Hence E.L.A.S.-E.A.M. has come to be viewed
as the champion of democracy fighting against British backing
of the royal cause. Though this is false, world reaction has
been very damaging. Now is the time, I suggest, to give a true
picture of the situation, and the Press should paint E.L.A.S. in
its true colours. So that the world will see that Britain, as friend
and ally, had no choice, a factual exposure should now be
made of the bitter suffering inflicted on the Greek people, the
dynamiting of property, the ruthless destruction and extortion,
the rounding up and execution of innocent hostages, the
coercion of the civilian population by terroristic methods in
true Nazi style. Following immediately on your courageous
mission, a full and accurate statement of the facts may lead

to a wholesome reversal of public opinion. Our Intelligen
and Information agencies in London and Athens shou
publish now the facts that must be in their possession.

Our own troops had no illusions. General Alexander h
previously sent me a censorship report on their letters home
was so struck by what I read that I had it printed and circulat
to the War Cabinet. It completely disposed of the lie spread
Communist circles that their sympathies were with E.L.A.S.

*   *   *

The continuous fighting in Athens during December at la
drove the insurgents from the capital, and by mid-Janua
British troops controlled all Attica. The Communists could
nothing against our men in open country, and a truce was sign
on January 11. All E.L.A.S. forces were to withdraw well cle
of Athens, Salonika, and Patras. Those in the Peloponnese we
to be given a safe-conduct to return to their homes. Briti
troops would cease fire and stand fast. Prisoners would be r
leased on both sides. These arrangements came into force
the 15th.

Thus ended the six weeks' struggle for Athens, and, as it ul
mately proved, for the freedom of Greece from Commun
subjugation. When three million men were fighting on eith
side on the Western Front and vast American forces we
deployed against Japan in the Pacific the spasms of Greece ma
seem petty, but nevertheless they stood at the nerve-centre
power, law, and freedom in the Western world.